Learning
JAVA 7

Other Titles by the Same Authors

- Learning PageMaker 7
- Learning 3D Max
- Learning Computer Fundamentals
- Learning Java 7
- Learning Internet & E-mail
- Learning HTML 5
- Learning JavaScript with HTML 5
- Learning Visual Basic 6
- Learning SQL
- Learning Web Designing
- Learning Multimedia
- Learning Networking
- Learning PC Hardware
- Learning Desk Top Publishing
- Learning C
- Learning C++
- Learning Windows XP
- Learning Windows Vista
- Learning Windows 7
- Learning Windows XP, Vista, Office 2007 & Internet & E-mail
- Learning MS Office XP
- Learning MS Access 2003
- Learning MS Excel 2003
- Learning MS Word 2003
- Learning MS Office 2003
- Learning MS Access 2007
- Learning MS Excel 2007
- Learning MS Word 2007
- Learning MS Office 2007
- Learning Tally 9.0
- Learning Dreamweaver CS4
- Learning CorelDRAW X4
- Learning Photoshop CS4
- Learning Flash CS4
- Learning Illustrator CS4
- Learning Microsoft Access 2010
- Learning Microsoft Excel 2010
- Learning Microsoft Word 2010
- Learning Microsoft Office 2010
- Learning AutoCAD 2010
- Learning Dreamweaver CS5
- Learning CorelDraw X5
- Learning Flash CS5
- Learning Illustrator CS5
- Learning Photoshop CS5
- Learning ASP.Net 4.0
- Learning C# 4.0
- Learning ASP.Net and C#.Net
- Learning Tally 9.0 (Hindi)
- Learning Internet & E-mail (Hindi)
- Learning Desk Top Publishing (Hindi)

Learning
JAVA 7

Ramesh Bangia

B.Sc., Comp. Sc. (IIT - Delhi)

Formerly Managing Editor, Software Today

Formerly Incharge Computer Centre, Hindustan Copper Ltd., New Delhi

KHANNA BOOK PUBLISHING CO. (P) LTD.

::: *Publisher of Engineering and Computer Books* :::

Head Office : 4C/4344, Ansari Road, Darya Ganj, New Delhi-110002
Phone: 011-23244447/48 Fax: 011-23244447

Regd. Office : 1694-95, Nai Sarak, Delhi-110006
Phone: 011-23283211 Fax: 011-23256658

E-Mail : contact@khannabooks.com
Website : www.khannabooks.com

Learning **JAVA 7**

Ramesh Bangia

First Edition : 2013

Published by:
KHANNA BOOK PUBLISHING CO. (P) LTD.
Head Off.: 4C/4344, Ansari Road, Darya Ganj, New Delhi-110 002
Phone: 011-23244447-48 **Fax:** 011-23244447
E-mail: contact@khannabooks.com
Website: www.khannabooks.com

Regd. Off: 1694-95, 1st Floor, Nai Sarak, Delhi-110006 (India)
Phone: 011-23283211 Telefax: 011-23256658

Printed in India by:
SPS Printers and Binders, Delhi

PREFACE

Learning of a software is both easy and difficult. It depends upto what level you are planning to learn. If you are learning only for the working use, then it is very easy. But, when you try to go deep into it, then you realise how difficult it is to master it.

This book has been written in mind to make you aware of the options available in the software and how they can be used. It is like telling the child about the steps and stairs. You are the one who is to climb the stair. This book will just guide you how to use the stairs.

I am indeed debited to my publishers Khanna Book Publishing Co. Pvt. Ltd. for their suggestions and encouragement given in producing this book.

Suggestions for improvement of the book are indeed welcome.

Author

CONTENTS

CHAPTER 1

Introduction to JAVA

In this chapter you will read about:

- Keywords of Java.
- Java and C++.
- Converting C++ program to Java.
- Converting Default Arguments.
- Converting Arrays based Pointers.

History of Java

In 1991, while working at Sun Microsystems, James Gosling, Patrick Naughton, Chris Warth, Ed Frank, and Mike Sheridan conceived Java. It took them 18 months to develop the first working version of the software language. This was initially called "Oak" but was renamed "Java" in 1995. Between the initial implementation of Oak in 1992 and the public announcement of Java in 1995, many more people contributed to the design and evolution of the language. Bill Joy, Arthur van Hoff, Jonathan Payne, Frank Yellin, and Tim Lindholm were the key players.

When Java was developed, no body thought of it for a platform like Internet. Instead, the primary motivation was the need for a platform-independent language that could be used to create software to be embedded in various consumer electronic devices, such as microwave ovens and remote controls. As you can probably guess, many different types of CPUs are used as controllers. The trouble with C and C++ (and most other languages) is that they are designed to be compiled for a specific target. Although it is possible to compile a C++ program for just about any type of CPU, to do so requires a full C ++ compiler targeted for that CPU. The problem is that compilers are expensive and time-consuming to create. An easier—and more cost—efficient-solution was needed.

In an attempt to find such a solution, work began on a portable, platform-independent language that could be used to produce code that would run on a variety of CPUs under differing environments. This effort ultimately led to the creation of Java. Around the same time that the details of Java were being worked out, a second, and ultimately more important, factor was emerging that would play a crucial role in the future of Java. This second force was, of course, the World Wide Web. Had the Web not taken shape at about the same time that Java was being implemented, Java might have remained a useful but obscure language for programming consumer electronics.

However, with the emergence of the World Wide Web, Java was propelled to the forefront of computer language design, because the Web, too, demanded portable programs. Most programmers learn early in their careers that portable programs are as elusive as they are desirable. While the quest for a way to create efficient, portable (platform-independent) programs is nearly as old as the discipline of programming itself, it had taken a back seat to other, more pressing problems.

Further, because much of the computer world had divided itself into the three competing camps of Intel, Macintosh and UNIX, most programmers stayed within their fortified boundaries, and the urgent need for portable code was reduced. However, with the advent of the Internet and the Web, the old problem of portability returned with a vengeance. After all, the Internet consists of a diverse, distributed universe populated with many types of computers, operating systems, and CPUs. Even though many types of platforms are attached to the Internet, users would like them all to be able to run the same program.

What was once an irritating but low-priority problem had become a high-profile necessity. During 1993, it became obvious to members of the Java design team that the problems of portability frequently encountered when creating code for embedded controllers are also found when attempting to create code for the Internet.

In fact, the same problem that Java was initially designed to solve on a small scale could also be applied to the Internet on a large scale. This realization caused the focus of Java to switch from consumer electronics to Internet programming. So, while the desire for an architecture-neutral programming language provided the initial spark, the Internet ultimately led to Java's large-scale success.

Java, as said before, derives much of its character from C and C++. This is so because, the Java designers knew that using the familiar syntax of C and echoing the object-oriented features of C++ would make their language appealing to the legions of experienced C/C++ programmers. In addition to the surface similarities, Java shares some of the other attributes that helped make C and C++ successful.

Firsty, Java was designed, tested, and refined by real, working programmers. It is a language grounded in the needs and experiences of the people who devised it. Thus, Java is also a programmer's language.

Secondly, Java is cohesive and logically consistent.

Thirdly, except for those constraints imposed by the Internet environment, Java gives you, the programmer, full control. If you program well, your programs reflect it. If you program poorly, your programs reflect that, too.

Putting differently, Java is not a language with training wheels. It is a language for professional programmers. Because of the similarities between Java and C++, it is tempting to think of Java as simply the "Internet version of C++." However, to do so would be a large mistake. Java has significant practical and philosophical differences. While it is true that Java was influenced by C++, it is not an enhanced version of C++. For example, Java is neither upwardly nor downwardly compatible with C++. Of course, the similarities with C++ are significant, and if you are a C++ programmer, then you will feel right at home with Java. One other point: Java was not designed to replace C++. Java was designed to solve a certain set of problems. C++ was designed to solve a different set of problems. Both will coexist for many years to come.

The environmental change that prompted Java was the need for platform-independent programs destined for distribution on the Internet. However, Java also embodies changes in the way that people approach the writing of programs.

Specifically, Java enhances and refines the object-oriented paradigm used by C++. Thus, Java is not a language that exists in isolation. Rather, it is the current instance of an ongoing process begun many years ago. This fact alone is enough to ensure Java a place in computer language history. Java is to Internet programming what C was to systems programming: a revolutionary force that will change the world.

Java as Internet Language?

As mentioned earlier, Java programming is the key factor of Internet programming. This is so because Internet helped catapult Java to the forefront of programming, and Java, in turn, has had a profound effect on the Internet. The reason for this is quite simple: Java expands the universe of objects that can move about freely in cyberspace. In a network, two very broad categories of objects are transmitted between the server and your personal computer: passive information and dynamic, active programs. For example, when you read your e-mail, you are viewing passive data.

Even when you download a program, the program's code is still only passive data until you execute it. However, a second type of object can be transmitted to your computer: a dynamic, self-executing program. Such a program is an active agent on the client computer, yet is initiated by the server. For example, a program might be provided by the server to display properly the data that the server is sending. As desirable as dynamic, networked programs are, they also present serious problems in the areas of security and portability. Prior to Java, cyberspace was effectively closed to half the entities that now live there. Java addresses those concerns and, by doing so, has opened the door to an exciting new form of program: the applet.

Keywords of Java

As in any other software or programming language, it is very important to understand the keywords first and then jump on to using it. Although the fundamental forces that necessitated the invention of Java are portability and security, other factors also played an important role in moulding the final form of the language. The key considerations were summed up by the Java team in the following list of keywords:

Simple

As the computer programming has grown over the years the language itself has taken care of most of the aspects leaving programmer with less and less work. I remember, in way back in 1970s, we used to languages like AutoCoder, FORTRAN, etc, which would need a real complicated programming. As we grew, the computer languages not only became easier to code but simple to use. So keeping the tradition going Java is also simple to use.

Assuming that you have some programming experience, you will not find Java hard to master. If you already understand the basic concepts of object-oriented programming, learning Java will be even easier. Best of all, if you are an experienced C++ programmer, moving to Java will require very little effort.

Because Java inherits the C/C++ syntax and many of the object-oriented features of C++, most programmers have very little trouble learning Java. Also, some of the more confusing concepts from C++ are either left out of Java or implemented in a cleaner, more approachable manner. Besides its similarities with C/C++, Java has another attribute that makes it easy to learn: it makes an effort not to have surprising features. In Java, there are a small number of clearly defined ways to accomplish a given task.

Object-Oriented

Java was never designed to be source-code compatible with any other language. This allowed the Java team the freedom to design with a blank slate. One outcome of this was a clean, usable, pragmatic approach to objects. Borrowing liberally from many seminal object-software environments of the last few decades, Java manages to strike a balance between the purist's "everything is an object" paradigm and the pragmatist's "stay out of my way" model. The object model in Java is simple and easy to extend, while simple types, such as integers, are kept as high-performance nonobjects.

Security

This one factor is probably the important factor why Java is more popular with the Internet. As you are aware, every time you download a normal program, you are risking a viral infection. Prior to Java, most users did not download executable programs frequently, and those who did scanned them for viruses prior to execution. Even so, most users still worried about the possibility of infecting their systems with a virus. In addition to viruses, another type of malicious program exists that must be guarded against. This type of program can gather private information, such as credit card numbers, bank account balances, and passwords, by searching the contents of your computer's local file system.

Java answers both of these concerns by providing a firewall between a networked application and your computer. When you use a Java-compatible Web browser, you can safely download Java applets without fear of viral infection or malicious intent. Java achieves this protection by confining a Java program to the Java execution environment and not allowing it access to other parts of the computer. The ability to download applets with confidence that no harm will be done and that no security will be breached is considered by many to be the single most important aspect of Java.

Portable

Many types of computers and operating systems are in use throughout the world—and many are connected to the Internet. For programs to be dynamically downloaded to all the various types of platforms connected to the Internet, some means of generating portable executable code is needed. The same mechanism that helps ensure security also helps create portability.

Robust

As mentioned earlier, Java is platform free and works on most of the platforms. To make it so makes extraordinary demands on a program, because the program must execute reliably in a variety of systems. Thus, the ability to create robust programs was given a high priority in the design of Java. To gain reliability, Java restricts you in a few key areas, to force you to find your mistakes early in program development.

At the same time; Java frees you from having to worry about many of the most common causes of programming errors. Because Java is a strictly typed language, it checks your code at compile time. However, it also checks your code at run time. In fact, many hard-to-track-down bugs that often turn up in hard-to-reproduce run-time situations are simply impossible to create in Java. Knowing that what you have written will behave in a predictable way under diverse conditions is a key feature of Java. To better understand how Java is robust, consider two of the main reasons for program failure: memory management mistakes and mishandled exceptional conditions (that is, run-time errors).

Memory management can be a difficult, tedious task in traditional programming environments. For example, in C/C++, the programmer must manually allocate and free all dynamic memory. This sometimes leads to problems, because programmers will either forget to free memory that has been previously allocated or, worse, try to free some memory that another part of their code is still using. Java virtually eliminates these problems by managing memory allocation and deallocation for you. In fact, deallocation is completely automatic, because Java provides garbage collection for unused objects. Exceptional conditions in traditional environments often arise in situations such as "division by zero" or "file not found," and they must be managed with clumsy and hard-to-read constructs. Java helps in this area by providing object-oriented exception handling. In a well-written Java program, all run-time errors can—and should—be managed by your program.

Multithreaded

Java was designed to meet the real-world requirement of creating interactive, networked programs. To accomplish this, Java supports multithreaded programming, which allows you to write programs that do many things simultaneously. The Java run-time system comes with an elegant yet sophisticated solution for multiprocess synchronization that enables you to construct smoothly running interactive systems. Java's easy-to-use approach to multithreading allows you to think about the specific behaviour of your program, not the multitasking subsystem.

Architecture-Neutral

One of the main problems facing programmers is that no guarantee exists that if you write a program today, it will run tomorrow-even on the same machine. Remember what happened to programs written in 70s to 90s which would not run in 2000, leading to a massive Y2K problem. Operating system upgrades, processor upgrades, and changes in core system resources can all combine to make a program malfunction.

The Java designers made several hard decisions in the Java language and the Java Virtual Machine in an attempt to alter this situation. Their goal was "write once; run anywhere, any time, forever." To a great extent, this goal has been accomplished.

Interpreted and High Performance

As described earlier, Java enables the creation of cross-platform programs by compiling into an intermediate representation called Java bytecode. This code can be interpreted on any system that provides a Java Virtual Machine. Most previous attempts at cross-platform solutions have done so at the expense of performance. Other interpreted systems, such as BASIC, Tcl, and PERL, suffer from almost insurmountable performance deficits.

Java, however, was designed to perform well on very low-power CPUs. As explained earlier, while it is true that Java was engineered for interpretation the Java bytecode was carefully designed so that it would be easy to translate directly into native machine code for very high performance by using a just-in-time compiler; Java run-time systems that provide this feature lose none of the benefits of the platform-independent code. "High-performance cross-platform" is no longer an oxymoron.

Distributed

Java is designed for the distributed environment of the Internet, because it handles TCP /IP protocols. Infact, accessing a resource using a URL is not much different from accessing a file. The original version of Java (Oak) included features for intra-address-space messaging. This allowed objects on two different computers to execute procedures remotely.

Java has recently revived these interfaces in a package called Remote Method Invocation (RMI). This feature brings an unparalleled level of abstraction to client/server programming.

Dynamic

Java programs carry with them substantial amounts of run-time type information that is used to verify and resolve accesses to objects at run time. This makes it possible to dynamically link code in a safe and expedient manner. This is crucial to the robustness of the applet environment, in which small fragments of bytecode may be dynamically updated on a running system.

Java and C++

Let us first see how we can compare C++ and Java. This can be divided into 3 categories.

- Java features which were not there in C++
- C++ features not supported by Java
- Features common to them by different

Let us see them one by one.

Java features which were not there in C++

There are a number of features in Java that have no equivalent in C++. Perhaps the 3 most important are multithreading, packages, and interfaces, but there are several others that enrich the Java programming environment as well.

- **Multithreading:** Multithreading allows two or more pieces of the same program to execute concurrently. Further, this approach to concurrence is supported at the language level. There is no parallel for this in C++. If you need to multithread a C++ program, you will need to do so manually, using operating system functions. While both methods allow for concurrent execution of two or more threads, Java's approach is cleaner and easier to use.
- **Library functions:** There is no feature in C++ that directly corresponds to a Java package. The closest similarity is a set of library functions that use a common header file. However, constructing and using a library in C++ is completely different from constructing and using a package in Java.

- **Abstract class:** The Java interface is somewhat similar to a C++ abstract class. (An *abstract class* in C++ is a class that contains at1east one pure virtual function.) For example, it is impossible to create an instance of a C++ abstract class or a Java interface. Both are used to specify a consistent interface that subclasses will implement. The main difference is that an interface more clearly represents this concept.
- **Memory allocation:** Java has a streamlined approach to memory allocation. Like C++, it supports the new keyword. However, it does not have delete. Instead, when the last reference to an object is destroyed, the object, itself, is automatically deleted the next time that garbage collection occurs.
- **API library:** Java "removes" the C++ standard library, replacing it with its own set of API classes. While there is substantial functional similarity, there are significant differences in the names and parameters. Also, since all of the Java API library is object-oriented, and only a portion of the C++ library is, there will be differences in the way library routines are invoked.
- **Break and Continue:** The break and continue statements have been enhanced in Java to accept labels as targets.
- **Character type:** The char type in Java declares 16-bit-wide Unicode characters. This makes them similar to C++'s **wchar_t** type. The use of Unicode helps ensure portability.
- **>>> operator:** Java adds the >>> operator, which performs an unsigned right shift.
- **Documentation comment:** In addition to supporting single-line and multiline comments, Java adds a third comment form: the *documentation comment*. Documentation comments begin a /** and end with a */.
- **String:** Java contains a built-in string type called String. String is somewhat similar to the standard string class type provided by C++. Of course, in C++ string is only available if you include its class declarations in your program. It is not a built-in type.

C++ Features not supported by Java

Java does not support a number of C++ features. In some cases, a specific C++ feature simply didn't relate to the Java environment. In other cases, the designers of Java eliminated some of the duplication of features that exists in C++. In still other instances, a feature of C++ is not supported by Java because it was deemed too dangerous for Internet applets.

Perhaps the single biggest difference between Java and C++ is that Java does not support pointers. As a C++ programmer you know that the pointer is one of C++'s most powerful and important language features. It is also one of its most dangerous when used improperly. Pointers don't exist in Java for two reasons:

- Pointers are very dangerous to use. For example, using a C++ style pointer, it is possible to gain access to memory addresses outside a program's code and data. A malicious program could make use of this fact to damage the system, perform unauthorized accesses (such as obtaining passwords), or otherwise violate security restrictions.
- Even if pointers could be restricted to the confines of the Java run-time system (which is theoretically possible, since Java programs are interpreted), the designers of Java believed that they were inherently troublesome.

Some of the other features not supported by Java are:

- **Structures and unions:** Java does not include structures or unions. These were felt to be redundant since the class encompasses them.

- **Operator overloading:** Java does not support operator overloading. It is sometimes a source of ambiguity in a C++ program, and the Java design team felt that it causes more trouble than benefit.
- **Preprocessor:** Java does not include a preprocessor nor does it support the preprocessor directives. The preprocessor plays a less important role in C++ than it does in C. The designers of Java felt that it was time to eliminate it entirely.
- **Conversions:** Java does not perform any automatic type conversions that result in a loss of precision. For example, a conversion from long integer to integer must be explicitly cast.
- **Code:** All the code in a Java program is encapsulated within one or more classes. Therefore, Java does not have what you normally think of as global variables or global functions.
- **Default arguments:** Java does not allow default arguments. In C++, you may specify a value that a parameter will have when there is no argument corresponding to that parameter when the function is invoked. This is not allowed in Java.
- **Multiple superclass:** Java does not support the inheritance of multiple superclasses by a subclass.
- **Constructors:** Although Java supports constructors, it does not have destructors. It does, however, add the **finalize( )** function.
- **Typedef:** Java does not support **typedef**.
- **Unsigned integers:** It is not possible to declare unsigned integers in Java.
- **Goto:** Java does not allow the **goto**.
- **Delete:** Java does not have the **delete** operator.
- **I/O operations:** The **<<** and **>>** in Java are not overloaded for I/O operations.
- **Objects:** In Java, objects are passed by reference only. In C++, objects may be passed by value or by reference.

Features Common to them but Different

There are some features common to both C++ and Java that each language handles a bit differently:

- **True and False:** While both C++ and Java support a Boolean data type, Java does not implement true and false in the same way as C++. In C++, true is any nonzero value. False is zero. In Java, true and false are predefined literals, and these are the only values that a Boolean expression may have.

  While C++ also defines true and false, which may be assigned to a **bool** variable, C++ automatically converts nonzero values into true and zero values into false. This does not occur in Java.
- **Class:** When you create a C++ class, the access specifiers apply to groups of statements. In Java, access specifiers apply only to the declarations that they immediately precede.
- **Exception handling:** C++ supports exception handling that is fairly similar to Java's. However, in C++ there is no requirement that a thrown exception be caught.

Converting C++ program to Java

When you convert a C++ program into Java, perhaps the greatest number of changes will be caused by pointers. Most C++ code is heavily dependent upon pointers for its operation. You can't program anything very significant in C++ without using a pointer. There are 4 general categories of pointer usage that you will encounter in C++ code:

- **As parameters to functions:** Although C++ supports the reference parameter, there is a large base of legacy code that was originally written in C, which does not support reference parameters. In C, if a function needs to change the value of an argument, it is necessary to explicitly pass a pointer to that argument. Therefore, it is still common to find pointer parameters used in C++ code that was originally ported from C.

  Also, in some cases the same function library will need to be shared by both C and C++ code, which prevents the use of reference parameters. Additionally, many of the standard library functions supported by C++ are holdovers from C.

  When one of these C-based functions requires the address of an argument, a pointer to the argument is used. Inside the function, the argument is then accessed through its pointer.

- **To provide a more efficient means of implementing certain constructs-especially array indexing:** For example, it is often more efficient to sequentially move through an array using a pointer rather than an array index. While modem compilers implement highly efficient optimizations, pointers can still provide a significant performance boost. Thus, the use of pointers to access arrays is ubiquitous in C++ code.

- **To support memory allocation:** In C++, when you allocate memory, an address (that is, a pointer) to that memory is returned. This address must be assigned to a pointer variable. Once this has been done, the pointer can point to any part of the allocated memory—or anywhere else, for that matter—by means of pointer arithmetic.

  In Java, when an object is allocated by new, a reference to the object is returned. This reference must be assigned to a reference variable of a compatible type. While Java reference variables do implicitly point to the object that was allocated by the new operator, they cannot be manipulated in, the same way as C++ pointers. And they cannot point to memory outside of the Java run-time context.

- **To provide access to any arbitrary machine address, possibly to call a ROM routine or to read/write directly to memory:** Since Java purposely disallows such actions, this use of pointers has no direct parallel. If you are writing applications, not applets, you can always use Java's native capabilities to gain access to native code routines that would be allowed access to such system resources.

Let's look at two examples in which pointer-based C++ code is converted to Java.

Converting Pointer Parameters

For example, consider this C++ program that reverses the signs of a Coord object, which stores a pair of Cartesian coordinates. The function **reverseSign**( ) is passed a pointer to the Coord object that will be reversed. As you can see, C++'s*, &, and -> pointer operators are used to perform the operation.

```
// Reverse the signs of a coordinate C++ version
#include <iostream>
using namespace std;

class Coord {
public:
    int x;
    int y;
};
```

```
// Reverse the sign of the coordinates
void reverseSign(Coord *ob) {
    ob->x = -ob->x;
    ob->y = -ob->y;
}

int main()
{
    Coord ob;

    ob.x = 10;
    ob.y = 20;

    cout << "Original values for ob: ";
    cout << ob.x << ", " << ob.y << "\n";
    reverseSign(&ob);

    cout << "Sign reversed values for ob: ";
    cout << ob.x << ", " << ob.y << "\n";

    return 0;
}
```

This program can be recoded into the following Java version. As you can see, most of the conversion involves the deletion of the C++ pointer operators. Since Java passes objects by reference, changes to the parameter automatically affect the argument.

```
// Reverse the signs of a coordinate Java version
class Coord {
    int x;
    int y;
};

class DropPointers {
    // Reverse the sign of the coordinates.
    static void reverseCoord(Coord ob) {
        ob.x = -ob.x;
        ob.y = -ob.y;
    }
    public static void main(String args[ ]) {
        Coord ob = new Coord();

        ob.x = 10;
        ob.y = 20;

        System.out.println("Original values for ob: "+
            ob.x + ",  " + ob.y);
```

```
        reverseCoord(ob);

        System.out.println("Sign reversed values for ob:    " + ob.x + "  ,  " +
ob.y) ;
    }
}
```

The output from both of these programs is the same and is shown here:

```
Original values for ob:    10, 20
Sign reversed values for ob:       -10,    -20
```

Converting Arrays based Pointers

Pointer-based array accessing can be a bit difficult to follow, because the normal C + + coding style encourages rather dense, complex expressions. For example, this short C + + program copies the contents of one array to another. It uses *0* to mark the end of the arrays. Even in this simple example, if you did not know that this program copied the contents of **nums** to **copy** (and later displayed the arrays), it would require some careful thought before you were completely sure that you knew what the code was doing.

```
// Copy an array in C++ using pointers.
#include <iostream>
using namespace std;

int main ( )
{
    int nums[ ] = {10, 12, 24, 45, 23, 19, 44,
                          88, 99, 65, 76, 12, 89, 0};
    int copy[20];

    int *p1, *p2; II integer pointers

    // copy array
    p1 = nums; // p1 points to start of nums array
    p2 = copy;
    while (*p1) *p2++ = *p1++;
    *p2 = 0; // terminate copy with zero

    // Display contents of each array.
    cout << "Here is the original array: \n";
    p1 = nums;
    while(*p1) cout << *p1++ << " ";
    cout << endl;

    cout << "Here is the copy: \n";
    p1 = copy;
    while(*p1) cout << *p1++ << " ";
    cout << endl;

    return 0;
```

```
}
```

Even though it is quite simple for C+ + code, at first glance the line

```
While (*p1) *p2++ = *p1++;
```

still requires a moment of thought to decipher its exact operation. One of the advantages of Java is that it does not encourage the creation of such expressions in the first place. Here is the Java version of the program. As you can see, its purpose and effects are transparent.

```
// Array copy without pointers using Java.
class CopyArray {
  public static void main(String args[ ]) {
    int nums[ ]   =   {10, 12, 24, 45, 23, 19, 44
                      88, 99, 65, 76, 12, 89, 0}
    int copy[ ] = new int{14];
    int i;

    // copy array
    for(I = 0; nums[i] ! = 0; i++)
       copy[i] = nums[i];
    nums[i] = 0; // terminate copy with zero

    // Display contents of each array.
    System.out.println("Here is the original array:");
    for(I = 0; numsli] ! = 0; i++)
       System.out.print(nums{i] + " ");
    System.out.println();

    System.out.println("Here is the copy:");
    for(I = 0; nums[i] ! = 0; i++)
       System.out.print(copy[il + " ");
    System.out.println();
  }
}
```

Both versions of the program produce the following results:

```
Here is the original array:
10 12 24 45 23 19 44 88 99 65 76 12 89
Here is the copy:
10 12 24 45 23 19 44 88 99 65 76 12 89
```

Converting C+ + Abstract Classes into Java Interfaces

One of the most innovative aspects of Java is the interface. It specifies the form of its various methods without specifying any implementation details. Each class that implements an interface does so by creating the actual methods declared by the interface. Thus, in Java an interface is the means by which you can define the general form of a class while ensuring that all specific versions of the class conform to the same set of rules. The interface is one of the ways that Java provides support for polymorphism.

Abstract classes in C+ + are similar to abstract classes in Java: they do not contain a full set of implementation details. In C++, an abstract class contains at least one pure virtual function. A pure virtual function defines no implementation; it only defines the function prototype. Thus, a pure virtual function in C++ is essentially the same as an abstract method in Java.

In C++, abstract classes serve a function similar to interfaces in Java. While not all C++ abstract classes can be converted into Java interfaces, many can. Here is a short C++ program that uses an abstract class called **IntList** to define the form of an integer list. An implementation of this class is created by **IntArray**, which uses an array to implement a list of integers.

```
// A C++-style abstract class and its implementation.
#include <iostream>
#include <cstdlib>
using namespace std;

// An abstract class that defines the form of an   integer list.
class IntList {
public:
   virtual int getNext() = 0; // pure virtual functions
   virtual void putOnList(int i) = 0;
};

// Create an implementation of an integer list.
class IntArray : public IntList {
   int storage [100] ;
   int putIndex, getIndex;
public:
   IntArray() {
      putlndex = 0;
      getlndex = 0;
}

// Return next integer in list.
int getNext() {
   if(getIndex >= 100) {
      cout << "List Underflow";
      exit (1) ;
   }
   getIndex++;
   return storage[getIndex-1];
}

// Put an integer on the list
void putOnList(int i) {
   if(putlndex < 100) {
      storage [putlndex] = i;
      putIndex++;
   }
   else {
      cout << "List Overflow";
```

```
        exit (1);
    }
}

int main()
{
    IntArray nums;
    int i;

    for(i = 0; i<10; i++) nums.putOnList(i);

    for(i = 0; i<10; i++)
        cout << nums.getNext( ) << endl;

    return 0;
}
```

In this program, the abstract class **IntList** defines only the form of an integer list. It contains only pure virtual functions and does not declare any data. For these reasons, it can be made into an interface when the program is converted into Java, as shown here:

```
// Here, IntList is made into an interface which IntArray implements.

// Define interface for an integer list.
interface IntListIF {
    int getNext();
    void putOnList(int i);
}

// Create an implementation of an integer list.
class IntArray implements IntListIF {
    private int storage[ ];
    private int putlndex, getlndex;

    IntArray() {
        storage = new int[1001];
        putIndex = 0;
        getIndex = 0;
}

// Create an implementation of an integer list.
public int getNext() {
    if(getIndex >= 100) {
        System.out.println("List Underflow");
        System.exit(1);
    }
    getIndex++;
    return storage[getIndex - 1};
```

```
}

// Put an integer on the list.
public void putOnList(int i) {
   if(putlndex < 100) {
      storage [putlndex] = i;
      putlndex++;
   }
   else {
      System.out.println("List Overflow");
      System.exit(1);
   }
}

class ListDemo {
   public static void main(String args[ ]) {
      IntArray nums = new IntArray();
      int i;

      for(I = 0; I < 10; i++) nums.putOnList(i);

      for(I = 0; I < 10; i++1
         System.out.println(nums.getNext());
   }
}
```

As you can see, there is nearly a one-to-one correspondence between the C++ abstract class **IntList** and the Java interface **IntListIF**. It is possible to convert **IntList** into **IntList1F** because it contained only pure virtual functions. This is the key. If **IntList** had contained any data or function implementations, then it would not have qualified for conversion into an interface.

When you convert or adapt C++ code into Java, look for examples of abstract classes that contain only pure virtual functions. These are prime candidates for conversion to Java interfaces. But don't overlook abstract C++ classes that contain a small number of implemented functions or data.

It is possible that these items don't really belong in the abstract class to begin with and should be defined by individual implementations. Since C++ does not define an interface construct, there was no reason for C++ programmers to think in terms of one.

Sometimes a concrete member is contained in an otherwise abstract class simply for expedience—not because it is the most logical place for it. For example, consider the following abstract C++ class:

```
// An abstract C++ class.
class SomeClass {
   bool isOK;
public:
   virtual int f1() = 0;
   virtual void f2(int i) = 0;
   virtual double f3() = 0;
   virtual int f4(int a, char ch) = 0
```

```
};
```


The only reason that this class cannot be made into a Java interface is the existence of **isOK**. Presumably, **isOK** is used to indicate some status associated with the class. However, if you think about it, there really is no reason for **isOK** to be defined as a variable. Instead, you could specify a method called **isOK()** that returns the status. In this approach, **isOK( )** will be defined, along with the other methods, by any implementing class. Thus, you could convert the preceding C++ abstract class into the following Java interface:

```
interface SomeClass {
    int f1();
    void f2(int i);
    double f3 ();
    int f4(int a, char ch);
    boolean isOK();
}
```

Many abstract classes in C++ can—and should—be converted into interfaces when you move code to Java. In doing so, you will probably find that it clarifies the structure of the class hierarchy.

Converting Default Arguments

One extensively used feature of C++ that Java does not support is default function arguments, For example, the area( ) function shown in the following C++ program computes the area of a rectangle if called with two arguments, or the area of a square if called with one argument,

```
// C++ program that uses default arguments.
#include <iostream>
using namespace std;

/* Compute area of a rectangle. For a square, pass only one argument.
*/
double area(double 1, double w = 0) {
    if(w == 0) return 1 * 1;
    else return 1 * w;
}

int main ()
{
    cout << " Area of 2.2 by 3.4 rectangle: " ;
    cout << area(2.2, 3.4) << endl;
    cout << "Area of 3.0 by 3.0 square: ";
    cout << area(3.0) << endl;
    return 0 ;
}
```

As you can see, when **area( )** is called with only one argument, the second defaults to zero. When this happens, the function simply uses the first argument for both the length and the width of the rectangle.

While convenient, default arguments are not, of course, necessary. In essence, default arguments are actually a shorthand form of function overloading in which one form of the function has a different number of parameters than the other.

Thus, to convert a C++ function that contains one or more default arguments into Java, simply create overloaded methods that handle each case. In this example, you need a version of **area( )** that takes two arguments and another that takes only one argument. Using this approach, here is the preceding program rewritten for Java:

```
// Java version of area program.
class Area {
    // Compute area of a rectangle.
    static double area(double l, double w) {
        if (w==0) return l * l;
        else return l * w;
    }

    // Overload area( ) for a square.
    static double area(double l) {
        return l * l;
    }
    public static void main(String args[ ]) {
        System.out.println("Area of 2.2 by 3.4 rectangle:    " + area(2.2,
3.4));
        System.out.println("Area of 3.0 by 3.0 square:
area(3.0));
    }
}
```

Reference Parameters of C++ and Java

Earlier you had seen how a pointer parameter becomes a reference parameter in Java. Of course, C++ also supports reference parameters. As mentioned, most pointer parameters found in C++ code are simply holdovers from C. Nearly all new C++ code will use reference parameters when a function needs access to the argument, itself.

Since both Java and C++ support reference parameters, you might think that the conversion of a C++ function that uses reference parameters to a Java method would involve few changes. Unfortunately, this is not always the case.

To understand why, let's convert the following C++ program, which swaps the contents of two Coord objects using reference parameters:

```
// Swap coordinates — C++ version.
#include <iostream>
using namespace std;

class Coord {
public:
    int x;
```

```
    int y;
};

// Swap contents of two Coord objects.
void swap(Coord &a, Coord &b) {
    Coord temp;

    // Swap contents of objects
    temp = a;
    a = b;
    b = temp;
}

int main()
{
    Coord ob1, ob2;

    ob1.x = 10;
    ob1.y = 20;

    ob2.x = 88;
    ob2.y = 99;

    cout << "Original values:\n";
    cout << "ob1: "<< ob1.x << ", " << ob1.y << "\n";
    count << ob2; " << ob2.x << ", " << ob2.y << "\n";
    cout << "\n";
    swap(ob1, ob2);

    cout << "Swapped values:\n";
    cout << "ob1: " << ob1.x << ", " << ob1.y << "\n";
    cout << "ob2: " << ob2.x << ", " << ob2.y << "\n";

    return 0;
}
```

Following is the output produced by this program. As you can see, the contents of **ob1** and **ob2** have been exchanged:

```
Original values:
ob1 : 10, 20
ob2 : 88, 99

Swapped values:
ob1: 88, 99
ob2 : 10, 20
```

In Java, all objects are accessed via an object reference variable. Thus, when an object is passed to a method, only its reference is passed. This means that all objects are automatically passed by reference to a Java method. Without thinking any deeper about what is actually occurring, someone might initially try the following (incorrect) conversion of the preceding program:

```
// Swap program incorrectly converted to Java.
class Coord {
  int x;
  int y;
};

class SwapDemo {
 static void swap(Coord a, Coora b) {
  Coord temp = new Coord( );

  // this won't swap contents of a and b!
  temp = a;
  a = b. ,
  b= temp;
 }

 public static void main(String args[ ]) {
  Coord ob1 = new Coord();
  Coord ob2 = new Coord();

  ob1.x = 10;
  ob1.y = 20;

  ob2.x = 88;
  ob2.y = 99;

  system:out.prifitln("Original values:");
  System.out;println("ob1: " +
      ob1.x + ", " + ob1.y);
  System.out.println("ob2: " +
      ob2 .x + ", " + ob2.y + "\n");

  swap (ob1, ob2);

  System.out.println("Swapped values:");
  System.out.println("ob1: " +
      ob1. x + ", " + ob1.y);
  System.out.println("ob2: " +
      ob2.x + ", " + ob2.y + "\n");
 }
}
```

The output produced by this incorrect program is shown here:

```
Original values:
ob1: 10, 20
ob2 : 88, 99
```

```
Swapped values:
ob1: 10, 20
ob2: 88, 99
```

As you can see, the values of **ob1** and **ob2** in main() have not been exchanged! Although a bit counterintuitive at first, the reason is actually obvious, once you understand precisely what happens when an object reference is passed to a method. Java passes all arguments to methods using call-by-value,

This means that a copy of the argument is made, and what occurs to the copy inside the method has no effect on the argument used to call the method, However, this situation is blurred a bit in the case of object references, When an object reference is passed to a method, a copy of the reference variable is made, as just explained.

This means that the parameter inside the method will refer to the same object as does the reference variable used as an argument outside the method. Therefore, operations on the object through the parameter will affect the object referred to by the argument (since they are one and the same).

But operations on the reference parameter, itself, affect only that parameter. Thus, when the preceding program attempts to swap the objects by exchanging the objects pointed to by a and b, all that is happening is that the parameters (that is, the copies of the arguments) are exchanging what they are referring to, but this does not alter what **ob1** and **ob2** refer to back in main(),

To 'fix the program, swap() needs to be rewritten so that the contents of the objects are exchanged, not what the parameters refer to. Here is the corrected version of swap():

```
// Corrected version of swap().
static void swap(Coord a, Coord b) {
    Coord temp = new Coord();

    // swap contents of objects
    temp.x = a.x;
    temp.y = a.y;
    a.x = b.x;
    a.y = b.y;
    b.x = temp.x;
    b.y = temp.y;
}
```

If you substitute this version of swap() into the preceding program, the correct results will be achieved.

Converting Multiple-Inheritance Hierarchies of C++

C++ allows one class to inherit two or more base classes at the same time. Java does not. Since C++ supports multiple inheritance and Java does not, you may have to deal with this issue when porting C++ applications to Java. While every situation is different, two general pieces of advice can be offered. First, in many cases, multiple inheritance is employed in a C++ program when there is actually no need to do so. When this is the case, just convert the class structure to a single-inheritance hierarchy.

For example, consider this C++ class hierarchy that defines a class called House:

```
class Foundation {
    // ...
};

class Walls {
    // ...
};
```

```
class Rooms {
    // ...
} ;

class House : public Foundation, Walls, Rooms {
    // ...
} ;
```

Notice that **House** multiply inherits **Foundation, Walls**, and **Rooms**. While there is nothing wrong with structuring a C++ hierarchy like this, it is not necessary. For example, here is the same set of classes structured for Java:

```
class Foundation {
    // ...
} ;

class Walls extends Foundation {
    // ...
} ;

class Rooms extends Walls {
    // ...
} ;

class House extends Rooms {
    // ...
} ;
```

Here, each class extends the preceding one, with **House** becoming the final extension. Sometimes a multiple inheritance hierarchy is more readily converted by including objects of the multiply inherited classes in the final object. For example, here is another way that **House** could be constructed in Java:

```
class Foundation {
    // ...
} ;

class Walls {
    // ...
} ;

class Rooms {
    // ...
} ;

/* Now, House includes Foundation, Walls, and Rooms as object members.
*/
class House {
    Foundation f;
    Walls w;
    Rooms r;
    // ...
}
```

Here, **Foundation**, **Walls**, and **Rooms** are objects that are part of **House** rather than inherited by **House**. One other point: sometimes a C++ program will contain a multiple-inheritance hierarchy simply because of poor initial design. A good time to correct this type of design flaw is when you port to Java.

Destructors Versus Finalization

When you move from C++ to Java, one of the more important issues you will face is the difference between a C++ destructor and a Java **finalize()** method. Although similar in many respects, their actual operation is distinctively different. Let's begin by reviewing the purpose and effect of a C++ destructor and the Java **finalize()** method. In C++, when an object goes out of scope, it is destroyed. Just prior to its destruction, its destructor function is called (if it has one). This is a hard-and-fast rule. There are no exceptions. Let's look more closely at each part of this rule:

- **Every object is destroyed where it goes out of scope.** Thus, if you declare a local object inside a function, when that function returns, that local object is automatically destroyed. The same goes for function parameters and for objects returned by functions.
- **Just before destruction, the object's destructor is called.** This happens immediately, and before any other program statements will execute. Thus, a C++ destructor will always execute in a deterministic fashion. You can always know when and where a destructor will be executed.

While the deterministic behavior of a C++ constructor and the somewhat probabilistic aspect of finalization are of little concern in most cases, they will have an impact on others. For example, consider the following C++ program:

```
// This C++ program can call f() indefinitely.
#include <iostream>
#include <cstdlib>
using namespace std;

const int MAX = 5;
int count = 0;

class X {
public:
    // constructor
    X() {
    if(count<MAX) {
        count++;
    }
    else {
        cout << "Error - can't construct";
        exit (1);
    }
}

    // destructor
    -X() {
        count-;
    }
};
void f()
```

```
{
    x ob; // allocate an object
    // destruct on way out
}

int main()
{
    int i

    for(i = 0; i < (MAX*2); i++) {
        f() ;
        cout << "Current count is: " << count << endl;
    }
    return 0;
}
```

Here is the output generated by this program:

```
Current count is: 0
Current count is: 0
Current count is: 0
Current count is: 0
Current count is: 0
Current count is: 0
Current count is: 0
Current count is: 0
Current count is: 0
Current count is: 0
```

Look carefully at the constructor and destructor for **X**. The constructor increments the value of count as long as count is less than **MAX**. The destructor decrements count.

Thus, count is incremented when an **X** object is created and decremented when an **X** object is destroyed. But no more than **MAX** objects can exist at anyone time. However, in **main()**, **f()** is called **MAX*2** times without causing an error!

Here is why. Inside **f( )**, an object of type **X** is created, causing count to be incremented, and then the function returns. This causes the object to immediately go out of scope and its destructor to be called, which decrements count.

Thus, calling f( ) has no net effect on the value of count. This means that it can be called indefinitely. However, this is not the case when this program is converted to Java.

Here is the Java version of the preceding program:

```
// This Java program will fail after 5 calls to f().

class X {
    static final int MAX = 5;
    static int count = 0;

    // constructor
    X() {
        if(count<MAX) {
            count++;
```

```
    }
        }
        else {
            System.out.println("Error – can't construct");
            System.exit(1);
        }
    }

    // finalization
    protected void finalize() {
        count–;
    }

    static void f()
    {
        x ob = new X(); // allocate an object
        // destruct on way out
    }
    public static void main(String args[ ]) {
        int i

        for(i=0; i < (MAX*2); i++) {
            f() ;
            System.out.println("Current count is: " +
    count);
        }
    }
}
```

This program will fail after five calls to **f( )**, as this output shows:

```
Current count is: 1
Current count is: 2
Current count is: 3
Current count is: 4
Current count is: 5
Error -can't construct
```

The reason the program fails is that garbage collection does not occur each time **f( )** returns. Thus, **finalize()** is not invoked, and the value of **count** is not decremented. After five calls to the method, count reaches its maximum value and the program fails. It is important to emphasize that precisely when garbage collection occurs is implementation dependent.

It is possible that for some implementation of Java, on some platform, the preceding program will function similarly to its C+ + version. However, the point of the example remains: In C+ +, you know when and where a destructor will be called. In Java, you do not know when or where **finalize( )** will be executed.

Therefore, when porting code from C+ + to Java, you will need to watch for instances in which the precise timing of the execution of a destructor is relied upon. With this it ends the discussion on C+ + and now the discussion would concentrate totally on Java.

CHAPTER 2

JAVA Programming

In this chapter you will read about:

- Reserve Words.
- Format of the Program.
- Compilation of the Program.
- Decision making statements.
- Classes and Objects.

Introduction

In this chapter you will learn about the simple Java programming and learn to write programs in Java. You will also learn to compile and run them.

Writing the Program

As they say that the best way to learn swimming is to jump into the swimming pool. So what we will do is that we will write a program in Java and learn about it by making various changes side by side. Like other software, java too has its own extension called .java. So each Java program will have a .java extension at the end of it. At stage I assume that you are computer literate and know the basic operations of computer, like creating a file.

Let us create our first Java program called test1.java. Simply type the following lines in your word processor and save it with the above name and make sure that it is in text mode.

```
Class test1
{
    public static void main (string args[ ])
    {
    System.out.println("Sachin Tendulkar);
    }
}
```

This program, as you might have guessed will print the words, Sachin Tendulkar. This type of program can be used to print anything and everything. This part is called the coding of the program. Next we will learn how to compile it, i.e., to convert it into the language of the computer.

As you have noticed that the class is followed by the name of the program name which you are writing. In the above example, the name of the class is test1. This name has to be unique for this program. If you are not new to programming then you know that each program has some data and some processing in it. In the above program however, there is no data and there is no processing. Just print out the name.

The processing is nothing but the instructions given to the computer to do certain actions. A processing method definition begins with { and ends with }, similar to the class definition which also begins with { and ends with }.

Reserved Words

It is not that you can write your program using any or all words. Some words have been reserved by Java for its own use. They in fact form part of the instructions. Thus, they cannot be used by the programmer. A complete list of the reserved words is given below. Java treats the upper and lower cases separately. Replacing class with Class or CLASS is not allowed. If you write Class or CLASS, the compiler will treat it as some ordinary word, and would not recognize your intention to use it as the reserved word class.

Here is a complete list of reserve words:

abstract	boolean	break	byte	case
cast	catch	char	class	const
continue	default	do	double	else
extends	final	finally	float	for
future	generic	goto	if	implements
import	inner	instanceof	int	interface
long	native	new	null	operator

outer	package	private	protected	public
rest	return	short	static	super
switch	synchronized this	throw	throws	
transient	try	var	void	volatile
while.				

Identifiers

They are the words which are used to identify something. The word test1, used as a class name above, is called an identifier in the terminology of computer programming. In Java an identifier can start with a letter, an underscore (_), or a dollar sign ($). They cannot start with a number, although numbers are allowed inside the identifiers. Symbols such as:

@	#	%	"	&
*	:	+	-	=
«	»	;	,	I
!	'	"	'	0
]	0	a	~	|

are reserved for operators in Java. You should avoid using such cryptic symbols in your identifier, even though some of them may be allowed. Apart from this, you are free to choose any names.

Format of the Program

Those familiar with the other programming languages know about the format of the program writing. In fact, Java is a free format language. When compiler reads a Java program, it gives no importance to the number of words put in a line.

It ignores extra blanks, which are also called spaces in computer terminology, at the beginning and at the end of a line, and between two consecutive words. It treats the end of line (or beginning of a new line) as a blank. It also treats tab character as a blank. Also note that the punctuation symbols (;), ({) and a) are not part of the words, and therefore need not be separated explicitly from the adjacent words.

Keeping with all these things in mind, you can write the above program in several different ways as follows:

```
class test1
{
public static void main(String args[ ])
    {System.out.println("Sachin Tendulkar"); }
}
```

```
class test1 { public static void main(String args[ ])
    {System.out.println("Sachin Tendulkar"); } }
```

```
class test1
        public static void
main(String
    args[ ])
```

```
{
   System.out.println("Sachin Tendulkar")
} }


      class test1 {
   public static void main(string args[ ])
{
   System.out.println("Sachin Tendulkar")
      ; } }
class
test1
{
public
static
void
main
(
String
args
[
]
)
{
System
.
out
.
println
(
"Sachin Tendulkar"
)
;
}
}
```

If you compile and run these programs the result will be the same, as before, Sachin Tendulkar. The main thing is that you have written a program, someone else should also be able to understand it by just looking at it. Note that the text between the double quotes is called a string, and should be treated like a single word. Breaking a string over the lines would be an error.

Adding Comments to the Program

Let us now extend this program by adding comments in it:

```
class test1
{
   public static void main(String args[ ])
   {
```

```
    // This is a single line comment.
    System.out.println("Sachin Tendulkar");
    /*  Between these
        two indicators you
        can write anything. ...*/
    }
}
```

The resultant output of the program will remain the same irrespective of the comment lines. Anything that appears after // until the end of that line is called a comment and is ignored by the compiler. In addition, anything that appears after /* up to */ is also a comment.

The first style is used only for writing short comments (up to one line) whereas the later, form is used to write big descriptions as comments. The single line comment (//) can be inside a multi-line comment (/*...*/) like this

```
/*something // anything */
```

But inverse of this, that is, a /**/ inside a // like

```
// anything /* something */ everything
```

or

```
// something /* anything
    else    */
```

is not allowed. Also, a single-line comment inside another single-line comment like this is allowed:

```
// anything // everything
```

but serves hardly any purpose. Multi-line comment inside another multi-line comment like this is not allowed:

```
/* anything
     /* everything
   else
     */
   something
   everything */
```

These comments are added for the reader of the program to understand the program better; they are of no use to the machine. The machine/compiler ignores comments. As mentioned in the earlier chapter, we expect Java to last more and more years to come. So when you see the program after few years you would not have difficulty in understanding the program if you have put good comments in it.

Compilation the Program

Java programs have to be compiled first to run them later. After seeing the results obtained from the compiled program, you can revise your program if needed and compile it again.

Cycle of Edit-Compile-Run

When Java is loaded on your system, in an appropriate directory, files named java, javac, appletviewer, javadoc, javah, javap, jdb, etc. are stored which act as system commands. After you have written your program in the file, say test1.java, type this command:

```
javac test1.java
```

and press enter. The system will do the compilation (**javac** is a short name for Java compiler), and create another file named test1.class. This file is an intermediate stabe in the total Java process. Once you get this, type another command

```
java.test1
```

Note that here the command is just **java** and not **javac** or **javap**, etc. Also note that only test1 is typed, and not test1.class or test1.java, etc. In case you make any mistake, the machine will point it out to you. So please follow the instructions on the monitor. Please take care of the upper/lower cases as Java is very particular about it. So typing **Javac** or **JAVAC** in place of **javac** would be a big mistake for the system, although a human being can understand such things better.

The program in the test1.java file looks like this:

```
class test1
{
    public static void main(String args[ ])
    {
    System.out.println("Sachin Tendulkar"); }
    }
}
```

This program can now be compiled using the following command

```
javac test1.java
```

This will result in a file named test1.class in your directory. To run this program, now type the following command

```
java test1
```

and will result in giving the following on the screen

```
Sachin Tendulkar
```

You can edit the program by using the word processor again to include some other name instead of Sachin Tendulakr. Now the program will look like this:

```
class test1
{
    public static void main(String args[ ])
    {
    System.out.println("Rahul Dravid" );
    }
}
```

Now compile this too using the command javac test1.java, and then run the test1 class using java test1 as before to see this output:

```
Rahul Dravid
```

Supposing now we change the class name to test2. Add Mohan to the name to see the change in the output:

```
class test2
{
    public static void main(string args[ ])
```

```
    {
    System.out.println("Rahul Mohan Dravid");
    }
}
```

This program can also be compiled and run. This time the file in the directory is test2.class. The old file test1.class is also there. This time, the output of compilation is collected in test2.class instead of test1.class, mainly because you have replaced the class name by test2. This indicates that the class files are named after the class names, and have no relevance with the initial file name. If you run the test1 class (by typing java testl) the old output will be shown. But if you run the test2 class (by typing java test2) you will see the following output with Mohan appearing between Rahul and Dravid.

```
Rahul Mohan Dravid
```

Debugging of the Program

It is not possible that you write a program and it runs on the first instance only. You may need to run it 2-3 times before making it perfect. Let us now see the type of mistakes you can make and how to correct them. These mistakes are called bugs in the computer terminology. The act of removing or fixing a bug is called debugging. Various aids are available to detect bugs. Generally the Java compiler points out bugs in most of the cases. Consider our earlier program once again:

```
class testl
    {
    public static void main(String args[ ])
    {
    System.out.println
        ("Rahul Mohan Dravid");
    .}
}
```

A typical mistake is to forget the class name (the first line). In this case, when you compile the above program using javac, you will get an error:

```
testl.java:1: Class or interface declaration expected.
{
^
1 error
```

In the error message the file name, the line number, etc., are reported, and the error is pointed out.

Another common mistake is to forget the semicolon (;) at the end of the statement.

```
class testl
{
    public static void main(String args[ ])
    {
    System.out.println("Rahul Mohan Dravid")
    }
}
```

This gives an error like this:

```
test1.java:6: ';' expected.
    System.out.println("Rahul Mohan Dravid")
^
1 error
```

Another mistake would be of forgetting the closing parenthesis (}).

```
class test1
{
    public static void main(String args[ ])
    {
    System.out.println("Rahul Mohan Dravid")
}
```

This gives:

```
test1.java:4: '}' expected
}
^
1 error
```

Another common error is to forget the closing double quote at the end of a string.

```
class test1
{
    public static void main(String args[ ])
    {
    System.out.println("Rahul Mohan Dravid)
    }
}
```

This gives

```
test1.java:3: String not terminated at end of line.
    {
    System.out.println("Rahul Mohan Dravid);
    }
        ^
test1.java:4: ')' expected
}
^
test1.java:4: '}' expected
}
^
3 errors
```

As the string is not closed, the) and } are treated as part of the string, and on line 4 both these are expected. This is an example where one error has cascading effect on to the rest of the program.

So now you know the type of errors you can make and how to correct them.

Data Variables

So far we have not talked about the data which can be given in the program. This data can be either stored in the computer or can be manipulated or calculated using different arithmetic operations. Such stored numbers are called variables in the computer terminology. The variable facility provided in computers is as follows: a variable is a place in the computer's memory where a value can be stored (recorded). This value can be changed in the course of calculations by overwriting it. A name can be given to a variable, so that you can refer to it by this name.

The rules in Java for choosing a name for a variable are the same as those for choosing identifiers. After choosing the name of a variable, you need to declare the type of value this variable is going to store. This is called the type of variable, or just the type. In mathematics, there are two types of numbers: **Integers**, such as 0, 1, 2, –1, –2, –3, etc. and **Real numbers** like 2.33, –35.8967680954, the number π, irrational numbers like 2, etc. In Java, the first type is called **int** (short name for integer) and the second type is called **double** (double precision floating point number). Inside the machine, these two numbers are stored differently. The double takes much more space than the int. So you have to tell the computer precisely whether the number is an int or a double. If **x** is an int number and **yy** is a double, you declare them as

```
int x;
double yy;
```

Assignments

If you want to give or assign a value of 5 to an int variable y, you write

```
y = 5;
```

Please note that 'equal to' sign (=) is not the same as in mathematics; this operator takes value from the right hand side (rhs) and puts that into the left hand side (lhs). If you turn the sides and write

```
5 = y;
```

the compiler will assume here that you are trying to change the value of 3 which is absurd and will throw the command out. You may also write

```
y = 5 + 6;
```

in which case the rhs calculation is done first and the value 11 is assigned to lhs, i.e., y. The values of variables can be printed to the terminal screen in a much straightforward way as shown by this program:

```
class testl
    {
    public static void main(String args[ ])
    {
    int y;
    y = 5 + 6;
    System.out.println("y is " + y );
    }
}
```

The output is

```
y is 11
```

In the above **println** statement, you are requesting the system to print two things one after another—the string "y is ", and the string "11" (as the value of y). In fact, by putting a + sign between two strings, you have actually made one combined string and passed it to the **System.out.println** command.

Two strings can be combined in Java by putting a + sign between them. The same symbol + is also used to add two numbers in mathematics. Do not get confused unnecessarily. Looking at the things around the + sign, it is always clear whether it is the + of numbers' addition or the + of strings' combination! The following program will make it more clear:

```
class testl
   {
   public static void main(String args[ ])
   {
   int y;
   y = 5 + 6;
   System.out.println("y is " + y +y);
   }
}
```

The output is

```
y is 1111
```

This is a consequence of juxtaposition. The computer has printed 3 arguments one after another. If you want to perform the arithmetic sum y + y and then print 22 as the result, your print line command should have been

```
System.out.println(" y is " + (y + y) );
```

In this case, the expression in the inner brackets is looked at before other things. Thus (y + y) gives 22 (current value of y is 11) and then the string becomes like

```
System.out.println("y is " + "22");
```

and produces the output as

```
y is 22
```

Variable Values

The value stored in a variable is automatically read when you refer to it as if it is a number of that type. For example, if you assign

```
x = 7;
```

and then write

```
y = 5 + x;
```

then the x in the rhs will be replaced by its value 7, and so y will get the value 12. You can even use the same name x in both lhs and rhs:

```
x = x + 3;
```

In lhs it is the variable name to which you are assigning the value; in rhs, it is the current value of x is being used. Note the importance of the word current. With so many assignments, the current value of any variable keeps on changing, and you need to keep a track of it! As an example consider this program:

```
class testl
   {
   public static void main(String args [ ])
```

```
    {
    int y;
    y = 7;
    System.out.println("y now is " + y);
    y = y + y
    System.out.println("y now is " + y);
    y = y + y
    System.out.println("y now is " + y);
    y = y + y
    System.out.println("y now is " + y);
    }
}
```

The values printed are all different as shown by this output:

```
x now is 7
x now is 14
x now is 21
x now is 28
```

Swapping Values of Variables

In programming, swapping of two variables is quite a tricky issue, particularly if you forget that the current value of a variable keeps changing. In order to swap (exchange) the values of two variables x and y, consider this program with comments explaining what is being done:

```
class testl
    {
    public static void main(string args[])
    {
    int x, y; // You can combine
       // declarations of the same type.
    x = 3;      // Assignment
    y = 4;      // Assignment
    x = y;      // Swapping
    y = x;      // Swapping
    System.out.println("x is "  +  x);
    System.out.println("y is "+ y);
    }
}
```

The output:

```
x is 4
y is 4
```

Can you explain why both the variables, x and y, have the same value 4 when y should have been 3? If not, try to print values of both x and y after every assignment in the program. Once x = y; is done, original value of x is lost! In order to prevent it you should modify the program as follows:

```
class testl
```

```
{
public static void main(String args[ ])
{
int x, y, temp;  // New variable temp
x = 3;      // Assignment
y = 4;      // Assignment
temp = y; // Swapping;
    // preserving original y value
y = x;      // Swapping
x = temp;
    // Swapping; using stored value
System.out.println("x now is " + x);
System.out.println("y now is " + y);
}
}
```

The output, as expected, is

```
x now is 4
y now is 3
```

Decision Making

So far we have talked about storing and printing. But, this is not all. Computer can be used to take decisions too. It can pick up alternatives between the two. Every programming language offers a facility to write down alternatives to be followed, and Java is no exception to that. Java provides two constructs, **if** and **switch** statements.

The if Statement

It is like saying that if this happens I will do this else I will do this. Not clear, lets take an example: If Ram gets 60% marks his father will give him a wrist watch, else, he would be given a fountain pen. The 'if' statement in Java is much the same as the word 'if' in English language. It takes a condition, or logical statement, which is either true or false, depending on the situation. Based on the current value, it takes different actions. In its simplest form it is defined as follows:

```
if (condition)
    action;
```

This means that if the condition is TRUE, only then the action is performed; otherwise no action is taken. As an example, consider

```
if (marks < 50)
    system.out.println{"3rd division");
```

The **int** variable **marks** is used to store the marks of the student, and this statement is a part of generating result. The brackets around the condition are necessary; within them, the condition itself can be a very long statement like this:

```
if (    (sub1marks >= 50)   &&
    (sub2marks >= 50) &&
    (sub3marks >= 50) &&
    (sub4marks >= 50) &&
    (sub5marks >= 50) )
System.out.println("Passed");
```

where && means and, and > = means greater than or equal to. Observe how brackets are carefully arranged so that you can match the opening-closing pairs clearly. Similarly, the action part can also be complicated, typically consisting of two or more statements like this:

```
if (marks < 50)
    {
    System.out.println("Failed");
    TotalFailures = TotalFailures + I;
    }
```

In which case all statements are put one after another in the curly brackets {and}, so that, for the 'if' statement, it is like only a single action, from { to }. One of these statements can itself be another 'if' statement like this:

```
if (marks >= 50)
    {
    System.out.println("Passed");
    if (marks >= 60)
        System.out.println("in First Class");
    }
```

This can happen any number of times:

```
if (marks >= 50)
    {
    System.out.println("Passed");
    if (marks >= 60)
        {
        System.out.println(" in First Class");
        if (marks >= 70)
            System.out.println
                (" With Distinction");
        }
    }
```

The else Part

In Java, the 'if' construct can be used in two different styles:

```
    if (condition)
        action1;  // condition evaluates to true.
```

or

```
    if (condition)
        action1;  // condition evaluates to true.
```

else

```
        action2;  // condition evaluates to false.
```

You may write

```
    if (marks < 50)
    System.out.println("Failed");
```

else

```
    System.out.println("Passed");
```

Such a statement is symmetric in the sense that you can achieve the same effect even if you write

```
if (marks >= 50)
```

```
        System.out.println("Passed");
    else
        System.out.println("Failed");
```

Consider now

```
        if (x > y)
            x = y;
        y = 0;
```

In this case y = 0; has nothing to do with the 'if' above. Irrespective of the condition (x > y) it will always be evaluated. If you want to set y = 0 only if x > y, then you should put the last two lines between the curly brackets like this:

```
    if (x > y)
        {
        x = y;
        y = 0;
        }
```

Now another example:

```
        if (condition1)
        if (condition2)
        action3;
        else
        action4;
```

The rule is that the 'else' will get attached to the nearest 'if'. With this rule, now, if condition1 is false, nothing happens. If it is true, either action3 or action4 will take place, depending upon condition2. Here action4 is an alternative to action3; only one of them would take place.

This code is quite different from the following:

```
        if (condition1)
        {
        if (condition2)
        action3;
        }
        else
        action4;
```

in which if condition1 is false, action4 will take place. If condition1 is true, then action3 will take place only if condition2 is true. When you write such codes, be careful in keeping indentation; with proper indentation both these codes would look like:

```
        if (condition1)
            if (condition2)
                action3;
            else
                action4;
```

And the other one:

```
        if (condition1)
            {
            if (condition2)
            action3;
            }
```

```
else
        action4;
```

The ?: Operator

Java provides a short hand notation for the 'if...else' statement, called the ?: operator. The statement

```
condition ? action1 : action 2;
```

is actually equivalent to

```
if (condition)
        action1;
else
        action2;
```

The **?:** operator is used when both action1 and action2 are single action statements rather than big blocks of statements enclosed in {and} brackets. This operator is generally used when you need to write a single-line code of 'if' statement. It is a single expression and can be used accordingly. For example, when x stores the maximum of a and b, using if you write

```
if (a>b)
    x = a;
else
    x = b;
```

But using ?: you write

```
x = a>b ? a : b;
```

so that x does not go inside the ?: operator, but the value calculated by ?: operator is assigned to x. Although you can always write using if...else, sometimes this operator turns out to be very handy.

The Switch Statement

The 'if' statement is useful when there are one or two actions, but is not so convenient when the actions are more. If you need to do different actions on different dates of a month, you may end up writing something like this (==) which means equal to; don't confuse it with =, which is assignment!

```
if (date == 1)
action1;
else
if (date == 2)
action2;
else
if (date == 3)
action3;
else
if (date == 4)
action4;
else
.......
```

In such a situation, it is convenient to use the switch statement as follows:

```
switch (date)
{ //  ──────────────────────  switch begins here.
```

```
        case 1:    { action1; break; }
        case 2:    { action2; break; }
        case 3:    { action3; break; }
        case4: { action4; break; }
        ......... ....................
        case 31:   { action3; break; }
        default:   { default-action; break; }
    } // ............................................. switch ends here.
```

The computer follows the case ...: parts one by one, keeping an eye on the current value of the date. If the date has value 3, for example, then the computer goes over case 1: and then skips everything between {and}. It then goes to case 2: and again does the same thing. It then goes to case 3: and realizes that this is the value of date. In this case, it follows all the statements between {and} brackets.

Here if you have included the 'break;' statement before }, the computer immediately stops further testing of cases and goes to the end of the switch statement. In case you don't mention break; as the last statement before }, the computer will keep on checking further cases down, entering into' case 4:' etc.

In case you do not have actions for every date, the computer may do the last case called default. Of course, giving default case is optional, but it is always better to have the default, at least to give a message that default case is entered (may be by mistake). This helps to detect any unexpected value given by mistake. For example, in case you set the value of date as 32 or 33, the default case will be performed. Do not forget that all the cases and their corresponding actions are enclosed in big curly brackets {and}.

Repetitions

Repeating a given task might be boring to human beings, but that is one of the great abilities due to which computers have become useful. In Java three different constructs are provided to perform repetitions, each one with a different style of telling the computer how long to perform, and when to stop. Repetition is also called a loop or looping in the language of computer science.

The while Statement

The 'while' statement has the form

```
while (condition)
    action1;
```

or, for more actions,

```
while (condition)
    {
    action1;
    action2;
    action3;
    .........
    }
```

As in the case of 'if,' the condition is a statement that evaluates to TRUE or FALSE, depending on the current values of the variables involved. The action part is repeated as long as the condition evaluates to true. This means, some of the variables must change values during the execution so that the condition becomes false at some point of time, and the statement will end. Here is an example followed by explanations, for you to understand the 'while' loop better:

```
class whileTest1
```

```
{   public static void main(String args[ ])
    {
    int i = 2;
    while (i < 15)
        {
        System.out.println(i);
        i = i * 2;
        }
    }
}
```

Its output is

```
2
4
8
```

Initially the declaration of int i is combined with the initialization statement i = 2; in a single statement int i = 2; In Java this is allowed, and is also convenient. So at the entry to 'while,' i has the value 2. the condition i < 15 is actually 2 < 15 here, which is true, and the body statements are evaluated. This prints 2, and performs i = i * 2. Recall that the i in rhs is the current value of i, which is 2. The sign * means multiplication in Java. So rhs is 2 * 2 = 4, and this value is now given to i.

Then the computer goes back to the word 'while,' and repeats the whole procedure. Now i is 4 and 4 < 15 is true, so that the value is printed and the statement i = i * 2; becomes i = 4 * 2; giving the value 8 to i. Computer prints this and then again goes back to the word 'while.' Now i is 16 and 16 < 15 is FALSE. Since the condition is FALSE, the 'while' statement is completed, without any further repetition. Thus only three values, 2, 4 and 8 are printed. One requirement of the 'while' statement is that the variables used in writing the condition must change values during the statement execution.

Another, perhaps more important requirement is that variables should change value in such a way that at some point of time, the condition will become FALSE. Otherwise the loop will continue infinitely. Consider this program:

```
class whileTest2
{   public static void main(String args[ ])
    {
    int i = 1;
    while (i ! = 6)
        {
        System.out.println(i);
        I = I + 2;
        }
    }
}
```

where i! = means not equal to in Java. The output is:

```
1
3
5
7
```

```
9
11
13
....
```

This goes on infinitely! This happens because no odd value can be 6, even if i changes each time. The right condition would have been i < 6, which will become FALSE when i becomes 7.

An important thing to remember is that there is no semicolon (;} after the condition in the 'while' statement (it was not there in 'if' statement also!}. So writing

```
while (condition);
    action1;
```

or,

```
while (condition);
    {
    action1;
    action2;
    .........
    }
```

is wrong. Actually, this semicolon makes it into two statements, and the first one causes problems as the action part is empty (absent), and the variables in the condition are not changed at all.

The DO Statement

The 'do' statement has the form

```
do
   action1;
while (condition)
```

or, for more actions,

```
do
    {
    action1;
    action2;
    action3;
    .........
    }
while (condition);
```

The condition is a statement that evaluates to TRUE or FALSE, depending on the current values of variable involved. The action part is repeated as long as the condition evaluates to TRUE. This means, some of the variables must change values during the execution so that the condition becomes FALSE at some point of time, and the statement ends.

For a 'do' loop, the action part is executed first, and then the condition is checked. This means that the actions are done at least once, irrespective of the initial values of the condition! This is the main difference between the 'while' statement and the 'do' statement. Otherwise there are not many conceptual differences between 'while' and 'do.'

The FOR Statement

The 'for' construct is convenient in representation because the three different parts of initializing variables, testing the condition, and changing variable values, are put in the header part; only the action part is in the body. A 'for' statement in Java looks like this:

```
for(initialize; condition; change) action;
```

or

```
for(initialize; condition; change)
    {
    action1;
    action2;
    .........
    }
```

The earlier program to print powers of 2 looks like this:

```
class forTest1
{
    public static void main(String args[ ])
    {
    for (int i = 2; i < 15; i = i * 2) system.out.println(i);
    }
}
```

Note that you can bring the declaration of the variable i along with its initialization inside the 'for' statement!

Many people find the 'for' statement much more convenient than using 'while' or 'do' statement. And it helps for debugging, because all the changing and controlling information is in the header line at the top. Although most of the time you will see changes in the condition variables only in the head, it is not a compulsion. The variable i in the above case can be changed inside the loop also:

```
class forTest2
{
    public static void main(string args[ ])
    {
    for (int i = 2; i < 15; i = i * 2)
        {
        system.out.println(i);
        i = i - 1;
        }
    }
}
```

It produces

```
2
3
5
9
```

as expected (you may examine the code line by line).

You may have different varieties:

```
class forTest3
{
    public static void main(String args[ ])
    {
    for (int i = 30; i > 5; ) // Last part empty.
        {
        System.out.println(i);
        i = i -5;
        }
    }
}
```

Output:

```
30
25
20
15
10
```

Or

```
class forTest4
{
    public static void main(string args[ ])
    {
    int i = 2;
    for ( ; i < 30; )
        // First and last part empty.
    {
    System.out.println(i);
    i = i * 2;
    }
}
```

Object Oriented Programming

I am quite sure that you must have heard about it without knowing about it. Well, Objected Oriented Programming, or simply OOPs, as it is called is the simplest form of programming. I wish all the programming for the computer was designed like this. All OOPs languages provides simple constructs to enable you to express your natural ideas efficiently. They also allow you to talk about various objects. They allow you to classify objects according to their properties and behaviours into various different classes. They allow you to define how your objects look, how your objects behave and also to define new objects as improvements or modification of old objects. They also allow your objects to pass messages to each other and get the work done in a systematic manner.

In fact, they allow you to write down programs that model natural behaviours and attributes in the best possible way, without regard to the capacity and limitations of your computers. Java is one of the OOP language, providing all these facilities. Java, is the latest OOP language, and so is one of the most advanced amongst all available OOP languages.

Classes and Objects

Object is like a thing which can do some work for you. A man is an object; so also are animals. How do these objects do your work? By your request! If you have any health problem, you go to a doctor and ask him to do the needful. You can think of the set (or collection) of all doctors as a set of men with special attributes and behaviours. Such a set, with attributes and behaviours together, is called a Class. Members of a class are called objects of the class. There is a class of doctors, a class of lawyers, a class of teachers, a class of bankers, and so on! All with different types of attributes and different behaviours. There is also a class of just human beings. All these other classes are derived from it.

An object of a class is also called an instance of that class. A doctor, Mr X, is one instance of the class of doctors; another doctor, Mr Y, is another instance of the class of doctors; a third doctor, Mr Z, is a third instance of the class of doctors; and so on. All these Mr X, Y and Z show characteristics of doctors, yet they are different objects. It is interesting to note the analogy of an object and its class with a variable and its type.

You have already learnt about the numeric types—byte, short, int, long, float and double, and other types char and boolean. Each of them actually is better described as a class rather than a type. The attributes of int are different from those of the long (their ranges are different), although their behaviours are same.

On the other hand, the class int and the class double have different attributes as well as different behaviours. In case of int, you have the method of calculating remainder through the operation of %, which is absent in the case of doubles. Hence, note that although all of them represent mathematical numbers, they are different classes. Each one can be viewed as a class, with its own attributes and behaviours. Similarly, even char and boolean can also be viewed as classes.

From the class of teachers, you may derive a subclass of principals. This mechanism of deriving a subclass from a given class is unlimited. All objects in a class share certain attributes and behaviours, which actually characterize (define) that class. In a subclass, all attributes and behaviours of the original class are adopted; in addition, some more attributes and behaviours get added that are not found in the original class.

Different additions define different subclasses. After you define a subclass, the original class is called its superclass. As an example, you can think of a general class of all numbers, with the four arithmetic operations +, -, * and / as methods indicating behaviour. Then you can view the fixed point numbers and floating point numbers as two subclasses of numbers.

The fixed point subclass has an additional operation % defined for its objects, which is not available to all the numbers. The floating point class objects can have scientific notation using E, which is not common to all numbers. You may go further from these two subclasses by defining byte, short, int and long as subclasses of fixed point numbers, and float and double as subclasses of floating point numbers. Each subclass has certain special properties (at least a different range) in addition to the properties of its superclass.

Here are the Java declarations for the class date:

```
class date
    {
    int day;
    int month;
    int year;
    }
```

or, you can combine to get

```
    class date
```

```
{
int day, month, year;
}
```

This is just the declaration about the attributes, or the data part of the date class. There is another part of behavioural description, called methods. What operations do you need to perform on a date? To set a date, to get a date, to print a date, to get the next date, to get the previous date, and so on. In Java, you need to provide a method to do each one of these operations. With methods, the definition of date class would look like:

```
class date
    {
    // ——Data (attributes).
    int day, month, year;
    // ——Methods (behaviour) .
    void set-date(int dd, int mm, int yy)
        { }; // Empty body for the time being.
    void print_date()
        { }; // Empty body for the time being.
    II Only two methods for the time being.
    }
```

For setting the given date, you need to supply the values of the day (dd), the month (mm) and the year (yy). This is indicated by declaring these three variables inside ( ) brackets after the name set-date(). For printing, you don't have to supply anything; you use the already set values. Both, the data and the methods, declared in this way are called members of the class.

Creating Objects

Once you have defined the class date, you can declare objects of that class. For example, when you define a class student (yes, students are also objects and they form a class), you may use the date like this:

```
class student
    {
    // ———————— Data
        String name;
        date birth_date, joining_date;
    // ————————Methods
    // ——No method for the time being.
    }
```

In this class there are two date objects, birth-date and joining_date. You may set the birth_date in the class student by sending a message to the birth-date object. This is done by writing a statement like

```
birth_date.set_date(20, 8, 1986);
```

The objects birth-date and joining-date are associated with two classes. One is the date class, which acts as their type; you say these two are instances of the date class. The other class is student for which these act as data. You say these objects are data of the student class. This situation in general occurs every time. An object is an instance of some class (type-variable relation) and is also used as data in some other class.

In Java, everything you write, either data or methods, always resides inside some class. In Pascal, FORTRAN, C, C++, such a restriction was not there, because these were not strict OOP languages. Due to this reason, in the earlier programs you had to declare some dummy class called test1.

The New Operator

When you declare an object of any class in Java, it is merely a declaration like

```
date birth_date;
```

but the object is not created in the memory of the computer. Java expects you to explicitly create it using the new operator as:

```
birth_date = new date();
```

After this, the required memory is allocated and this object birth_date is created. Note the () parentheses after the word date. These are essential. Do not forget to use the new operator, and don't forget the brackets () !

After you create an object, you can use it. The sequence of your statements should be:

```
date birth_date;
//........other code
birth_date = new date();
//........other code
birth_date.set-date(26, 8, 1986);
```

In Java, you may combine the declaration and creation in a single statement as:

```
date birth_date = new date();
```

You should try to combine in this way so that the chances of forgetting the creation are reduced. Note that, in the Java terminology, creation is also called initialization of an object.

As another special concession, whenever you deal with a pre-defined type, Java allows you to combine all the three actions (declare, create and set) into a single statement as

```
int x = 100; // new is not required !
```

Operations on Objects

Now I discuss various aspects of defining and using of methods in Java.

Consider a file testl.java containing the following code:

```
class date
{
// ——————————————— Data (attributes) .
int day, month, year;
// ————————————————Methods (behaviour).
void print-date()
    {
    system.out.println
    (day + "-" + month + "-" + year);
    }
void set_date(int dd, int mm, int yy)
    {
    day = dd; month = mm; year = yy;
    };
// Only two methods for the time being.
}
```

This is a complete definition for the class date. The date class has 3 variables (data items) of int type, called day, month and year. Setting a date is setting values for these data. There is a method set-date to do this setting. There is another method print-date to print the values of these variables. The actions of these methods are quite simple. The *header* of a method is the part before {. The body of a method is the part from {to}. The print-date method has nothing between (and) in its header. It doesn't generate any new object, and so the word 'void' precedes its name in its header. It just uses a println statement in its body. The method set-date needs to be supplied with the three values for the day, the month and the year variables. This is done by declaring three int variables in its header as shown. These variables are called parameters in programming languages.

These are also called dummy parameters, or just dummies, because it doesn't matter what name you use in place for dd, mm, yy while passing a message (invoking) to this method. You may pass actual int numbers, or int variables like xx, or int expressions like xx + yy in place of each of these dummies. Without dummies the header looks like

```
void set_date(int, int, int)
```

This is called the *signature* of the method in Java. Observe the message passed to this method in the testl class below. The dot of d0.set_date means you are talking about the set_date method of the d0 object. If you want the same method for some other d1 object, you would have used d1.set-date instead.

```
class testl
    {
    public static void main(String args[ ])
    {
    date d0 - new date();
    d0 set_date(20,8,1986) ;
    // setting to 20 Aug 1986
    d0.print_date();
    }
```

The first line of the main method in the test1 class declares d0 as a date object and creates it using 'new'. In the next line a message is passed to d0 to set its date to 20-8-1986. Next, a message is passed to print the set date. After, compiling and running this program, you get this output

```
20-8-1986
```

Now modify test1 class as

```
class testl
{
public static void main(String args[ ])
    {
    date d0 = new date()
    date d1 = new date();
    d0 set_date(20,8,1986);
    d1 = d0;
    d0.print_date();
    d1print_date();
    }
}
```

After, compiling and running it gives

```
20-8-1986
20-8-1986
```

Observe that you have defined another object d1 of class date, created it through 'new', but instead of setting a date for it using set_date method, assigned or copied the d0 date onto it. When you printed, both the dates were alike as expected.

Parameters

The standard way to pass information to any method is to declare parameters (dummies) in its heading and put values in the corresponding places while passing message to the method. The set-date method of the date class has three parameters dd, mm, and yy, all expecting an int type information, which will be assigned to the class variables date, month and year respectively during execution of the method set-date.

Thus you declare

```
void set_date(int dd, int mm, int yy)
```

and pass a message like

```
d0.set_date(20,8,1986);
```

Note that these parameters can be of any pre defined types: byte, short, int, long, float, double, char or Boolean. As such you need not always pass a literal value, but you can write a variable whose value will be used. Thus, if you have declared int xx; in your program, and have assigned value 20 to it, you can use the variable name xx in place of 20 and write the message like

```
d0.set_date(xx,8,1986);
```

You can say that whatever has been put here, will be assigned to the dummies dd, mm and yy. So writing 20 would be equivalent to the assignment xx = 20; and writing xx would be equivalent to the assignment dd = xx; in which xx appears in the rhs, and so, its value is used. Thus, both are equivalent.

As a matter of fact, you can write expression like 10+10, or 4+10+6 also. This is perfectly like an assignment. Other than the pre defined types, the parameters can be of some other class also. For example you may have some method declaration like

```
xyz(date dd11, dd22)
```

to which you may pass your dates d0 and d1. Note that, for these objects of general (other than pre defined) classes, it is not possible to assign a value, or an expression, because no such value or expressions are possible. The only thing you can put is the current value of some object of that class, like d0 and d1 here.

Returning Values

In the previous section you have seen that by declaring parameters you can pass information to a method while sending a message to it. But this is only a one way communication. The method cannot pass information back to the message sender through these parameters. Let us see how you can pass information back from a method to its message sender.

If you are dealing with a class of mathematical objects, you may need to define a method that calculates the square (third power) of a given number, and sends it back (returns) to the caller (message sender). In Java this is possible to do using the return statement as follows:

```
class testmath
{
// ————————Data (attributes) .
// ————————Methods (behaviour)
```

```
double testsquare(double nn)
    // return type double; not void.
    {
    return(nn*nn);
    }
    // Only one methods for the time being. }

class test1
{
public static void main(String args[ ])
    {
    testmath mm = new testmath();
    double xx;
    xx = mm.testsquare (3.0);
    System.out.println (xx);
    }
}
```

The output:

```
27
```

The method testsquare uses a statement return(...); to return the value of the expression in the brackets. You may directly give the expression like nn*nn as you have done above, in case the calculations are straightforward. Otherwise, you may use some method of calculations that stores the value into some temporary variable, and then put that variable as shown here:

```
double testsquare(double nn)
    {
    double temp;
    temp = nn*nn;
    return(temp);
    }
```

The calculations may be of any complexity, which might create some object of a class rather than a simple type. For example, you may develop a method to calculate the next date of a given date inside our class date. Such a method will have a code like this:

```
date next-date()
// return type is date; not double or void.
    {
    date temp = new date();
    // temp stores the calculated next date.
    // Do the actual calculations here ......
    return(temp);
    };
```

And you may call it by writing like this:

```
d1 = d0.next_date( );
```

so that d1 stores the next date of d0,

The return statement can occur anywhere in the method, any number of times. When it is executed, the control immediately transfers back to the message sender (invoker), and the code below the return statement is not executed.

For example,

```
class test1
    (
    int max(int a, int b)
        {
        return(a);
        return(b);
        }
    }
```

gives an error

```
test1.java:6: Statement not reached,
        return(b);
    1 error
```

If you intend to calculate maximum of two numbers, you may write like this':

```
class cc1
    {
    int max(int a, int b)
        {
        if (a > b)
            return(a) ;
        else
            return(b);
        }
    }
```

Depending on the values of a and b only one of the two return statements will be executed, After it the control will go back without any regard to the remaining code, The following modification will also have the same effect:

```
class cc1
    {
    int max(int a, int b)
        {
        if (a > b) return(a);
        return(b);
        }
    }
```

If the given 'a' is bigger than the given 'b,' the first return(a) statement will be executed, and the control will immediately pass back to the message sender, thereby the remaining statement return(b) will be automatically ignored.

On the other hand, if the given 'a' is lesser or equal to the given 'b,' the if condition will not allow the first return(a) statement to be executed. The control then goes to the next statement, which will correctly return 'b.'

Returning More Values

In Java, the only way to pass back information to the message sender (invoker) is through the return statement in the method code. But this allows you to pass exactly one object. What would you do in case you need to pass back more than one object? To appreciate the problem, consider a method get_xy() that calculates the x and y coordinates of a given point. The point is identified by both x and y coordinates together, and so each time you need to calculate both of them and return the calculated values from get_xy() method.

In Java, you cannot do so using two parameters, or two return statements. The solution lies in learning to think in an object oriented fashion. If the x and y (or any two or more) objects are totally unrelated, the solution is simple. Define a separate method to calculate each of them, and use an appropriate method as and when you need. So here, you may define get_x() and get_y() separately. But when the (two or more) objects to be returned are related to each other in some way, try to explain that relation.

In the example above, since these are coordinates of some point, both of them coexist. You should then define a class called 'point,' something like this:

```
class point
  {
  double x, y;
  //..........other things.
  }
```

and then define the method as get_point() rather than a method called get_xy(), which calculates both x and y coordinates of some point object, and returns this point object. The code would look something like this:

```
point get_point(. ..)
// This returns a point object.
  {
  point temp;
  //......actual code
      temp.x = . . . ;
      temp.y = . . . ;
  return(temp);
  }
```

which you can invoke by

```
point pp = new point();
//.....other code.
pp = get_point(...);
```

So if you are trapped in a situation in which you need to return more objects simultaneously, check the possibility of some non object oriented thinking, and try to avoid it.

Indirect Returning

In Java, it is possible to modify the object passed as a parameter. Thus, if you can have a method modify_point(point p) in which you may do the necessary calculations, and finally assign values to x and y of p. Thus

```
void modify_point{point p)
  {
  //  . .  .  .  your code.
      p.x = . . . ;
```

```
    p.y = . . . ;
  }
```

which you can be invoked by

```
point pp = new point();
//.......other code...
modify_point(pp);
```

Note carefully the difference between this method and get_point method above. Although this method works good for user defined (general) objects, it does not work for the pre defined types (byte, short...). So better avoid the style of returning values by using this indirect method.

The THIS Facility

Java provides a facility to refer to the object inside a method for which it (the method) is invoked. This is done by using the word **this**. For example, when you write

```
d0.set-date();
```

the **this** inside set-date() would refer to d0 object. On the other hand, if you have written

```
d1.set-date();
```

the word *this* would then mean d1 (and not d0) object. Generally the facility of **this** is required when you deal with two or more objects of the same class, and the method of one of them is invoked. As an example, consider a method to calculate the days elapsed between two dates:

```
int elapsed(date oth); {...};
```

This method is a member of class date. It returns the elapsed days as an int value. When d0 and d1 are two dates for whom you want to calculate the days elapsed, you may give a message like:

```
xx = d0.elapsed(d1);
```

where xx is an int variable in which you collect the result. Here you have invoked the elapsed() for d0. So inside the elapsed() method, the word **this** refers to d0 and the parameter oth refers to d1 you have passed. Since you have invoked elapsed of d0, you do not have to pass it as a parameter; system already knows about it.

Note that, since both d0 and d1 are date objects, you may alternatively pass the following message to do the same job:

```
xx = d1.elapsed(d0);
```

In this case, of course, the word **this** inside the elapsed() method would refer to d1. Using the word **this**, you may write elapsed as something like this:

```
elapsed(date oth)
    {
    if (this.year == oth.year)
        {
        //.......... details here. .
        };
    else
        if (this.year < oth.year)
        {
        // ..........details here...
        };
    // ..............details here.
    } // end of elapsed
```

CHAPTER 2

Overloading

Consider the date class defined earlier:

```
class date
   {
   // —Data (attributes).
   int dayJ month, year;
   // —Methods (behaviour).
   void set_date(int dd, int mm, int yy)
       {
       day = dd; month = mm; year = yy;
       };
   void print-date()
       {
       System.out.println
           (day + "-" + month + "-" + year);
       }
   // Only two methods for the time being.
   }
```

It has a method set_date, which takes all the three int values and sets the date. But often you might want to set a new date of the same month (and year), or often the year is the same although day and month keep changing. In such a situation, it becomes quite boring to supply 1996, 1996, 1996 each time! Fortunately, Java provides a facility called **overloading** a method that allows you to define the dates using default values.

Consider this method

```
void set_date(int dd, int mm)
    {
    day = dd; month = mm; year = 1996;
    };
```

It has the same name set_date, but has only two parameters for day and month. This method can reside in the date class along with the other method, without causing any confusion. If you pass a message to set the date of some object d0 using

```
d0.set-date(8,10,1996);
```

the system uses old set-date with 3 parameters. If you just write

```
d0.set-date(8,10);
```

the system understands your intention of using the newly defined set-date and goes accordingly. You may also define yet another set-date method as

```
void set_date(int dd)
    {
    day = dd; month = 10; year = 1996;
    };
```

and if you just give the call

```
d0.set-date(8);
```

it will set the date properly. All these overloaded methods will set the date to 8-10-1996. By writing multiple such methods, you are overloading their common name. In this case you have overloaded the set-date method. Note that all the overloaded methods should reside in the same class, and each one should have a different signature (style of parameters) than the other. The signature differs even if the number of parameters are the same but their types or classes are different. As an example, all the following methods have different signatures:

```
Set_date(int, int, int);
Set_date(double, int, int);
Set_date(int, double, int);
Set_date(int, int, double);
Set_date(double, double, int);
Set_date(int, double, double);
Set_date(double, double, double);
Set_date(int, int);
Set_date(double, int);
Set_date(int, double);
Set_date(double, double);
Set_date(int);
Set_date(double);
Set_date();
```

Overloading methods provide convenience due to two reasons:

1. You have a choice of different signatures.
2. After defining the class you can always modify it by introducing one more overloading which adds a facility without disturbing earlier working code.

Constructor

In Java, a new object is created when you use the operator called new. During this creation, the system invokes (and executes) a method called constructor, by which it creates appropriate memory for the object. You may not have written this constructor, but the system has done that job for you. Note that the constructor has the same name as the class. In Java, you can also define your own constructor. This will have the same name as of the class, and it will do all the things you want it to do, in addition to the things done by the system's default constructor.

As an example, our set-date method in the date class actually does the job of setting the date, and should have been a constructor. You need just to change its name to date and remove the word 'void.' With this, our class date looks like this:

```
class date
    {
    // Data (attributes).
    int day, month, year;
    // Methods (behaviour).
    date(int dd, int mm, int yy)
    // constructor
        {
        day = dd; month = mm; year = yy;
        };
    void print-date()
```

```
        {
        System.out.println
            (day + "-" + month + "-" + year);
        }
  // Only two methods for the time being.
  }
```

Other than its special name, the constructor is just like any other method in Java. You can also overload the constructor. With some of them, the class of date looks like this

```
class date
{
// Data (attributes).
int day, month, year;
// Methods (behaviour).
// One method & 3 constructors.
date(int dd,int mm, int yy)
// constructor 1
{
day = dd; month = mm; year = yy;
} ;
date(int dd) // ————————-constructor 2
{
day = dd; month = 10; year = 1996;
} ;
date(int dd, int mm) // ——————constructor 3
{
day = dd; month = mm; year = 1996;
} ;
void print-date()
   {
   System.out.println
       (day + "-" + month + "-" + year);
   }
}
```

The FINALIZE Method

Java provides a facility to define a special method called **finalize** in every class that you define. During run time, Java automatically calls this method whenever it is about to reclaim the memory allocated to an object of the class.

In the finalize method, you should: Write code to release any external resource like an open file or a loaded special font, which otherwise would remain hanging forever. Also, you do not have to release or free any memory because Java anyway does that for you. Generally you may not need this facility in your day-to-day programming, but in case a need arises, it is there. The method looks like this:

```
finalize( ...)
{
```

```
//. ...write your code.
}
```

Static Data and Methods

In general you define a class (date for example) and declare, create and use objects of this class in some other classes (d0 and d1 in the test1 class for example). Each of these objects have their own data and methods. The value of d0.month might be 10 whereas the value of d1.month be 6 at the same time. When you write d0.set_date, you are using the set-date method of d0, which is expected to change the d0.day, d0.month, and d0.year values. It would not touch the same values of d1, i.e. d1.day, d1.month, and d1.year.

However, it is possible to define some data and methods in a class as common data/methods for all objects of that class. A common example of this is a class representing a family. All the members would have the same surname, and there is no point in declaring the surname as an object variable. It should be defined as a class variable, common to all objects of the class.

Another example is the count of the number of objects of the class, of say lawyers. This count needs to be defined as a variable of the whole class, and should show the same value to all objects of the class. In order to do this, you need to put a word 'static' before such a datum (variable or object). When dealing with the students' marks obtained in a subject, the maximum possible marks are the same for all of them, and should be treated as the class datum rather than the datum for individual students.

You may define the class marksheet something like this:

```
class marksheet
{
static int max_marks;
int marks_obtained;
//.....other things
  }
```

And you should initialize this variable max_marks by stating

```
marksheet.max_marks = 100;
```

somewhere in your code. You can also combine the declaration and initialization in one stroke by defining the class like this:

```
class marksheet
{
static int max_marks = 100;
// defined and initialized also.
int marks-obtained;
//.....other things
}
```

To illustrate the point, consider this example. For an organization, the foundation date of the organization is the same for all employees. So while defining the class employee, this should be declared as the class variable. This is done by putting a word 'static' as:

```
class employee
```

CHAPTER 2

```
{
// ............................Data
String name;
date birth_date, joining-date;
static date FoundationDate;
// ...................... Methods
//...........No method for the time being.
}
```

If you have declared a variable ee1 of the employee class somewhere in your code like

```
employee ee1;
```

and you want to set the FoundationDate, you can write

```
employee.FoundationDate.set_date(20,8,1986);
```

When you print or do anything with the static variable, you can use the class name instead of the object name. However, this is not a compulsion. A class datum is also available for the object datum, and writing

```
ee1.FoundationDate.set-date(20,8,1986);
```

is also allowed! Similar remarks apply to static methods also.

Here is a more detailed example using methods:

```
class cc1
{
void xx()
{System.out.println("xx invoked"); }
static void yy()
{System.out.println("yy invoked"); }
    }
class testl
{
public static void main(String args[1)
{
cclobj1c = new cc1();
System.out.print
("Using object obj1. ...");
objl.xx();
System.out.print
( "Using object obj1 " ) ;
objl.yy();
System.out.print
("Using class ccl. ...");
cc 1 .yy ( ) ; } }
```

Output:

```
Using object objl. ...xx invoked
Using object obj 1: yy invoked
Using class ccl.....yy invoked
```

The method yy0 is static, and so, can be invoked either by sending message to an object or to the class, as shown. On the other hand, xx() is a non-static method. If you try to access a non-static datum or method by sending message to the class instead of an object, the compiler detects this error:

```
testl.java:20: Can't make static reference to method void xx() in class cc1.
Cc1.xx();
^
1 error
```


Now here is another aspect of 'static' through an example:

```
class cc1
{
int value;
void yy()
{
system.out.println("value = " + value);
    }
class cc2
{
static ccl iiii, hhhh; // Declaration.
// -—Creation inside a block.
static {hhhh=new ccl(); hhhh.value = 4;}
// --Creation inside another block.
static {iiii=new cc1(); iiii.value=5;}
    }
class testl
{
public static void main(String args[ ])
    {
cc2 obj2 = new cc2();
system.out.print
("Using object obj2 and object hhhh");
obj2:hhhh.yy();
system.out.print
("Using class cc2 and object iiii");
cc2 .iiii. yy ( ) ;
    }
}
```

Output:

```
Using object obj2 and object hhhh value =4
Using class cc2 and object iiii value =5
```

Class cc2 has data hhhh and iiii of class cc1. Both are defined static. Both are declared at one place, and initialized at other places inside static blocks.

This is something new and so observe it carefully. Such a static block can appear anywhere in the class after the declaration of a static datum. It is not attached to any method of the class. You can have multiple such static blocks to initialize more data, at different places inside the class as shown in the example above.

You can also put all of them in a single static block without affecting the output, like:

```
class cc2
{
static ccl iiii, hhhh; // Declaration.
// —Creation inside a block.
static
{
hhhh = new cc1(); hhhh.value = 4;
iiii = new cc1 ( ); iiii.value = 5;
} // end of static block
    }
```

CHAPTER 3

Collecting Objects

In this chapter you will read about:

- Introduction to objects.
- Lterator and the Enhanced For Statement.
- AutoBoxing and Unboxing.
- Utilities.

Introduction

Applications often must manage collections of objects. Although you can use arrays for this purpose, they are not always a good choice. For example, arrays have fixed sizes, making it tricky to determine an optimal size when you need to store a variable number of objects. Also, arrays can be indexed by integers only, which make them unsuitable for mapping arbitrary objects to other objects.

Java's standard class library provides the Collections Framework and legacy APIs to manage collections on behalf of applications. The *Collections Framework* is a standard architecture for representing and manipulating *collections,* which are groups of objects stored in instances of classes designed for this purpose. After presenting an overview of this framework's architecture, this section introduces you to the various types (mainly located in the Java. util package) that contribute to this architecture.

Overview

The Collection Framework's architecture is divided into three sections:

- *Core interfaces:* The framework provides core interfaces for manipulating collections independently of their implementations.
- *Implementation classes:* The framework provides classes that provide different core interface implementations to address performance and other requirements.
- *Utility classes:* The framework provides utility classes whose methods let you sort arrays, obtain synchronized collections, and perform other operations.

The core interfaces include java.lang.Iterable, Collection, List, Set, SortedSet, NavigableSet, Queue, Deque, Map, SortedMap, and NavigableMap. Collection extends Iterable; List, Set, and Queue each extend Collection; SortedSet extends Set; NavigableSet extends SortedSet; Deque extends Queue; SortedMap extends Map; and NavigableMap extends SortedMap.

The framework's implementation classes include ArrayList, LinkedList, TreeSet, HashSet, LinkedHashSet, EnumSet, PriorityOueue, ArrayDeque, TreeMap, HashMap, LinkedHashMap, IdentityHashMap, WeakHashMap, and EnumMap. The name of each concrete class ends in a core interface name, identifying the core interface on which it is based.

The framework's implementation classes also include the abstract AbstractCollection, AbstractList, AbstractSequentialList, AbstractSet, AbstractOueue, and AbstractMap classes. These classes offer skeletal implementations of the core interfaces to facilitate the creation of concrete implementation classes.

Finally, the framework provides two utility classes: Arrays and Collections.

Comparable Versus Comparator

A collection implementation stores its elements in some *order* (arrangement). This order may be unsorted, or it may be sorted according to some criterion (such, as alphabetical, numerical, or chronological).

A sorted collection implementation defaults to storing its elements according to their *natural ordering.* For example.'the natural ordering of String objects is *lexicographic or dictionary* (also known as alphabetical) order.

A collection cannot rely on equals () to dictate natural ordering because this method can only determine if two elements are equivalent. Instead, element classes must implement the Java.lang.Comparable<T> interface and its int compareTo( ) method.

A sorted collection uses compareTo( ) to determine the natural ordering of this method's element argument o in a collection. compareTo( ) compares argument o with the current element (which is the element on which compareTo( ) was called) and does the following:

- It returns a negative value when the current element should precede o.

- It returns a zero value when the current element and o are the same.
- It returns a positive value when the current element should succeed o.

When you need to implement Comparable's compareTo( ) method, there are some rules that you must follow. These rules, listed next, for implementing the equals ( ) method:

- *compareTo( ) must be reflexive:* For any nonnull reference value x, x. compareTo(x) must return 0.
- *compareTo( ) must be symmetric.* For any nonnull reference values x andy, x.compareTo(y) = = -y.compareTo(x) musthold.
- *compareTo ( ) must be transitive.* For any nonnull reference values x, y, and z, if < x. compareTo (y) > 0 is true, and if y.compareTo(z) > 0 is true, then x.compareTo(z) > 0 must also be true.

Also, compareTo( ) should throw NullPointerException when the null reference is passed to this method. However, you do not need to check for null because this method throws NullPointerException when it attempts to access a null reference's members.

You might occasionally need to store in a collection objects that are sorted in some order that differs from their natural ordering. In this case, you would supply a comparator to provide that ordering.

A *comparator is* an object whose class implements the Comparator interface. This interface, whose generic type is Comparator<T>, provides the following pair of methods:

- int compare (T o1, T o2) compares both arguments for order. This method returns 0 when ol equals o2, a negative value when ol is less than 02, and a positive value when ol is greater than 02.
- boolean equals (Object o) returns true when o "equals" this Comparator in that o is also a Comparator and imposes the same ordering. Otherwise, this method returns false.

Iterable and Collection

Most of the core interfaces are rooted in Iterable and its Collection subinterface. Their generic types are Iterable<T> and Collection<E>.

Iterable describes any object that can return its contained objects in some sequence. This interface declares an Iterator<T> iterator () method that returns an Iterator instance for iterating over all the contained objects.

Collection represents a collection of objects that are known as *elements.* This interface provides methods that are common to the Collection subinterfaces on which many collections are based. The following table describes these methods.

Table Collection Methods

Method	Description
boolean add(E e)	Add element e to this collection. Return true if this collection was modified as a result; otherwise, return false. (Attempting to add e to a collection that does not permit duplicates and already contains a same-valued element results in e not being added.) This method throws java.lang. UnsupportedOperationException when add( )is not supported, ClassCastException when e's class is not appropriate for this collection, java.lang.IllegalArgumentException when some property of e prevents it from being added to this collection, java.lang.NullPointerException when e contains the null reference and this collection does not support null elements,

	and java.lang.IllegalStateException when the element cannot be added at this time because of insertion restrictions. IllegalStateException signals that a method has been invoked at an illegal or inappropriate time. In other words, the Java environment or Java application is not in an appropriate state for the requested operation. It is often thrown when you try to add an element to a bounded queue (a queue with a maximum length) and the queue is full.
boolean addAll(Collection<? extends E> c)	Add all elements of collection c to this collection. Return true if this collection was modified as the result; otherwise, return false. This method throws UnsupportedOperationException when this collection does not support addAllQ, ClassCastException when the class of one of c's elements is inappropriate for this collection, IllegalArgumentException when some property of an element prevents it from being added to this collection, NullPointerException when c contains the null reference or when one of its elements is null and this collection does not support null elements, and IllegalStateException when not all the elements can be added at this time because of insertion restrictions.
void clearQ	Remove all elements from this collection. This method throws UnsupportedOperationException when this collection does not support clear().
boolean contains(Object o)	Return true when this collection contains o; otherwise, return false. This method throws ClassCastException when the class of o is inappropriate for this collection, and NullPointerException when o contains the null reference and this collection does not support null elements.
boolean containsAll(Collection<?> c)	Return true when this collection contains all the elements that are contained in the collection specified by c; otherwise, return false. This method throws ClassCastException when the class of one of c's elements is inappropriate for this collection, and NullPointerException when c contains the null reference or when one of its elements is null and this collection does not support null elements.
boolean equals(Object o)	Compare o with this collection and return true when o equals this collection; otherwise, return false.
int hashCode( )	Return this collection's hash code. Equal collections have equal hash codes.
boolean isEmpty( )	Return true when this collection contains no elements; otherwise, return false.
Iterator<E> iterator( )	Return an Iterator instance for iterating over all of the elements contained in this collection. There are no guarantees concerning the order in which the elements are returned (unless this collection is an instance of some class that provides a guarantee). This Iterable method is redeclared in Collection for convenience.
boolean remove(Object o)	Remove the element identified as o from this collection. Return true when the element is removed; otherwise, return false. This method'throws UnsupportedOperationException when this collection does not support remove( ), ClassCastException when the class of o is inappropriate for this

Method	Description
	collection, and NullPointerException when o contains the null reference and this collection does not support null elements.
boolean removeAll(Collection<?> c)	Remove all the elements from this collection that are also contained in collection c. Return true when this collection is modified by this operation; otherwise, return false. This method throws UnsupportedOperationException when this collection does not support removeAHQ, ClassCastException when the class of one of c's elements is inappropriate for this collection, and NullPointerException when c contains the null reference or when one of its elements is null and this collection does not support null elements.
boolean retainAll(Collection<?> c)	Retain all the elements in this collection that are also contained in collection c. Return true when this collection is modified by this operation; otherwise, return false. This method throws UnsupportedOperationException when this collection does not support retainAll( ), ClassCastException when the class of one of c's elements is inappropriate for this collection, and NullPointerException when c contains the null reference or when one of its elements is null and this collection does not support null elements.
int size( )	Return the number of elements contained in this collection, or Java. lang. Integer.MAX_VALUE when there are more than Integer.MAX_VALUE elements contained in the collection.
Object[ ] toArray( )	Return an array containing all the elements stored in this collection. If this collection makes any guarantees as to what order its elements are returned in by its iterator, this method returns the elements in the same order. The returned array is "safe" in that no references to it are maintained by this collection. (In other words, this method allocates a new array even when this collection is backed by an array.) The caller can safely modify the returned array.
<T> T[ ] toArray(T[ ] a)	Return an array containing all the elements in this collection; the runtime type of the returned array is that of the specified array. If the collection fits in the specified array, it is returned in the array. Otherwise, a new array is allocated with the runtime type of the specified array and the size of this collection. This method throws NullPointerException when null is passed to a, and java.lang.ArrayStoreException when a's runtime type is not a supertype of the runtime type of every element in this collection.

The above table reveals three exceptional things abput various Collection methods. First, some methods can throw instances of the UnsupportedOperationException class. For example, add() throws UnsupportedOperationException when you attempt to add an object to an *immutable* (unmodifiable) collection.

Second, some of Collection's methods can throw instances of the ClassCastException class. For example, removeQ throws ClassCastException when you attempt to remove an entry (also known as mapping) from a tree-based map whose keys are Strings, but specify a non-String key instead.

Finally, Collection's add( ) and addAll( ) methods throw IllegalArgumentException instances when some *property* (attribute) of the element to be added prevents it from being added to this collection. For example, a third-party collection class's add( ) and addAll( ) methods might throw this exception when they detect negative Integer values.

Iterator and the Enhanced For Statement

By extending Iterable, Collection inherits that interface's iterator( ) method, which makes it possible to iterate over a collection, iterator( ) returns an instance of a class that implements the Iterator interface, whose generic type is expressed as Iterator<E> and which declares the following three methods:

- boolean hasNext( ) returns true when this Iterator instance has more elements to return; otherwise, this method returns false.
- E next( ) returns the next element from the collection associated with this Iterator instance, or throws java.util.NoSuchElementException when there are no more elements to return.
- void remove( ) removes the last element returned by next() from the collection associated with this Iterator instance. This method can be called only once per next() call. The behavior of an Iterator instance is unspecified when the underlying collection is modified while iteration is in progress in any way other than by calling remove( ). This method throws UnsupportedOperationException when it is not supported by this Iterator, and IllegalStateException when remove () has been called without a previous call to next( ) or when multiple remove () calls occur with no intervening next () calls.

The following example shows you how to iterate over a collection after calling iterator () to return an Iterator instance:

```
Collection<String> col = ... // This code does not compile because of the
"...".
// Add elements to col.
Iterator iter = col.iterator( );
while (Iter.hasNext( ))
    System.out.println(iter.next());
```

The while loop repeatedly calls the iterator's hasNext( ) method to determine whether or not iteration should continue, and (if it should continue) the next( ) method to return the next element from the associated collection.

Because this idiom is commonly used, Java 5 introduced syntactic sugar to the for statement to simplify iteration in terms of the idiom. This sugar makes this statement appear like the foreach statement found in languages such as Perl, and is revealed in the following simplified equivalent of the previous example:

```
Collection<String> col = ... // This code does not compile because of the
"...". //
Add elements to col.
for (String s: col)
    System.out.println(s);
```

This sugar hides col. iterator( ), a method call that returns an Iterator instance for iterating over col's elements. It also hides calls to Iterator's hasNext( ) and next( ) methods on this instance. You interpret this sugar to read as follows: "for each String object in col, assign this object to s at the start of the loop iteration."

The enhanced for statement is limited in that you cannot use this statement where access to the iterator is required to remove an element from a collection. Also, it is not usable where you must replace elements in a collection/array during a traversal, and it cannot be used where you must iterate over multiple collections or arrays in parallel.

Autoboxing and Unboxing

Developers who believe that Java should support only reference types have complained about Java's support for primitive types. One area where the dichotomy of Java's type system is clearly seen is the Collections Framework: you can store objects but not primitive type-based values in collections.

Although you cannot directly store a primitive type-based value in a collection, you can indirectly store this value by first wrapping it in an object created from a primitive type wrapper class such as Integer, and then storing this primitive type wrapper class instance in the collection—see the following example:

```
Collection<Integer> col = ...; // This code does not compile because of the
"...".
int x = 27;
col.add(new Integer(x)); // Indirectly store int value 27 via an Integer
object.
```

The reverse situation is also tedious. When you want to retrieve the int from col, you must invoke Integer's intValue( ) method (which, if you recall, is inherited from Integer's Java. lang. Number superclass). Continuing on from this example, you would specify int y = col. iterator( ). next( ). intValue( ); to assign the stored 32-bit integer to y.

To alleviate this tedium, Java 5 introduced autoboxing and unboxing, which are a pair of complementary syntactic sugar-based language features that make primitive values appear more like objects. (This "sleight of hand" is not complete because you cannot specify expressions such as 27.doubleValue( ).)

Autoboxing automatically *boxes* (wraps) a primitive value in an object of the appropriate primitive type wrapper class whenever a primitive type is specified but a reference is required. For example, you could change the example's third line to col. add(x); and have the compiler box x into an Integer object.

Unboxing automatically *unboxes* (unwraps) a primitive value from its wrapper object whenever a reference is specified but a primitive type is required. For example, you could specify int y = col. iterator( ). next ( ); and have the compiler unbox the returned Integer object to int value 27 prior to the assignment.

Although autoboxing and unboxing were introduced to simplify working with primitive values in a collections context, these language features can be used in other contexts, and this arbitrary use can lead to a problem that is difficult to understand without knowledge of what is happening behind the scenes. Consider the following example:

```
Integer il = 127;
Integer i2 = 127;
System.out.println(il == i2); // Output: true
System.out.println(il < i2); // Output: false
System.out.println(il > i2); // Output: false
System.out.println(il+i2); // Output: 254
11 = 30000;
12 = 30000;
System.out.println(il == i2); // Output: false
System.out.println(il < i2); // Output: false
System.out.println(il > i2); // Output: false
i2 = 30001;
System.out.println(il < i2); // Output: true
System.out.println(il+i2); // Output: 60001
```

With one exception, this example's output is as expected. The exception is the il = = i2 comparison where each of il and i2 contains 30000. Instead of returning true, as is the case where each of il and i2 contains 127, il = = i2 returns false. What is causing this problem?

Examine the generated code and you will discover that Integer il = 127; is converted to Integer il = Integer.valueOf (127); and Integer i2 = 127; is converted to Integer i2 = Integer. valueOf (127);. According to valueOf( )'s Java documentation, this method takes advantage of caching to improve performance.

Integer maintains an internal cache of unique Integer objects over a small range of values. The low bound of this range is -128, and the high bound defaults to 127. However, you can change the high bound by assigning a different value to system property Java. lang. Integer. IntegerCache. high (via the java.lang.System class's String setProperty(String prop. String value) method.

Because of the cache, each Integer. valueOf (127) call returns the same Integer object reference, which is why il = = i2 (which compares references) evaluates to true. Because 30000 lies outside of the default range, each Integer. valueOf (30000) call returns a reference to a new Integer object, which is why il = = i2 evaluates to false.

In contrast to = = and ! =, which do not unbox the boxed values prior to the comparison, operators such as <, >, and + unbox these values before performing their operations. As a result, il < i2 is converted to il.intValue( ) < i2.intValue() andil+i2 is converted to il.intValue( )+i2.intValue( ).

List

A list is an ordered collection, which is also known as a sequence. Elements can be stored in and accessed from specific locations via integer indexes. Some of these elements may be duplicates or null (when the list's implementation allows null elements). Lists are described by the List interface, whose generic type is List<E>.

List extends Collection and redeclares its inherited methods, partly for convenience. It also redeclares iterator( ), add( ), remove( ), equals( ), and hashCode( ) to place extra conditions on their contracts. For example, List's contract for add( ) specifies that it appends an element to the end of the list, rather than adding the element to the collection.

List also declares the following table list-specific methods.

Table List-specific Methods

Method	Description
void add(int index, E e)	Insert element e into this list at position index. Shift the element currently at this position (if any) and any subsequent elements to the right. This method throws UnsupportedOperationException when this list does not support add( ), ClassCastException when e's class is inappropriate for this list, IllegalArgumentException when some property of e prevents it from being added to this list, NullPointerException when e contains the null reference and this list doesn't support null elements, and java.lang.IndexOutOfBoundsException when index is less than 0 or index is greater than size( ).
boolean addAll(int index, Collection<? extends E> c)	Insert all c's elements into this list starting at position index and in the order that they are returned by c's iterator. Shift the element currently at this position (if any) and any subsequent elements to the right. This method throws UnsupportedOperationException when this list does not support addAHQ, ClassCastException when the class of one of c's elements is

inappropriate for this list, IllegalArgumentException when some property of an element prevents it from being added to this list, NullPointerException when c contains the null reference or when one of its elements is null and this list does not support null elements, and IndexOutOf BoundsException when index is less than 0 or index is greater than size().

E get(int index)
: Return the element stored in this list at position index. This method throws IndexOutOf BoundsException when index is less than 0 or index is greater than or equal to size().

int indexOf(Object o)
: Return the index of the first occurrence of element o in this list, or -1 when this list does not contain the element. This method throws ClassCastException when o's class is inappropriate for this list, and NullPointerException when o contains the null reference and this list does not support null elements.

int lastIndexOf(Object o)
: Return the index of the last occurrence of element o in this list, or -1 when this list does not contain the element. This method throws ClassCastException when o's class is inappropriate for this list, and NullPointerException when o contains the null reference and this list does not support null elements.

ListIterator<E> listIterator()
: Return a list iterator over the elements in this list. The elements are returned in the same order as they appear in the list.

ListIterator<E> listIterator(int index)
: Return a list iterator over this list's elements starting with the element at index. Elements are returned in the same order as they appear in the list. IndexOutOf BoundsException is thrown when index is less than 0 or index is greater than size( ).

E remove(int index)
: Remove the element at position index from this list, shift any subsequent elements to the left, and return this element. UnsupportedOperationException is thrown when this list does not support remove( ); IndexOutOfBoundsException is thrown when index is less than 0, or greater than or equal to size( ).

E set(int index, E e)
: Replace the element at position index in this list with element e and return the element previously stored at this position. This method throws

UnsupportedOperationException when this list does not support set(), ClassCastException when e's class is inappropriate for this list, IllegalArgumentException when some property of e prevents it from being added to this list, NullPointerException when e contains the null reference and this list does not support null elements, and IndexOutOf BoundsException when index is less than 0 or index is greater than or equal to size().

List<E> subList(int fromIndex, int toIndex)
: Return a view (discussed later) of the portion of this list between fromIndex (inclusive) and toIndex (exclusive). (If fromIndex and toIndex are equal, the returned list is empty.) The returned listjis backed by this list, so nonstructural changes in the returned list are reflected in this list and vice-versa. The returned list supports all the optional list methods (those methods that can throw

UnsupportedOperationException) supported by this list. This method throws IndexOutOf BoundsException when fromIndex is less than 0, toIndex is greater than size(), or fromIndex is greater than toIndex.

CHAPTER 3

The above table refers to the ListIterator interface, which is more flexible than its Iterator superinterface in that ListIterator provides methods for iterating over a list in either direction, modifying the list during iteration, and obtaining the iterator's current position in the list.

ListIterator declares the following methods:

- void add(E e) inserts e into the list being iterated over. This element is inserted immediately before the next element that would be returned by next (), if any, and after the next element that would be returned by previous (), if any. This method throws UnsupportedOperationException when this list iterator does not support add(), ClassCastException when e's class is inappropriate for this list, and IllegalArgumentException when some property of e prevents it from being added to this list.
- boolean hasNext( ) returns true when this list iterator has more elements when traversing the list in the forward direction.
- boolean hasPrevious( ) returns true when this list iterator has more elements when traversing the list in the reverse direction.
- E next( ) returns the next element in this list and advances the cursor position. This method throws NoSuchElementException when there is no next element.
- int nextIndex( ) returns the index of the element that would be returned by a subsequent call to next (), or the size of the list when at the end of the list.
- E previous () returns the previous element in this list and moves the cursor position backwards. This method throws NoSuchElementException when there is no previous element.
- int previousIndex( ) returns the index of the element that would be returned by a subsequent call to previous( ), or -1 when at the beginning of the list.
- void remove () removes from the list the last element that was returned by next( ) or previous( ). This call can be made only once per call to next( ) or previous( ). Furthermore, it can be made only when add( ) has not been called after the last call to next( ) or previous( ). This method throws UnsupportedOperationException when this list iterator does not support remove( ), and IllegalStateException when neither next( ) norprevious( ) has been called, orremove( ) oradd( ) has already been called after the last call to next( ) or previous( ).
- void set(E e) replaces the last element returned by next( ) or previous( ) with element e. This call can be made only when neither remove( ) noradd( ) has been called after the last call to next( ) or previous( ). This method throws UnsupportedOperationException when this list iterator does not support set( ), ClassCastException when e's class is inappropriate for this list, IllegalArgumentException when some property of e prevents it from being added to this list, and IllegalStateException when neither next( ) nor previous( ) has been called, or remove( ) or add( ) has already been called after the last call to next( ) or previous( ).

A ListIterator instance does not have the concept of a current element. Instead, it has the concept of a *cursor for* navigating through a list. The nextIndex( ) and previousIndex( ) methods return the *cursor position,* which always lies between the element that would be returned by a call to previous( ) and the element that would be returned by a call to next( ). A list iterator for a list of length *n* has *n* + 1 possible cursor positions, as illustrated by each caret (^) as shown here:

```
                  Element(o)     Element(l)     Element(2)      ... Element(n-l)
cursor positions: ^            ^             ^                ^                  ^
```

The remove( ) and set( ) methods are not defined in terms of the cursor position; they are defined to operate on the last element returned by a call to next( ) or previous( ).

The last table's description of the subList( ) method refers to the concept of a *view*, which is a list that is backed by another list. Changes that are made to the view are reflected in this backing list. The view can cover the entire list or, as subList( )'s name implies, only part of the list.

The subList( ) method is useful for performing *range- view* operations over a list in a compact manner. For example, list. subList (fromIndex, toIndex). clear( ); removes a range of elements from list where the first element is located at fromIndex and the last element is located at toIndex-1.

ArrayList

The ArrayList class provides a list implementation that is based on an internal array. As a result, access to the list's elements is fast. However, because elements must be moved to open a space for insertion or to close a space after deletion, insertions and deletions of elements is slow. ArrayList supplies three constructors:

- ArrayList( ) creates an empty array list with an initial *capacity* (storage space) of ten elements. Once this capacity is reached, a larger array is created, elements from the current array are copied into the larger array, and the larger array becomes the new current array. This process repeats as more elements are added to the array list.
- ArrayList(Collection < ? extends E > c) creates an array list containing c's elements in the order in which they are returned by c's iterator. NullPointerException is thrown when c contains the null reference.
- ArrayList(int initialCapacity) creates an empty array list with an initial capacity of initialCapacity elements. IllegalArgumentException is thrown when initialCapacity is negative.

The following demonstrates an array list.

A demonstration of an array-based list

```
import Java.util.ArrayList;
import Java.util.List;

class ArrayListDemo
   public static void main(String[] args)
   {
      List<String> Is = new ArrayListoQ;
      String[] weekDays = {"Sun", "Mon", "Tue", "Wed", "Thu", "Fri", "Sat"};
      for (String weekDay: weekDays)
         1s.add(weekDay);
      dump("1s:". Is);
      Is.set(Is.indexOf("Wed"), "Wednesday");
      dump("1s:", Is);
      Is.remove(1s.lastlndexOf(" Fri"));
      dumpC'1s:", Is);
   }
   static void dump(String title, List<String> Is)
   {
      System. out. print (title+" ");
      for (String s: Is)
         System. out. print(s+" ");
      System.out.println();
```

The List<String> Is = new ArrayListo( ); assignment reveals a couple of items to note:

- I've declared variable Is to be of List<String> interface type, and have assigned to this variable a reference to an instance of the Array List class that implements this interface. When working with the Collections Framework, it is common practice to declare variables to be of interface type. Doing so eliminates extensive code changes when you need to work with a different implementation class; for example, List<String> Is = new LinkedListo( );.
- The *diamond operator* < > (which is new in Java 7) reduces verbosity by forcing the compiler to infer actual type arguments for the constructors of generic classes. Without this operator, I would need to specify String as the actual type argument passed to ArrayList<E>, resulting in the more verbose List<String> Is = new ArrayList<String>(); instead of the shorter List<String> Is = new Array Listo( );.

The dump() method's enhanced for statement uses iterator( ), hasNext( ), and next( ) behind the scenes. When you run this application, it generates the following output:

```
Is: Sun Mon Tue Wed Thu Fri Sat
Is: Sun Mon Tue Wednesday Thu Fri Sat
Is: Sun Mon Tue Wednesday Thu Sat
```

LinkedList

The LinkedList class provides a list implementation that is based on linked nodes. Because links must be traversed, access to the list's elements is slow. However, because only node references need to be changed, insertions and deletions of elements is fast. (I will introduce you to nodes later in this chapter.) LinkedList supplies two constructors:

- LinkedList( ) creates an empty linked list.
- LinkedList(Collection<? extends E> c) creates a linked list containing c's elements in the order in which they are returned by c's iterator. NullPointerException is thrown when c contains the null reference.

The following listing demonstrates a linked list.

A demonstration of a linked list of nodes

```
import Java. util. LinkedList;
import Java. util. List;
import Java. util. Listlterator;

class LinkedListDemo
{
   public static void main(String[] args)
   {
      List<String> Is = new LinkedListoQ;
      String[] weekDays = {"Sun", "Mon", "Tue", "Wed", "Thu", "Fri", "Sat"};
      for (String weekDay: weekDays)
         Is.add(weekDay);
      dump("ls:", Is);
      ls.add(1, "Sunday");
      ls.add(3, "Monday");
      ls.add(5, "Tuesday");
      Is. add (7, "Wednesday");
      ls.add(9, "Thursday");
      ls.add(11, "Friday");
```

```
        Is.add(13, "Saturday");
        dump("ls:", Is);
        ListIterator<String> li = ls.listlterator(ls.size());
        while (li.hasPreviousQ)
            System . out . pr int (li . previous ( )+" " ) ;
        System . out . println ( ) ;
    }
    static void dump(String title, List<String> Is)
    {
        System. out. print (title+" ");
        for (String s: Is)
            System. out. print (s+" ");
        System . out . println ( ) ;
    }
}
```

This application demonstrates that each successive add () method call must increase its index by 2 to account for the previously added element when adding longer weekday names to the list. It also shows you how to output a list in reverse order: return a list iterator with its cursor initialized past the end of the list and repeatedly call previous ().

When you run this application, it generates the following output:

```
Is: Sun Mon Tue Wed Thu Fri Sat
Is: Sun Sunday Mon Monday Tue Tuesday Wed Wednesday Thu Thursday Fri Friday
Sat Saturday
Saturday Sat Friday Fri Thursday Thu Wednesday Wed Tuesday Tue Monday Mon
Sunday Sun
```

Set

A *set is* a collection that contains no duplicate elements. In other words, a set contains no pair of elements *el* and *e2* such that *el* .equals *(e2)* returns true. Furthermore, a set can contain at most one null element. Sets are described by the Set interface, whose generic type is Set<E>.

Set extends Collection and redeclares its inherited methods, for convenience and also to add stipulations to the contracts for add( ), equals( ), and hashCode( ), to address how they behave in a set context. Also, Set's documentation states that all constructors of implementation classes must create sets that contain no duplicate elements.

Set does nor introduce new methods.

TreeSet

The TreeSet class provides a set implementation that is based on a tree data structure. As a result, elements are stored in sorted order. However, accessing these elements is somewhat slower than with the other Set implementations (which are not sorted) because links must be traversed.

TreeSet supplies four constructors:

- TreeSet( ) creates a new, empty tree set that is sorted according to the natural ordering of its elements. All elements inserted into the set must implement the Comparable interface.
- TreeSet (Collection<? extends E> c) creates a new tree set containing c's elements, sorted according to the natural ordering of its elements. All elements inserted into the new set must implement the Comparable interface. This constructor throws ClassCastException when c's elements do not implement Comparable or are not mutually comparable, and NullPointerException when c contains the null reference.

- TreeSet (Comparator? super E> comparator) creates a new, empty tree set that is sorted according to the specified comparator. Passing null to comparator implies that natural ordering will be used.
- TreeSet(SortedSet<E> s) creates a new tree set containing the same elements and using the same ordering as s. This constructor throws NullPointerException when s contains the null reference.

The following listing demonstrates a tree set.

A demonstration of a tree set with String elements sorted according to their natural ordering

```
import Java.util.Set;
import Java.util.TreeSet;

class TreeSetDemo
{
    public static void main(String[] args)
    {
        Set<String> ss = new TreeSetoQ;
        String[] fruits = {"apples", "pears", "grapes", "bananas", "kiwis"};
        for (String fruit: fruits)
            ss.add(fruit);
        dumpC'ss:", ss);
    }
    static void dump(String title, Set<String> ss)
    {
    System. out. print (title+" ");
    for (String s: ss)
        System. out. print(s+" ");
    System . out . println ( ) ;
    }
}
```

Because String implements Comparable, it is legal for this application to use the TreeSetQ constructor to insert the contents of the fruits array into the set. When you run this application, it generates the following output:

```
ss: apples bananas grapes kiwis pears
```

HashSet

The HashSet class provides a set implementation that is backed by a hashtable data structure (implemented as a HashMap instance, discussed later, which provides a quick way to determine if an element has already been stored in this structure). Although this class provides no ordering guarantees for its.elements, HashSet is much faster than TreeSet. Furthermore, HashSet permits the null reference to ' be stored in its instances.

HashSet supplies four constructors:

- HashSet( ) creates a new, empty hashset where the backing HashMap instance has an initial capacity of 16 and a load factor of 0.75. You will learn what these items mean when I discuss HashMap later in this chapter.
- HashSet (Collection<? extends E> c) creates a new hashset containing c's elements. The backing HashMap has an initial capacity sufficient to contain c's elements and a load factor of 0.75. This constructor throws NullPointerException when c contains the null reference.

- HashSet(int initialCapacity) creates a new, empty hashset where the backing HashMap instance has the capacity specified by initialCapacity and a load factor of 0.75. This constructor throws IllegalArgumentException when initialCapacity's value is less than 0.
- HashSet(int initialCapacity, float loadFactor) creates a new, empty hashset where the backing HashMap instance has the capacity specified by initialCapacity and the load factor specified by loadFactor. This constructor throws IllegalArgumentException when initialCapacity is less than 0 or when loadFactor is less than or equal to 0.

The following listing demonstrates a hashset.

A demonstration of a hashset with String elements unordered

```
import java.util.HashSet;
import Java.util.Set;

class HashSetDemo
{
    public static void main(String[] args)
    {
        Set<String> ss = new HashSet<>();
        String[] fruits = {"apples", "pears", "grapes", "bananas", "kiwis",
                           "pears", null};
        for (String fruit: fruits)
            ss.add(fruit);
        dumpC'ss:", ss);
    }
    static void dump(String title, Set<String> ss)
    {
        System.out.print(title+" ");
        for (String s: ss)
            System.out.print(s+" ");
        System.out.println();
    }
}
```

In last listing TreeSetDemo application, I did not add null to the fruits array because TreeSet throws NullPointerException when it detects an attempt to add this element. In contrast, HashSet permits null to be added, which is why this listing includes null in HashSetDemo's fruits array.

When you run this application, it generates unordered output such as the following:

```
ss: null grapes bananas kiwis pears apples
```

Suppose you want to add instances of your classes to a hashset. As with String, your classes must override equals () and hashCode (); otherwise, duplicate class instances can be stored in the hashset. For example, the following listing presents the source code to an application whose Planet class overrides equals( ) but fails to also override hashCode( ).

A custom Planet class not overriding hashCode ()

```
import java.util.HashSet;
import Java.util.Set;

class CustomClassAndHashSet
{
    public static void main(String[] args)
```

```
    {
        Set<Planet> sp = new HashSet<>();
        sp.add(new Planet("Mercury"));
        sp.add(new Planet("Venus"));
        sp.add(new Planet("Earth"));
        sp.add(new Planet("Mars"));
        sp.add(new Planet("]upiter"));
        sp.add (new Planet("Saturn"));
        sp.add(new Planet("Uranus"));
        sp.add(new Planet("Neptune")):
        sp.add(new Planet("Fomalhaut b"));
        Planet pi = new Planet ("51 Pegasi b");
        sp.add(pl);
        Planet p2 = new Planet("51 Pegasi b");
        sp.add(p2);
        System. out. println(pl.equals(p2));
        System. out. println(sp);
    }
}
class Planet
{
    private String name;
    Planet(String name)
    {
        this. name = name;
    }
    @Override
    public boolean equals(Object o)
    {
        if (!(o instanceof Planet))
            return false;
        Planet p = (Planet) o;
        return p.name.equals(name);
    }
    String getNameQ
    {
        return name;
    }
    @Override
    public String toStringQ
    {
    return name;
    }
}
```

The above listing's Planet class declares a single name field of type String. Although it might seem pointless to declare Planet with a single String field because I could refactor this listing to remove Planet and work with String, I might want to introduce additional fields to Planet (perhaps to store a planet's mass and other characteristics) in the future.

When you run this application, it generates unordered output such as the following:

```
true
[Venus, Fomalhaut b, Uranus, Mars, Neptune, Jupiter, Earth, Mercury, Saturn,
51 Pegasi^ b, 51 Pegasi b]
```

This output reveals two 51 Pegasi b elements in the hashset. Although these elements are equal from the perspective of the overriding equals( ) method (the first output line, true, proves this point), overriding equals( ) is not enough to avoid duplicate elements being stored in a hashset: you must also override hashCode().

The easiest way to override hashCode() in Listing;5-5's Planet class is to have the overriding method call the name field's hashCode() method and return its value. (This technique only works with a class whose single reference field's class provides a valid hashCode( ) method.)

The following listing presents this overriding hashCode( ) method.

A custom Planet class overridinghashCode( )

```
import java.util.HashSet;
import Java.util.Set;

class CustomClassAndHashSet
{
    public static void main(String[] args)
    {
        Set<Planet> sp = new HashSet<>();
        sp.add(new Planet("Mercury"));
        sp.add(new Planet("Venus"));
        sp.add(new Planet("Earth"));
        sp.add(new Planet("Mars"));
        sp.add(new Planet("3upiter"));
        sp.add(new Planet("Saturn"));
        sp.add(new Planet("Uranus"));
        sp.add(new Planet("Neptune"));
        sp.add(new Planet("Fomalhaut b"));
        Planet pi = new Planet("51 Pegasi b");
        sp.add(pl);
        Planet p2 = new Planet("51 Pegasi b");
        sp.add(p2);
        System.out.println(pi.equals(p2));
        System.out.println(sp);
    }
}
class Planet
{
    private String name;
    Planet(String name)
    {
        this.name = name;
    }
    @Override
    public boolean equals(Object o)
    {
```

```
        if (!(o instanceof Planet))
            return false;
        Planet p = (Planet) o;
            return p. name. equals (name);
    }
    String getName()
    {
        return name;
    }
    @Override
    public int hashCodeQ
    {
        return name.hashCode();
    }
    @Override
    public String toString()
    {
        return name;
    }
}
```

Compile the above listing (javac CustomClassAndHashSet. Java) and run the application (Java CustomClassAndHashSet). You will observe output (similar to that shown below) that reveals no duplicate elements:

```
true
[Saturn, Earth, Uranus, Fomalhaut b, 51 Pegasi b, Venus, Dupiter, Mercury,
Mars,*-¹ Neptune]
```

EnumSet

An *enum* is an enumerated type that is expressed via reserved word enum. The following example demonstrates the traditional enumerated type:

```
static final int SUNDAY = 1;
static final int MONDAY = 2;
static final int TUESDAY = 4;
static final int WEDNESDAY = 8;
static final int THURSDAY = 16;
static final int FRIDAY = 32;
static final int SATURDAY = 64;
```

Although the enum has many advantages over the traditional enumerated type, the traditional enumerated type is less awkward to use when combining constants into a set; for example, static final int DAYS_OFF = SUNDAY | MONDAY;.

DAYS_OFF is an example of an integer-based, fixed-length *bitset,* which is a set of bits where each bit indicates that its associated member belongs to the set when the bit is set to 1, and is absent from the set when the bit is set to 0.

This bitset is formed by bitwise inclusive ORing the traditional enumerated type's integer constants together via the bitwise inclusive OR operator (|): you could also use +. Each constant must be a unique power of two (starting with one) because otherwise it is impossible to distinguish between the members of this bitset.

To determine if a constant belongs to the bitset, create an expression that involves the bitwise AND operator (&). For example, ((DAYS_OFF&MONDAY) = = MONDAY) bitwise ANDs DAYS_OFF (3) with MONDAY (2), which results in 2. This value is compared via = = with MONDAY (2), and the result of the expression is true: MONDAY is a member of the DAYS_OF F bitset.

You can accomplish the same task with an enum by instantiating an appropriate Set implementation class and calling the add() method multiple times to store the constants in the set. The following listing illustrates this more awkward alternative.

Creating the Set equivalent of DA YS_OFF

```
import Java. util. Set;
import Java. util. TreeSet;

enum Weekday
{
   SUNDAY, MONDAY, TUESDAY, WEDNESDAY, THURSDAY, FRIDAY, SATURDAY
}
class DaysOff
{
   public static void main(String[] args)
   {
      Set<Weekday> daysOff = new TreeSet<>();
      daysOff.add (Weekday.SUNDAY);
      daysOff.add (Weekday.MONDAY);
      System.out.println(daysOff );
   }
}
```

When you run this application, it generates the following output:

```
[SUNDAY, MONDAY]
```

As well as being more awkward to use (and verbose) than the bitset, the Set alternative requires more memory to store each constant and is not as fast. Because of these problems, EnumSet was introduced.

The EnumSet class provides a Set implementation that is based on a bitset. Its elements are constants that must come from the same enum, which is specified when the enum set is created. Null elements are not permitted; any attempt to store a null element results in a thrown NullPointerException.

The following listing demonstrates EnumSet.

Creating the EnumSet equivalent of DAYS_OFF

```
import Java.util.EnumSet;
import Java.util.Iterator;
import Java.util.Set;

enum Weekday
{
   SUNDAY, MONDAY, TUESDAY, WEDNESDAY, THURSDAY, FRIDAY, SATURDAY
}
class EnumSetDemo
{
   public static void main(String[] args)
   {
      Set<Weekday> daysOff = EnumSet.of(Weekday.SUNDAY, Weekday.MONDAY);
```

```
        Iterator<Weekday> iter = daysOff.iterator();
        while (iter.hasNext())
            System.out.println(iter.next()); }
    }
}
```

EnumSet, whose generic type is EnumSet<E extends Enum<E», provides various class methods for conveniently constructing enum sets. For example, <E extends Enum<E» EnumSet<E> of(E el, E e2) returns an EnumSet instance consisting of elements el and e2. In this example, those elements are Weekday. SUNDAY and Weekday. MONDAY.

When you run this application, it generates the following output:

```
SUNDAY
MONDAY
```

SortedSet

TreeSet is an example of a *sorted set,* which is a set that maintains its elements in ascending order, sorted according to their natural ordering or according to a comparator that is supplied when the sorted set is created. Sorted sets are described by the SortedSet interface.

SortedSet, whose generic type is SortedSet<E>, extends Set. With two exceptions, the methods it inherits from Set behave identically on sorted sets as on other sets:

- The Iterator instance returned from iterator() traverses the sorted set in ascending element order.
- The array returned by toArray( ) contains the sorted set's elements in order.

SortedSet's documentation requires that an implementation must provide the four standard constructors that I presented in my discussion of TreeSet. Furthermore, implementations of this interface must implement the methods that are described in the following table.

Table SortedSet-specific Methods

Method	Description
Comparator ? super E > comparator( )	Return the comparator used to order the elements in this set, or null when this set uses the natural ordering of its elements.
E first ()	Return the first (lowest) element currently in this set, or throw a NoSuchElementException instance when this set is empty.
SortedSet<E> headSet(E toElement)	Return a view of that portion of this set whose elements are strictly less than toElement. The returned set is backed by this set, so changes in the returned set are reflected in this set and vice versa. The returned set supports all optional set operations that this set supports. This method throws ClassCastException when toElement is not compatible with this set's comparator (or, when the set has no comparator, when toElement does not implement Comparable), NullPointerException when toElement is null and this set does not permit null elements, and IllegalArgumentException when this set has a restricted range and toElement lies outside of this range's bounds.
E last()	Return the last (highest) element currently in this set, or throw a NoSuchElementException instance when this set is empty.
SortedSet<E> subSet(E fromElement, E toElement)	Return a view of the portion of this set whose elements range from fromElement, inclusive, to toElement, exclusive.

(When fromElement and toElement are equal, the returned set is empty.) The returned set is backed by this set, so changes in the returned set are reflected in this set and vice versa. The returned set supports all optional set operations that this set supports. This method throws ClassCastException when fromElement and toElement cannot be compared to one another using this set's comparator (or, when the set has no comparator, using natural ordering), NullPointerException when fromElement or toElement is null and this set does not permit null elements, and IllegalArgumentException when fromElement is greater than toElement or when this set has a restricted range and fromElement or toElement lies outside of this range's bounds.

SortedSet<E> tailSet(E fromElement) — Return a view of that portion of this set whose elements are greater than or equal to fromElement. The returned set is backed by this set, so changes in the returned set are reflected in this set and vice versa. The returned set supports all optional set operations that this set supports. This method throws ClassCastException when fromElement is not compatible with this set's comparator (or, when the set has no comparator, when fromElement does not implement Comparable), NullPointerException when fromElement is null and this set does not permit null elements, and IllegalArgumentException when this set has a restricted range and fromElement lies outside of the range's bounds.

The set-based range views returned from headSet( ), subSet( ), and tailSet( ) are analogous to the list-based range view returned from List's subList( ) method except that a set-based range view remains valid even when the backing sorted set is modified. As a result, a set-based range view can be used for a lengthy period of time.

Each range view returned by headSet (), subset (), or tailSet () is *half open* because it does not include its high endpoint (headSet() and subSetQ) or its lowendpoint (tailSetQ). For the first two methods, the high endpoint is specified by argument toElement; for the last method, the low endpoint is specified by argument f romElement.

The following listing demonstrates a sorted set based on a tree set.

A sorted set of fruit and vegetable names

```
import java.util.SortedSet;
import java.util.TreeSet;

class SortedSetDemo
{
   public static void main(String[] args)
   {
      SortedSet<String> sss = new TreeSetoQ;
      String[] fruitAndVeg =
      {
      "apple", "potato", "turnip", "banana", "corn", "carrot", "cherry",
      "pear", "mango", "strawberry", "cucumber", "grape", "banana", "kiwi",
      "radish", "blueberry", "tomato", "onion", "raspberry", "lemon",
      "pepper", "squash", "melon", "zucchini", "peach", "plum", "turnip",
      "onion", "nectarine"
   };
```

```
System.out.println("Array size = "+fruitAndVeg.length);
for (String fruitVeg: fruitAndVeg)
   sss.add(fruitVeg);
dump("sss:", sss);
System.out.println("Sorted set size = "+sss.size());
System.out.printing"First element = "+sss.first());
System.out.println("Last element = "+sss.last());
System.out.println("Comparator = "+sss.comparator());
dumpC'hs:", sss.headSet("n"));
dump("ts:"., sss.tailSet("n"));
System.out.println("Count of p-named fruits & vegetables = "+
   sss.subSet("p", "q").size());
System.out.println("Incorrect count of c-named fruits & vegetables = "+
   sss. subSet ("carrot", ''cucumber").size());
System.out.println("Correct count of c-named fruits & vegetables = "+
   sss.subSet("carrot", "cucumber\0").size());
}
static void dump(String title, SortedSet<String> sss)
{
   System.out.print(title+" ");
   for (String s: sss)
      System.out.print(s+" ");
   System. out. println ();
}
}
```

When you run this application, it generates the following output:

```
Array size = 29
sss: apple banana blueberry carrot cherry corn cucumber grape kiwi lemon
mango melon
nectarine onion peach pear pepper plum potato radish raspberry squash
strawberry tomato
turnip zucchini
Sorted set size =26
First element = apple
Last element = zucchini
Comparator = null
hs: apple banana blueberry carrot cherry corn cucumber grape kiwi lemon mango
melon
ts: nectarine onion peach pear pepper plum potato radish raspberry squash
strawberry tomato
turnip zucchini
Count of p-named fruits & vegetables = 5
Incorrect count of c-named fruits & vegetables = 3
Correct count of c-named fruits & vegetables = 4
```

This output reveals that the sorted set's size is less than the array's size because a set cannot contain duplicate elements: the duplicate banana, turnip, and onion elements are not stored in the sorted set.

The comparator() method returns null because the sorted set was not created with a comparator. Instead, the sorted set relies on the natural ordering of String elements to store them in sorted order.

TheheadSet( ) andtailSet( ) methods are called with argument "n" to return, respectively, a set of elements whose names begin with a letter that is strictly less than n, and a letter that is greater than or equal to n.

Finally, the output shows you that you must be careful when passing an upper limit to subSet (). As you can see, ss.subSet("carrot", "cucumber") does not include cucumber in the returned range view because cucumber is subSet ()'s high endpoint.

To include cucumber in the range view, you need to form a *closed range* or *closed interval* (both endpoints are included). With String objects, you accomplish this task by appending \0 to the string. For example, ss.subSet("carrot", "cucumber\0") includes cucumber because it is less than cucumber\0.

This same technique can be applied wherever you need to form an *open range* or *open interval* (neither endpoint is included). For example, ss.subSet("carrot\o", "cucumber") does not include carrot because it is less than carrot\0. Furthermore, it does not include high endpoint cucumber.

You need to be careful when designing classes that work with sorted sets. For example, the class must implement Comparable when you plan to store the class's instances in a sorted set where these elements are sorted according to their natural ordering. Consider the following listing.

A custom Employee class not implementing Comparable

```
import java.util.SortedSet;
import java.util.TreeSet;

class CustomClassAndSortedSet
{
    public static void main(String[] args)
    {
        SortedSet<Employee> sse = new TreeSetoQ;
        sse.add(new Employee("Sally Doe"));
        sse.add(new Employee("Bob Doe")); // ClassCastException thrown here
        sse.add (new Employee("Dohn Doe"));
        System.out.println (sse);
    }
}
class Employee
{
    private String name;
    Employee (String name)
    {
        this. name = name; }
    }
    @Override
    public String toString()
    {
        return name;
    }
}
```

When you run this application, it generates the following output:

```
Exception in thread "main" Java. lang. ClassCastException: Employee cannot be
cast to*' Java . lang . Comparable
at Java. util.TreeMap. compare (TreeMap. Java: 1188)
at Java. util.TreeMap. put (TreeMap. Java: 531)
```

```
at Java. util.TreeSet.add(TreeSet. Java: 255)
at CustomClassAndSortedSet.main(CustomClassAndSortedSet.java:9)
```

The ClassCastException instance is thrown during the second add( ) method call because the sorted set implementation, an instance of TreeSet, is unable to call the second Employee element's compareToO method, because Employee does not implement Comparable.

The solution to this problem is to have the class implement Comparable, which is exactly what is revealed in the following listing.

Making Employee elements comparable

```
import java.util.SortedSet;
import Java. util. TreeSet;

class CustomClassAndSortedSet
{
    public static void main(String[] args)
    {
        SortedSet<Employee> sse = new TreeSetoQ;
        sse.add(new Employee(" Sally Doe"));
        sse.add (new Employee("Bob Doe"));
        Employee el = new Employee ("Dohn Doe");
        Employee e2 = new Employee("Dohn Doe");
        sse.add(el);
        sse.add(e2);
        System.out.println(sse);
        System.out.println (el.equals (e2 ));
    }
}
class Employee implements Comparable<Employee>
{
    private String name;
    Employee (String name)
    {
        this. name = name;
    }
    @Override
    public int compareTo( Employee e)
    {
        return name. compareTo(e. name);
    }
    @Override
    public String toString()
    {
    return name;
    }
}
```

This listing's main( ) method differs from earlier listing in that it also creates two Employee objects initialized to "John Doe", adds these objects to the sorted set, and compares these objects for equality via equals( ). Furthermore, the above listing declares Employee to implement Comparable, introducing a compareToQ method into Employee.

When you run this application, it generates the following output:

```
[Bob Doe, Dohn Doe, Sally Doe]
false
```

This output shows that only one "John Doe" Employee object is stored in the sorted set. After all, a set cannot contain duplicate elements. However, the false value (resulting from the equalsQ comparison) also shows that the sorted set's natural ordering is inconsistent with equals (), which violates SortedSet's contract:

The ordering maintained by a sorted set (whether or not an explicit comparator is provided) must be consistent with equals( ) if the sorted set is to correctly implement the Set interface. This is so because the Set interface is defined in terms of the equals ( ) operation, but a sorted set performs all element comparisons using its compareTo( ) (orcompare( )) method, so two elements that are deemed equal by this method are, from the standpoint of the sorted set, equal.

Because the application works correctly, why should SortedSet's contract matter? Although the contract does not appear to matter with respect to the TreeSet implementation of SortedSet, perhaps it will matter in the context of a third-party class that implements this interface.

The next listing shows you how to correct this problem and make Employee instances work with any implementation of a sorted set.

A contract-compliant Employee class

```
import Java.util.SortedSet;
import Java.util.TreeSet;

class CustomClassAndSortedSet
{
    public static void main(String[] args)
    {
        SortedSet<Employee> sse = new TreeSetoQ;
        sse.add(new Employee("Sally Doe"));
        sse.add(new Employee("Bob Doe"));
        Employee el = new Employee("Dohn Doe");
        Employee e2 = new Employee("Dohn Doe");
        sse.add(el);
        sse.add(e2);
        System.out.println(sse);
        System.out.println(el.equals(e2));
    }
}
class Employee implements Comparable<Employee>
{
    private String name;
    Employee(String name)
    {
        this.name = name;
    }
    @Override
    public int compareTo(Employee e)
    {
        return name. compareTo(e. name);
```

```
    }
    @Override
    public boolean equals (Object o)
    {
        if (!(o instanceof Employee))
            return false;
        Employee e = (Employee) o;
        return e. name. equals (name);
    }
    @Override
    public String toStringQ
    {
        return name;
    }
}
```

The above listing corrects the SortedSet contract violation by overriding equals( ) . Run the resulting application and you will observe [Bob Doe, John Doe, Sally Doe] as the first line of output and true as the second line: the sorted set's natural ordering is now consistent with equals ( ) .

NavigableSet

TreeSet is an example of a *navigable set,* which is a sorted set that can be iterated over in descending order as well as ascending order, and which can report closest matches for given search targets. Navigable sets are described by the NavigableSet interface, whose generic type is NavigableSet<E>, which extends SortedSet, and which is described in the following table.

Table NavigableSet-specific Methods

Method	Description
E ceiling(E e)	Return the least element in this set greater than or equal to e, or null when there is no such element. This method throws ClassCastException when e cannot be compared with the elements currently in the set, and NullPointerException when e is null and this set does not permit null elements.
Iterator<E> descendingIterator()	Return an iterator over the elements in this set, in descending order. Equivalent in effect to descendingSet().iterator().
NavigableSet<E> descendingSet()	Return a reverse order view of the elements contained in this set. The descending set is backed by this set, so changes to the set are reflected in the descending set and vice versa. If either set is modified (except through the iterator's own remove () operation) while iterating over the set, the results of the iteration are undefined.
E floor(E e)	Return the greatest element in this set less than or equal to e, or null when there is no such element. This method throws ClassCastException when e cannot be compared with the elements currently in the set, and NullPointerException when e is null and this set does not permit null elements.
NavigableSet<E> headSet(E toElement, boolean inclusive)	Return a view of the portion of this set whose elements are less than (or equal to, when inclusive is true) toElement.

The returned set is backed by this set, so changes in the returned set are reflected in this set and vice versa. The returned set supports all optional set operations that this set supports. This method throws ClassCastException when toElement is not compatible with this set's comparator (or, when the set has no comparator, when toElement does not implement Comparable), NullPointerException when toElement is null and this set does not permit null elements, and IllegalArgumentException when this set has a restricted range and toElement lies outside of this range's bounds.

E higher(E e) — Return the least element in this set strictly greater than the given element, or null when there is no such element. This method throws ClassCastException when e cannot be compared with the elements currentiy in the set, and NullPointerException when e is null and this set does not permit null elements.

E lower(E e) — Return the greatest element in this set strictly less than the given element, or null when there is no such element. This method throws ClassCastException when e cannot be compared with the elements currently in the set, and NullPointerException when e is null and this set does not permit null elements.

E pollFirst( ) — Return and remove the first (lowest) element from this set, or return null when this set is empty.

E pollLast() — Return and remove the last (highest) element from this set, or return null when this set is empty.

NavigableSet<E> subSet(E fromElement, boolean fromInclusive, E toElement, boolean toInclusive)

Return a view of the portion of this set whose elements range from fromElement to toElement. (When fromElement and toElement are equal, the returned set is^ empty unless NavigableSet<E> tailSet(E fromElement, boolean inclusive) fromInclusive and toInclusive are both true.) The returned set is backed by this set, so changes in the returned set are reflected in this set and vice versa. The returned set supports all optional set operations that this set supports. This method throws ClassCastException when fromElement and toElement cannot be compared to one another using this set's comparator (or, when the set has no comparator, using natural ordering), NullPointerException when fromElement or toElement is null and this set does not permit null elements, and IllegalArgumentException when fromElement is greater than toElement or when this set has a restricted range and fromElement or toElement lies outside of this range's bounds.

NavigableSet<E> tailSet(E fromElement, boolean Inclusive) — Return a view of the portion of this set whose elements are greater than (or equal to, when inclusive is true) fromElement. The returned set is backed by this set, so changes in the returned set are reflected in this set and vice versa. The returned set supports all optional set operations that this set supports. This method throws ClassCastException when fromElement is not compatible with this set's comparator (or, when the set has no comparator, when fromElement does not implement Comparable), NullPointerException when fromElement is null and this set does not

	permit null elements, and IllegalArgumentException when this set has a restricted range and fromElement lies outside of this range's bounds.

Queue

A queue is a collection in which elements are stored and retrieved in a specific order. Most queues are categorized as one of the following:

- **First-in, flrst-out (FIFO) queue.** Elements are inserted at the queue's tail and removed at the queue's head.
- **Last-in, flrst-out (LIFO) queue.** Elements are inserted and removed at one end of the queue such that the last element inserted is the first element retrieved. This kind of queue behaves as a stack.
- **Priority queue.** Elements are inserted according to their natural ordering, or according to a comparator that is supplied to the queue implementation.

Queue, whose generic type is Queue<E>, extends Collection, redeclaring add() to adjust its contract (insert the specified element into this queue if it is possible to do so immediately without violating capacity restrictions), and inheriting the other methods from Collection. The following table describes add( ) and the other Queue-specific methods.

Table Queue-specific Methods

Method	Description
boolean add(E e)	Insert element e into this queue if it is possible to do so immediately without violating capacity restrictions. Return true on success; otherwise, throw IllegalStateException when the element cannot be added at this time because no space is currently available. This method also throws ClassCastException when e's class prevents e from being added to this queue, NullPointerException when e contains the null reference and this queue does not permit null elements to be added, and IllegalArgumentException when some property of e prevents it from being added to this queue.
E element()	Return but do not also remove the element at the head of this queue. This method throws NoSuchElementException when this queue is empty.
boolean offer(E e)	Insert element e into this queue if it is possible to do so immediately without violating capacity restrictions. Return true on success; otherwise, return false when the element cannot be added at this time because no space is currently available. This method throws ClassCastException when e's class prevents e from being added to this queue, NullPointerException when e contains the null reference and this queue does not permit null elements to be added, and IllegalArgumentException when some property of e prevents it from being added to this queue.
E peek ()	Return but do not also remove the element at the head of this queue. This method returns null when this queue is empty.
E poll ()	Return and also remove the element at the head of this queue. This method returns null when this queue is empty.

E remove ()	Return and also remove the element at the head of this queue. This method throws NoSuchElementException when this queue is empty. This is the only difference between remove( ) and poll( ).

The above table reveals two sets of methods: in one set, a method (such as add()) throws an exception when an operation fails; in the other set, a method (such as offer( )) returns a special value (false or null) in the presence of failure. The methods that return a special value are useful in the context of capacity-restricted Queue implementations where failure is a normal occurrence.

Java supplies many Queue implementation classes, where most of these classes are members of the Java.util.concurrent package: LinkedBlockingOueue, LinkedTransferOueue, and SynchronousQueue are examples. In contrast, the Java. util package provides LinkedList and PriorityOueue as its Queue implementation classes.

PriorityQueue

The PriorityOueue class provides an implementation of a *priority queue,* which is a queue that orders its elements according to their natural ordering or by a comparator provided when the queue is instantiated. Priority queues do not permit null elements, and do not permit insertion of non-Comparable objects when relying on natural ordering.

The element at the head of the priority queue is the least element with respect to the specified ordering. If multiple elements are tied for least element, one of those elements is arbitrarily chosen as the least element. Similarly, the element at the tail of the priority queue is the greatest element, which is arbitrarily chosen when there is a tie.

Priority queues are unbounded, but have a capacity that governs the size of the internal array that is used to store the priority queue's elements. The capacity value is at least as large as the queue's length, and grows automatically as elements are added to the priority queue.

PriorityQueue (whose generic type is PriorityOueue <E>) supplies six constructors:

- PriorityOueue( ) creates a PriorityQueue instance with an initial capacity of 11 elements, and which orders its elements according to their natural ordering.
- PriorityQueue(Collection <? extends'E> c) creates aPriorityQueueinstance containing c's elements. If c is a SortedSet or PriorityQueue instance, this priority queue will be ordered according to the same ordering. Otherwise, this priority queue will be ordered according to the natural ordering of its elements. This constructor throws ClassCastException when c's elements cannot be compared to one another according to the priority queue's ordering, and NullPointerException when c or any of its elements contain the null reference.
- PriorityQueue(int initialCapacity) creates a PriorityQueue instance with the specified initialCapacity, and which orders its elements according to their natural ordering. This constructor throws IllegalArgumentException when initialCapacity is less than 1.
- PriorityOueue(int initialCapacity, Comparator? super E > comparator) creates a PriorityQueue instance with the specified initialCapacity, and which orders its elements according to the specified comparator. Natural ordering is used when comparator contains the null reference. This constructor throws IllegalArgumentException when initialCapacity is less than 1.
- PriorityQueue(PriorityOueue <? extends E> pq) creates aPriorityQueueinstance containing pq's elements. This priority queue will be ordered according to the same ordering as pq. This constructor throws ClassCastException when pq's elements cannot be compared to one another according to pq's ordering, and NullPointerException when pq or any of its elements contains the null reference.
- PriorityQueue(SortedSet <? extends E> ss) creates aPriorityQueueinstance containing ss's

elements. This priority queue will be ordered according to the same ordering as ss. This constructor throws ClassCastException when sortedSet's elements cannot be compared to one another according to ss's ordering, and NullPointerException when sortedSet or any of its elements contains the null reference.

Deque

A *deque* (pronounced deck) is a double-ended queue in which element insertion or removal occurs at its *head* or *tail*. Deques can be used as queues or stacks. Deque, whose generic type is Deque < E >, extends Queue, in which the inherited add(E e) method inserts e at the deque's tail. The following table describes Deque-specific methods.

Table Deque-specific Methods

Method	Description
void addFirst(E e)	Insert e at the head of this deque if it is possible to do so immediately without violating capacity restrictions. When using a capacity-restricted deque, it is generally preferable to use method offer Fir st(). This method throws IllegalStateException when e cannot be added at this time because of capacity restrictions, ClassCastException when e's class prevents e from being added to this deque, NullPointerException when e contains the null reference and this deque does not permit null elements to be added, and IllegalArgUmentException when some property of e prevents it from being added to this deque.
void addLast(E e)	Insert e at the tail of this deque if it is possible to do so immediately without violating capacity restrictions. When using a capacity-restricted deque, it is generally preferable to use method offerLast(). This method throws IllegalStateException when e cannot be added at this time because of capacity restrictions, ClassCastException when e's class prevents e from being added to this deque, NullPointerException when e contains the null reference and this deque does not permit null elements to be added, and IllegalArgUmentException when some property of e prevents it from being added to this deque.
Iterator < E > descendingIterator()	Return an iterator over the elements in this deque in reverse sequential order. The elements will be returned in order from last (tail) to first (head). The inherited Iterator < E > iterator () method returns elements from the head to the tail.
E element()	Retrieve hut do not remove die first element of this deque (at me head). This method differs from peekQ only in that it throws NoSuchEleWntException when this deque is empty. This method is equivalent to getFirstQ.
E getFirst()	Retrieve but do not remove the first element of this deque. This method differs from peekFirstQ only in that it throws NoSuchElementException when this deque is empty.
E getLast()	Retrieve but do not remove the last element of this deque. This method differs from peekLast () only in that it throws NoSuchElementException when this deque is empty.

boolean offer(E e)	Insert e at the tail of this deque if it is possible to do so immediately without violating capacity restrictions, returning true upon success and false when no space is currently available. When using a capacity-restricted deque, this method is generally preferable to the add() method, which can fail to insert an element only by throwing an exception. This method throws ClassCastException when e's class prevents e from being added to this deque, NullPointerException when e contains the null reference and this deque does not permit null elements to be added, and IllegalArgumentException when some property of e prevents it from being added to this deque. This method is equivalent to offerLast().
boolean offerFirst(E e)	Insert the specified element at the head of this deque unless it would violate capacity restrictions. When using a capacity-restricted deque, this method is generally preferable to the addFirst () method, which can fail to insert an element only by throwing an exception. This method throws ClassCastException when e's class prevents e from being added to this deque, NullPointerException when e contains the null reference and this deque does not permit null elements to be added, and IllegalArgumentException when some property of e prevents it from being added to this deque.
boolean offerLast(E e)	Insert e at the tail of this deque unless it would violate capacity restrictions. When using a capacity-restricted deque, this method is generally preferable to the addLast () method, which can fail to insert an element only by throwing an exception. This method throws ClassCastException when e's class prevents e from being added to this deque, NullPointerException when e contains the null reference and this deque does not permit null elements to be added, and IllegalArgumentException when some property of e prevents it from being added to this deque.
E peek()	Retrieve but do npt remove the first element of this deque (at the head), or return null when this deque is empty. This method is equivalent to peekFirstQ.
E peekFirst ()	Retrieve but do not remove the first element of this deque (at the head), or return null when this deque is empty.
E peekLastQ	Retrieve but do not remove the last element of this deque (at the tail), or return null when this deque is empty.
E poll ()	Retrieve and remove the first element of this deque (at the head), or return null when this deque is empty. This method is equivalent to pollFirstQ.
E pollFirstQ	Retrieve and remove the first, element of this deque (at the head), or return null when this deque is empty.
E pollLastQ	Retrieve and remove the last element of this deque (at the tail), or return null when this deque is empty.
E pop ()	Pop an element from the stack represented by this deque. In other words, remove and return the first element of this deque. This method is equivalent to removeFirst().

void push(E e)	Push e onto the stack represented by this deque (in other words, at the head of this deque) if it is possible to do so immediately without violating capacity restrictions, returning true upon success and throwing IllegalStateException when no space is currendy available. This method also throws ClassCastException when e's class prevents e from being added to this deque, NullPointerException when e contains the null reference and this deque does not permit null elements to be added, and IllegalArgumentException when some property of e prevents it from being added to this deque. This method is equivalent to addFirst ().
E removeQ	Retrieve and remove the first element of this deque (at the head). This method differs from poll() only in that it throws NoSuchElementException when this deque is empty. This method is equivalent to removeFirst().
E removeFirstQ	Retrieve and remove the first element of this deque. This method differs from pollFirst () only in that it throws NoSuchElementException when this deque is empty.
boolean removeFirstOccurrence(Object o)	Remove the first occurrence of o from this deque. If the deque does not contain o, it is unchanged. Return true when this deque contained o (or equivalently, when this deque changed as a result of the call). This method throws ClassCastException when o's class prevents o from being added to this deque, and NullPointerException when o contains the null reference and this deque does not permit null elements to be added. The inherited boolean remove(Object o) method is equivalent to this method.
E removeLast()	Retrieve and remove the last element of this deque. This method differs from pollLastQ only in that it throws NoSuchElementException when this deque is empty.
boolean removeLastOccurrence(Object o)	Remove the last occurrence of o from this deque. If the deque does not contain o, it is unchanged. Return true when this deque contained o (or equivalently, when this deque changed as a result of the call). This method throws ClassCastException when o's class prevents o from being added to this deque, and NullPointerException when o contains the null reference and this deque does not permit null elements to be added.

As the above table reveals, Deque declares methods to access elements at both ends of the deque. Methods are provided to insert, remove, and examine the element. Each of these methods exists in two forms: one throws an exception when the operation fails, the other returns a special value (either null or false, depending on the operation). The latter form of the insert operation is designed specifically for use with capacity-restricted Deque implementations; in most implementations, insert operations cannot fail.

ArrayDeque

The ArrayDeque class provides a resizable-array implementation of the Deque interface. It prohibits null elements from being added to a deque, and its iterator() method returns fail-fast iterators. ArrayDeque supplies three constructors:

- ArrayDeque() creates an empty array list with an initial capacity of 16 elements.
- ArrayDeque(Collection<? extends E> c) creates an array deque containing c's elements in the order in which they are returned by c's iterator. (The first element returned by c's iterator becomes the first element, or front of the deque.) NullPointerException is thrown when c contains the null reference.
- ArrayDeque(int numElements) creates an empty array deque with an initial capacity sufficient to hold numElements elements. No exception is thrown when the argument passed to numElements is less than or equal to zero.

Map

A *map is* a group of key /value pairs (also known as *entries).* Because the *key* identifies an entry, a map cannot contain duplicate keys. Furthermore, each key can map to at most one value. Maps are described by the Map interface, which has no parent interface, and whose generic type is Map<K, V> (K is the key's type; V is the value's type) .

The following table describes Map's methods.

Table Map-specific Methods

Method	Description
void clear()	Remove all elements from this map, leaving it empty. This method throws UnsupportedOperationException when clear () is not supported.
boolean containsKey(Object key)	Return true when this map contains an entry for the specified key; otherwise, return false. This method throws ClassCast Except ion when key is of an inappropriate type for this map, and NullPointerException when key contains the null reference and this map does not permit null keys.
boolean containsValue(Object value)	Return true when this map maps one or more keys to value. This method throws ClassCastException when value is of an inappropriate type for this map, and NullPointerException when value contains the null reference and this map does not permit null values.
Set<Map.Entry<K,V» entrySetQ	Return a Set view of the entries contained in this map. Because this map backs the view, changes that are made to the map are reflected in the set and vice versa.
boolean equals(Object o)	Compare o with this map for equality. Return true when o is also a map and the two maps represent the same entries; otherwise, return false.
V get(0bject key)	Return the value to which key is mapped, or null when this map contains no entry for key. If this map permits null values, then a return value of null does not necessarily indicate that the map contains no entry for key; it is also possible that the map explicitly maps key to the null reference. The containsKey() method maybe used to distinguish between these two cases. This method throws ClassCastException when key is of an inappropriate type for this map, and NullPointerException when key contains the null reference and this map does not permit null keys.

Method	Description
int hashCode()	Return the hash code for this map. A map's hash code is defined to be the sum of the hash codes for the entries in the map's entry Set () view.
boolean isEmpty()	Return true when this map contains no entries; otherwise, return false.
Set<K> keySet()	Return a Set view of the keys contained in this map. Because this map backs the view, changes that are made to the map are reflected in the set and vice versa.
V put(K key.V value)	Associate value with key in this map. If the map previously contained an entry for key, the old value is replaced by value. This method returns the previous value associated with key, or null when there was no entry for key. (The null return value can also indicate that the map previously associated the null reference with key, if the implementation supports null values.) This method throws UnsupportedOperationException when put() is not supported, ClassCastException when key's or value's class is not appropriate for this map, IllegalArgumentException when some property of key or value prevents it from being stored in this map, and NullPointerException when key or value contains the null reference and this map does not permit null keys or values.
void putAll(Map<? extends K,? extends V> m)	Copy all the entries from map m to this map. The effect of this call is equivalent to that of calling put (k, v) on this map once for each mapping from key k to value v in map m. This method throws UnsupportedOperationException when putAHQ is not supported, ClassCastException when the class of a key or value in map m is not appropriate for this map, IllegalArgumentException when some property of a key or value in map m prevents it from being stored in this map, and NullPointerException when m contains the. null reference or when m contains null keys or values and this map does not permit null keys or values.
V remove(Object key)	Remove key's entry from this map if it is present. This method returns the value to which this map previously associated with key, or null when the map contained no entry for key. If this map permits null values, then a return value of null does not necessarily indicate that the map contained no entry for key; it is also possible that the map explicitly mapped key to null. This map will not contain an entry for key once the call returns. This method throws UnsupportedOperationException when removeQ is not supported, ClassCastException when the class of key is not appropriate for this map, and NullPointerException when key contains the null reference and this map does not permit null keys.
int size()	Return the number of key/value entries in this map. If the map contains more than Integer.MAX_VALUE entries, this method returns Integer.MAXJ/ALUE.
Collection<V> valuesQ	Return a Collection view of the values contained in this map. Because this map backs the view, changes that are made to the map are reflected in the collection and vice versa.

Unlike List, Set, and Queue, Map does not extend Collection. However, it is possible to view a map as a Collection instance by calling Map's keySet (), values (), and entrySet () methods, which respectively return a Set of keys, a Collection of values, and a Set of key/value pair entries.

The entrySet() method returns a Set of Map. Entry objects. Each of these objects describes a single entry as a key/value pair and is an instance of a class that implements the Map. Entry interface, where Entry is a nested interface of Map. The following table describes Map. Entry's methods.

Table Map. Entry Methods

Method	Description
boolean equals(Object o)	Compare o with this entry for equality. Return true when o is also a map entry and the two entries have the same key and value.
K getKey()	Return this entry's key. This method optionally throws IllegalStateException when this entry has previously been removed from the backing map.
V getValue()	Return this entry's value. This method optionally throws IllegalStateException when this entry has previously been removed from the backing map.
int hashCodeQ	Return this entry's hash code.
V setValue(V value)	Replace this entry's value with value. The backing map is updated with the new value. This method throws UnsupportedOperationException when setValue() is not supported, ClassCastException when value's class prevents it from being stored in the backing map, NullPointerException when value contains the null reference and the backing map does not permit null, IllegalArgumentException when some property of value prevents it from being stored in the backing map, and (optionally) IllegalStateException when this entry has previously been removed from the backing map.

TreeMap

The TreeMap class provides a map implementation that is based on a red-black tree. As a result, entries are stored in sorted order of their keys. However, accessing these entries is somewhat slower than with the other Map implementations (which are not sorted) because links must be traversed.

TreeMap supplies four constructors:

- TreeMap () creates a new, empty tree map that is sorted according to the natural ordering of its keys. All keys inserted into the map must implement the Comparable interface.
- TreeMap(Comparator<? super K> comparator) creates a new, empty tree map that is sorted according to the specified comparator. Passing null to comparator implies that natural ordering will be used.
- TreeMap(Map<? extends K, ? extends V> m) creates a new tree map containing m's entries, sorted according to the natural ordering of its keys. All keys inserted into the new map must implement the Comparable interface. This constructor throws ClassCastException when m's keys do not implement Comparable or are not mutually comparable, and NullPointerException when m contains the null reference.

- TreeMap(SortedMap<K, ? extends V> sm) creates a new tree map containing the same entries and using the same ordering as sm. (I discuss sorted maps later in this chapter.) This constructor throws NullPointerException when sm contains the null reference.

HashMap

The HashMap class provides a map implementation that is based on a hashtable data structure. This implementation supports all Map operations, and permits null keys and null values. It makes no guarantees on the order in which entries are stored.

A hashtable maps keys to integer values with the help of a *hash function*. Java provides this function in the form of Object's hashCodeQ method, which classes override to provide appropriate hash codes.

A *hash* code identifies one of the hashtable's array elements, which is known as a *bucket* or *slot*. For some hashtables, the bucket may store the value that is associated with the key.

When storing a value in a hashtable, the hashtable uses the hash function to hash the key to its hash code, and then searches the appropriate linked list to see if an entry with a matching key exists. If there is an entry, its value is updated with the new value. Otherwise, a new node is created, populated with the key and value, and appended to the list.

When retrieving a value from a hashtable, the hashtable uses the hash function to hash the key to its hash code, and then searches the appropriate linked list to see if an entry with a matching key exists. If there is an entry, its value is returned. Otherwise, the hashtable may return a special value to indicate that there is no entry, or it might throw an exception.

The number of buckets is known as the hashtable's *capacity*. The ratio of the number of stored entries divided by the number of buckets is known as the hashtable's *load factor*. Choosing the right load factor is important for balancing performance with memory use:

- As the load factor approaches 1, the probability of collisions and the cost of handling them (by searching lengthy linked lists) increase.
- As the load factor approaches 0, the hashtable's size in terms of number of buckets increases with little improvement in search cost.
- For many hashtables, a load factor of 0.75 is close to optimal. This value is the default for HashMap's hashtable implementation.

HashMap supplies four constructors:

- HashMap() creates anew, empty hashmap with an initial capacity of 16 and a load factor of 0.75.
- HashMap(int initialCapacity) creates a new, empty hashmap with a capacity specified by initialCapacity and a load factor of 0.75. This constructor throws IllegalArgumentException when initialCapacity's value is less than 0.
- HashMap(int initialCapacity, float loadFactor) creates a new, empty hashmap with a capacity specified by initialCapacity and a load factor specified by loadFactor. This constructor throws IllegalArgumentException when initialCapacity is less than 0 or when loadFactor is less than or equal to 0.
- HashMap(Map<? extends K, ? extends V> m) creates a new hashmap containing m's entries. This constructor throws NullPointerException when m contains the null reference.

IdentityHashMap

The IdentityHashMap class provides a Map implementation that uses reference equality (= =) instead of object equality (equals()) when comparing keys and values. This is an intentional violation of Map's general contract, which mandates the use of equals () when comparing elements.

IdentityHashMap obtains hash codes via System's static int identityHashCode(Object x) method instead of via each key's hashCodeQ method. identityHashCodeQ returns the same hash code for x as returned by Object's hashCodeQ method, whether or not x's class overrides hashCodeQ. The hash code for the null reference is zero.

These characteristics give IdentityHashMap a performance advantage over other Map implementations. Also, IdentityHashMap supports *mutable keys* (objects used as keys and whose hash codes change when their field values change while in the map).

WeakHashMap

The WeakHashMap class provides a Map implementation that is based on weakly reachable keys. Because each key object is stored indirectly as the referent of a weak reference, the key is automatically removed from the map only after the garbage collector clears all weak references to the key (inside and outside of the map).

In contrast, value objects are stored via strong references (and should not strongly refer to their own keys, either directiy or indirectiy, because doing so prevents their associated keys from being discarded). When a key is removed from a map, its associated value object is also removed.

EnumMap

The EnumMap class provides a Map implementation whose keys are the members of the same enum. Null keys are not permitted; any attempt to store a null key results in a thrown NullPointerException. Because an enum map is represented internally as an array, an enum map approaches an array in terms of performance.

EnumMap supplies the following constructors:

- EnumMap(Class<K> key Type) creates an empty enum map with the specified key Type. This constructor throws NullPointerException when key Type contains the null reference.
- EnumMap(EnumMap<K, ? extends V> m) creates an enum map with the same key type as *m*, and with m's entries. This constructor throws NullPointerException when *m* contains the null reference.
- EnumMap(Map<K,? extends V> m) creates an enum map initialized with m's entries. If m is an EnumMap instance, this constructor behaves like the previous constructor. Otherwise, m must contain at least one entry in order to determine the new enum map's key type. This constructor throws NullPointerException when m contains the null reference, and IllegalArgumentException when m is not an EnumMap instance and is empty.

SortedMap

TreeMap is an example *of a sorted map,* which is a map that maintains its entries in ascending order, sorted according to the keys' natural ordering or according to a comparator that is supplied when the sorted map is created. Sorted maps are described by the SortedMap interface.

SortedMap, whose generic type is SortedMap<K, V>, extends Map. With two exceptions, the methods it inherits from Map behave identically on sorted maps as on other maps:

- The Iterator instance returned by the iterator () method on any of the sorted map's Collection views traverses the collections in order.
- The arrays returned by the Collection views' toArray () methods contain the keys, values, or entries in order. j

SortedMap's documentation requires that an implementation must provide the four standard constructors that I presented in my discussion of TreeMap. Furthermore, implementations of this interface must implement the methods that are described in the following table.

Table SortedMap-specific Methods

Method	Description
Comparator<? super K> comparator()	Return the comparator used to order the keys in this map, or null when this map uses the natural ordering of its keys.
Set<Map.Entry<K,V» entrySetQ	Return a Set view of the mappings contained in this map. The set's iterator returns these entries in ascending key order. Because this map backs the view, changes that are made to the map are reflected in the set and vice versa.
K firstKey()	Return the first (lowest) key currently in this map, or throw a NoSuchElementException instance when this map is empty.
SortedMap<K,V> headMap(K toKey)	Return a view of that portion of this map whose keys are strictly less than toKey. Because this map backs the returned map, changes in the returned map are reflected in this map and vice versa. The returned map supports all optional map operations that this map supports. This method throws ClassCastException when toKey is not compatible with this map's comparator (or, when the map has no comparator, when toKey does not implement Comparable), NullPointerException when toKey is null and this map does not permit null keys, and IllegalArgumentException when this map has a restricted range and toKey lies outside of this range's bounds.
Set<K> keySet()	Return a Set view of the keys contained in this map. The set's iterator returns the keys in ascending order. Because the map backs the view, changes that are made to the map are reflected in the set and vice versa.
K lastKey()	Return the last (highest) key currently in this map, or throw a NoSuchElementException instance when this map is empty.
SortedMap<K,V> subMap(K fromKey, K toKey)	Return a view of the portion of this map whose keys range from fromKey, inclusive, to toKey, exclusive. (When fromKey and toKey are equal, the returned map is empty.) Because this map backs the returned map, changes in the returned map are reflected in this map and vice versa. The returned map supports all optional map operations diat this map supports. This method throws ClassCastException when fromKey and toKey cannot be compared to one another using this map's comparator (or, when the map has no comparator, using natural ordering), NullPointerException when fromKey or toKey is null and this map does not permit null keys, and IllegalArgumentException when fromKey is greater than toKey or when this map has a restricted range and fromKey or toKey lies outside its bounds.
SortedMap<K,V> tailMap(K fromKey)	Return a view of that portion of this map whose keys are greater than or equal to fromKey. Because this map backs the returned map, changes in the returned map are reflected in this map and vice versa. The returned map supports all optional map operations that this

	map supports. This method throws ClassCastException when fromKey is not compatible with this map's comparator (or, when the map has no comparator, when fromKey does not implement Comparable), NullPointerException when fromKey is null and this map does not permit null keys, and IllegalArgumentException when this map has a restricted range and fromKey lies outside of the range's bounds.
Collection<V> values()	Return a Collection view of the values contained in this map. The collection's iterator returns the values in ascending order of the corresponding keys. Because the map backs the collection, changes that are made to the map are reflected in the collection and vice versa.

NavigableMap

TreeMap is an example of a navigable map, which is a sorted map that can be iterated over in descending order as well as ascending order, and which can report closest matches for given search targets. Navigable maps are described by the NavigableMap interface, whose generic type is NavigableMap<K,V>, which extends SortedMap, and which is described in the following table.

Table NavigableMap -specific Methods

Method	Description
Map.Entry<K,V> ceilingEntry(K key)	Return the key-value mapping associated with the least key greater than or equal to key, or null when there is no such key. This method throws ClassCastException when key cannot be compared with the keys currently in the map, and NullPointerException when key is null and this map does not permit null keys.
K ceilingKey(K key)	Return the least key greater than or equal to key, or null when there is no such key. This method throws ClassCastException when key cannot be compared with the keys currently in the map, and NullPointerException when key is null and this map does not permit null keys.
NavigableSet<K> descendingKeySet()	Return a reverse order navigable set-based view of the keys contained in this map. The set's iterator returns the keys in descending order. This map backs the set, so changes to the map are reflected in the set and vice versa. If the map is modified (except through the iterator's own remove() operation) while iterating over the set, the results of the iteration are undefined.
NavigableMap<K,V> descendingMap()	Return a reverse order view of the mappings contained in this map. This map backs the descending map, so changes to the map are reflected in the descending map and vice versa. If either map is modified while iterating over a collection view of either map (except through the iterator's own remove () operation), the results of the iteration are undefined.
Map.Entry<K,V> firstEntry()	Return a key-value mapping associated with the least key in this map, or null when the map is empty.
Map.Entry<K,V> floorEntry(K key)	Return a key-value mapping associated with the greatest key less than or equal to key, or null when there is no such key. This

	method throws ClassCastException when key cannot be compared with the keys currently in the map, and NullPointerException when key is null and this map does not permit null keys.
K floorKey(K key)	Return the greatest key less than or equal to key, or null when there is no such key. This method throws ClassCastException when key cannot be compared with the keys currently in the map, and NullPointerException when key is null and this map does not permit null keys.
NavigableMap<K,V> headMap(K toKey, boolean inclusive)	Return a view of the portion of this map whose keys are less than (or equal to, when inclusive is true) toKey. This map backs the returned map, so changes in the returned map are reflected in this map and vice versa. The returned map supports all optional map operations that this map supports. This method throws ClassCastException when toKey is not compatible with this map's comparator (or, when the map has no comparator, when toMap does not implement Comparable), NullPointerException when toMap is null and this map does not permit null keys, and IllegalArgumentException when this map has a restricted range and toKey lies outside of this range's bounds.
Map.Entry<K,V> higherEntry(K key)	Return a key-value mapping associated with the least key strictly greater than key, or null when there is no such key. This method throws ClassCastException when key cannot be compared with the keys currently in the map, and NullPointerException when key is null and this map does not permit null keys.
K higherKey(K key)	Return the least key strictly greater than key, or null when there is no such key. This method throws ClassCastException when key cannot be compared with the keys currently in the map, and NullPointerException when key is null and this map does not permit null keys.
Map.Entry<K,V> lastEntry()	Return a key-value mapping associated with the greatest key in this map, or null when the map is empty.
Map.Entry<K,V> lowerEntry(K key)	Return a key-value mapping associated with the greatest key strictly less than key, or null when there is no such key. This method throws ClassCastException when key cannot be compared with the keys currently in the map, and NullPointerException when key is null and this map does not permit null keys.
K lowerKey(K key)	Return the greatest key strictly less than key, or null when there is no such key. This method throws ClassCastException when key cannot be compared with the keys currently in the map, and NullPointerException when key is null and this map does not permit null keys.
NavigableSet<K> navigableKeySet()	Return a navigable set-based view of the keys contained in this map. The set's iterator returns the keys in ascending order. This map backs the set, so changes to the map are reflected in the set and vice versa. If the map is modified while iterating over the set (except through the iterator's own remove () operation), the results of the iteration are undefined.

Map.Entry<K,V> pollFirstEntry()	Remove and return a key-value mapping associated with the least key in this map, or null when the map is empty.
Map.Entry<K,V> pollLastEntry()	Remove and return a key-value mapping associated with the greatest key in this map, or null when the map is empty.
NavigableMap<K,V> subMap(K fromKey, boolean fromInclusive, K toKey, boolean toInclusive)	Return a view of the portion of this map whose keys range from fromKey to toKey. (When fromKey and toKey are equal, the returned map is empty unless fromInclusive and toInclusive are both true.) This map backs the returned map, so changes in the returned map are reflected in this map and vice versa. The returned map supports all optional map operations that this map supports. This method throws ClassCastException when fromKey and toKey cannot be compared to one another using this map's comparator (or, when the map has no comparator, using natural ordering), NullPointerException when fromKey or toKey is null and this map does not permit null elements, and IllegalArgumentException when fromKey is greater than toKey or when this map has a restricted range and fromKey or toMap lies outside of this range's bounds.
NavigableMap<K,V> tailMap(K fromKey, boolean inclusive)	Return a view of the portion of this map whose keys are greater than (or equal to, when inclusive is true) fromKey. This map backs the returned map, so changes in the returned map are reflected in this map and vice versa. The returned map supports all optional map operations that this map supports. This method throws ClassCastException when fromKey is not compatible with this map's comparator (or, when the map has no comparator, when fromKey does not implement Comparable), NullPointerException when fromKey is null and this map does not permit null keys, and IllegalArgumentException when this map has a restricted range and fromKey lies outside of this range's bounds.

The above table's methods describe the NavigableMap equivalents of the NavigableSet methods presented earlier, and even return NavigableSet instances in two instances.

Utilities

The Collections Framework would not be complete without its Arrays and Collections utility classes. Each class supplies various class methods that implement useful algorithms in the contexts of arrays and collections.

Following is a sampling of the Arrays class's array-oriented utility methods:

- static <T> List<T> asList(T... a) returns a fixed-size list backed by array a. (Changes to the returned list "write through" to the array.) For example, List<String> birds = Arrays.asList("Robin", "Oriole", "Bluejay"); converts the three-element array of Strings (recall that a variable sequence of arguments is implemented as an array) to a List whose reference is assigned to birds.
- static int binarySearch(int[] a, int key) searches array a for entry key using the binary search algorithm (explained following this list). The array must be sorted before calling this method; otherwise, the results are undefined. This method returns the index of the search key, if it is contained in the array; otherwise, (-(insertion point)-!) is returned. The insertion point is the

point at which key would be inserted into the array (the index of the first element greater than key, or a. length if all elements in the array are less than key) and guarantees that the return value will be greater than or equal to 0 if and only if key is found. Forexample,Arrays.binarySearch(new String[] {"Robin", "Oriole", "Bluejay"}, "Oriole") returns 1, "Oriole"'s index.

- static void fill(char[] a, char ch) stores ch in each element of the specified character array. For example, Arrays.fill(screen[i], ' '); fills the ith row of a 2D screen array with spaces.
- static void sort(long[] a) sorts the elements in long integer array a into ascending numerical order; for example, long lArray = new longf] { 20000L, 89L, 66L, 33L}; Arrays.sort(lArray);.
- static <T> void sort(T[] a, Comparator? super T> c) sorts the elements in array a using comparator c to order them. For example, when given Comparator<String> cmp = new Comparator<String>() { public int compare(String el, String e2) { return e2.compareTo(el); } }; String[] innerPlanets = { "Mercury", "Venus", "Earth", "Mars" };, Arrays.sort(innerPlanets, cmp); uses cmp to help in sorting innerPlanets into descending order of its elements: Venus, Mercury, Mars, Earth is the result.

There are two common algorithms for searching an array for a specific element. *Linear search* searches the array element by element from index 0 to the index of the searched-for element or the end of the array. On average, half of the elements must be searched; larger arrays take longer to search. However, the arrays do not need to be sorted.

In contrast, *binary search* searches ordered array *a's n* items for element e in a much faster amount of time. It works by recursively performing the following steps:

1. Set low index to 0.
2. Set high index to n-1.
3. If low index > high index, then Print "Unable to find " e. End.
4. Set middle index to (low index + high index) 12.
5. If e > a [middle index], then set low index to middle index + 1. Go to 3.
6. If e < a[middle index], then set high index to middle index-1. Go to 3.
7. Print "Found " e " at index" middle index.

The algorithm is similar to optimally looking for a name in a phone book. Start by opening the book to the exact middle. If the name is not on that page, proceed to open the book to the exact middle of the first half or the second half, depending on in which half the name occurs. Repeat until you find the name (or not).

Applying a linear search to 4,000,000,000 elements results in approximately 2,000,000,000 comparisons (on average), which takes time. In contrast, applying a binary search to 4,000,000,000 elements results in a maximum of 32 comparisons. This is why Arrays contains binarySearchQ methods and not also linearSearchQ methods.

Following is a sampling of the Collections class's collection-oriented class methods:

- static <T-extends Object&Comparable<? super T» T min(Collection<? extends T> c) returns the minimum element of collection c according to the natural ordering of its elements. For example, System.out.println(Collections.min(Arrays.asList(lOj 3, 18, 25))); outputs 3. All of c's elements must implement the Comparable interface. Furthermore, all elements must be mutually comparable. This method throws NoSuchElementException when c is empty.
- static void reverse(List<?> 1) reverses the order of list 1's elements. For example, List<String> birds = Arrays.asList("Robin", "Oriole", "Bluejay"); Collections.reverse(birds); System.out.println(birds); results in [Bluejay, Oriole, Robin] as the output

- static <T> List<T> singletonList(T o) returns an immutable list containing only object o. For example, list. removeAll(Collections.singletonList (null)); removes all null elements from list.
- static <T> Set<T> synchronizedSet(Set<T> s) returns a synchronized (thread-safe) set backed by set s; for example, Set<String> ss = Collections. synchronizedSet (new HashSet<String> ());. In order to guarantee serial access, it is critical that all access to the backing set is accomplished through the returned set.
- static <K,V> Map<K,V> unmodifiableMap(Map<? extends K,? extends V> m) returns an unmodifiable view of map m; for example, Map<String, Integer> msi = Collections.synchronizedMap(new HashMap<String, Integer>());. Query operations on the returned map "read through" to the specified map, and attempts to modify the returned map, whether direct or via its collection views, result in an UnsupportedOperationException.

You might be wondering about the purpose for the various "empty" class methods in the Collections class. For example, static final <T> List<T> empty List () returns an immutable empty list, as in List<String> ls = Collections. empty List();. These methods are present because they offer a useful alternative to returning null (and avoiding potential NullPointerExceptions) in certain contexts.

Legacy Collections APIs

Java 1.2 introduced the Collections Framework. Prior to the framework's inclusion in Java, developers had two choices where collections were concerned: create their own frameworks, or use the Vector, Enumeration, Stack, Dictionary, Hashtable, Properties, and BitSet types, which were introduced by Java 1.0.

Vector is a concrete class that describes a growable array, much like ArrayList. Unlike an ArrayList instance, a Vector instance is synchronized. Vector has been generified and also retrofitted to support the Collections Framework, which makes statements such as List<String> list = new Vector<String>(); legal.

The Collections Framework provides Iterator for iterating over a collection's elements. In contrast, Vector's elements () method returns an instance of a class that implements the Enumeration interface for *enumerating* (iterating over and returning) a Vector instance's elements via Enumeration's hasMoreElements() andnextElementQ methods.

Vector is subclassed by the concrete Stack class, which represents a LIFO data structure. Stack provides an E push(E item) method for pushing an object onto the stack, an E pop () method for popping an item off the top of the stack, and a few other methods, such as boolean empty () for determining whether or not the stack is empty.

Stack is a good example of bad API design. By inheriting from Vector, it is possible to call Vector's void add(int index, E element) method to add an element anywhere you wish, and violate a Stack instance's integrity. In hindsight, Stack should have used composition in its design: use a Vector instance to store a Stack instance's elements.

Dictionary is an abstract superclass for subclasses that map keys to values. The concrete Hashtable class is Dictionary's only subclass. As with Vector, HashTable instances are synchronized, HashTable has been generified, and HashTable has been retrofitted to support the Collections Framework.

Hashtable is subclassed by Properties, a concrete class representing a persistent set *of properties* (String-based key/value pairs that identify application settings). Properties provides Object setProperty(String key, String value) for storing a property, and public String get Property (String key) for returning a property's value.

Properties is another good example of bad API design. By inheriting from Hashtable, you can call Hashtable'sV put(K key, V value) method to store an entry with anon-String key and/or anon-String value.

In hindsight, Properties should have leveraged composition: store a Properties instance's elements in a Hashtable instance.

Finally, BitSet is a concrete class that describes a variable-length set of bits. This class's ability to represent bitsets of arbitrary length contrasts with the previously described integer-based, fixed-length bitset that is limited to a maximum number of members: 32 members for an int-based bitset, or 64 members for a long-based bitset.

BitSet provides a pair of constructors for initializing a BitSet instance: BitSet () initializes the instance to initially store an implementation-dependent number of bits, whereas BitSet (int nbits) initializes the instance to initially store nbits bits. BitSet also provides various methods, including the following:

- void and(BitSet bs) bitwise ANDs this bitset with bs. This bitset is modified such that a bit is set to 1 when it and the bit at the same position in bs are 1.
- void andNot(BitSet bs) sets all the bits in this bitset to 0 whose corresponding bits are set to 1 in bs.
- void c lear () sets all the bits in this bitset to 0.
- Object clone() clones this bitset to produce a new bitset. The clone has exactly the same bits set to one as this bitset.
- boolean get(int bitIndex) returns the value of this bitset's bit, as a Boolean true/false value (true for 1, false for 0) at the zero-based bitIndex. This method throws IndexOutOf BoundsException when bitIndex is less than 0.
- int length () returns the "logical size" of this bitset, which is the index of the highest 1 bit plus 1, or 0 when this bitset contains no 1 bits.
- void or(BitSet bs) bitwise inclusive ORs this bitset with bs. This bitset is modified such that a bit is set to 1 when it or the bit at the same position in bs is 1, or when both bits are 1.
- void set(int bitIndex, boolean value) sets the bit at the zero-based bitIndex to value (true is converted to 1; false is converted to 0). This method throws IndexOutOf BoundsException when bitIndex is less than 0.
- int size() returns the number of bits that are being used by this bitset to represent bit values.
- String toString () returns a string representation of this bitset in terms of the positions of bits that are 1; for example, {4, 5, 9, 10}.
- void xor (BitSet set) bitwise exclusive ORs this bitset with bs. This bitset is modified such that a bit is set to 1 when either it or the bit at the same position in bs (but not both) is 1.

CHAPTER 4

Creating Graphical User Interface

In this chapter you will read about:

- Abstract Window Toolkit.
- Components, Containers, Layout Managers, and Events.
- Images.
- Data Transfer.

Introduction

The applications presented in previous chapters featured Standard I/O-based user interfaces. Although these simple character-oriented user interfaces are convenient for demonstrating Java features or for interacting with small utility applications, they are inadequate for more sophisticated needs, such as filling out forms or viewing HTML pages. However, Java also provides APIs that let you create and enrich more sophisticated graphical user interfaces (GUIs).

Abstract Window Toolkit (AWT) is Java's original GUI-oriented API. After introducing AWT to Java, Sun Microsystems introduced Java Foundation Classes (JFC) as an AWT superset with many new capabilities. JFC's main APIs are Swing (for creating more sophisticated GUIs), Accessibility (for supporting assistive technologies), Java 2D (for creating high-quality graphics), and Drag and Drop (for dragging and dropping AWT/Swirig GUI components, such as buttons or textfields).

Abstract Window Toolkit

Abstract Window Toolkit (AWT) is Java's original windowing system-independent API for creating GUIs that are based on componerts, containers, layout managers, and events. AWT also supports graphics, colors, fonts, images, data transfer, and more.

The standard class library organizes AWT's many types into the Java. awt package and subpackages. However, not all Java. awt types and subpackages belong to AWT. For example, Java. awt. Graphics2D and Java. awt. geom belong to Java 2D. This arrangement exists because the Java. awt-based package structure provides a natural fit for various non-AWT types. (AWT is often viewed as part of JFC nowadays.)

Toolkits

AWT uses toolkits to abstract over windowing systems. A *toolkit is* a concrete implementation of AWT's abstract Java. awt. Toolkit class. AWT provides a separate toolkit for each windowing system used by the Windows, Solaris, Linux, and Mac OS platforms.

Toolkit declares various methods that AWT calls to obtain information about the platform's windowing system, and to perform various windowing system-specific tasks. For example, void beep () emits an audio beep.

Most applications should not call any of Toolkit's methods directly; they are intended for use by AWT. However, you might occasionally find it helpful to call some of these methods.

For example, you might want your application to sound one or more beeps when a long-running task finishes, to alert the user who might not be looking at the screen. You can accomplish this task by specifying code that's similar to the following:

```
Toolkit toolkit = Toolkit.getDefaultToolkit();
for (int i = o ; i < 5; i++)
{
toolkit.beep();
try { Thread.sleep(200); } catch (InterruptedException ie) {} }
```

This example reveals that you must obtain a Toolkit instance before you can call a Toolkit method, and that you do so by calling Toolkit's Toolkit getDef aultToolkit() class method. It also reveals that you might want to place a small delay between successive beeps to ensure that each beep is distinct.

Components, Containers, Layout Managers, and Events

AWT lets you create GUIs that are based on components, containers, layout managers, and events.

A *component is* a graphical widget that appears in a window on the screen; a label, a button, or a textfield is an example. A window is represented by a special component known as a *container.*

A *layout manager is* an object that organizes components and containers within a container. It is used to create useful GUIs (e.g., a form consisting of labels, textfields, and buttons).

An *eventis* an object describing a button click or other GUI interaction. Applications register *event listener* objects with components to listen for specific events so that application code can respond to them.

Components Overview

AWT provides a wide variety of component classes in the Java. awt package. The following is the class hierarchy for AWT's nonmenu component classes.

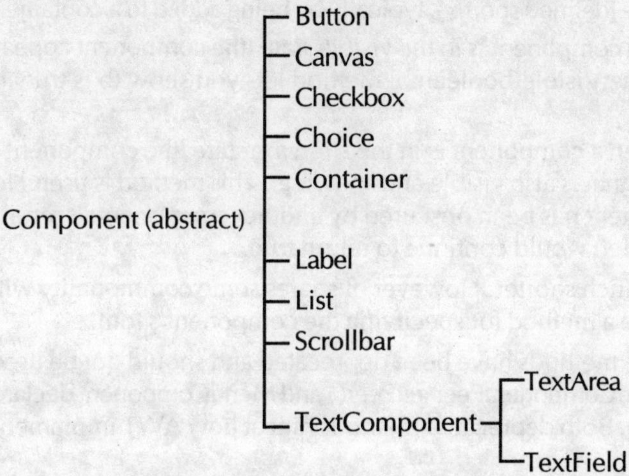

AWT's abstract Component class is the root class for all AWT nonmenu components (and Swing components). Directly beneath Component are Button, Canvas, Checkbox, Choice, Container, Label, List, Scrollbar, andTextComponent:

- Button describes a clickable label.
- Canvas describes a blank rectangular area. You would subclass Canvas to introduce your own AWT components.
- Checkbox describes a true/false choice. You can use Checkbox with Java. awt. CheckboxGroup to create a set of mutually exclusive radio buttons.
- Choice describes a drop-down list (also known as a pop-up menu) of strings.
- Container describes a component that stores other components. This nesting capability lets you create GUIs of arbitrary complexity and is very powerful.
- Label describes a single line of static text as a visual aid to the user.
- List describes a non-drop-down list of strings.
- Scrollbar describes a range of values.
- TextComponent describes any component that inputs text. Its TextArea subclass describes a text component for inputting multiple lines of text, whereas its TextField subclass describes a text component for inputting a single line of text.

AWT's abstract MenuComponent class (which doesn't extend Component) is the root class for all AWT menu components. Directly beneath MenuComponent are MenuBar and MenuItem:

- MenuBar encapsulates the windowing system concept of a menubar bound to a frame window. It contains a sequence of Menu components, where each Menu component contains a sequence of MenuItem components.

- MenuItem describes a single menuitem. Its CheckboxMenuItem subclass describes a menuitem that's implemented via a checkbox. Its Menu subclass describes a pull-down menu component that's deployed from a menu bar. (Menu extends MenuItem to create arbitrarily complex menus.) Menu is subclassed by PopupMenu to describe a menu that can be dynamically popped up at a specified position within a component.

Component declares many nonmenu component-oriented methods. For example, Component declares the following methods to inform the caller about the component's displayable, visible, and showing status:

- boolean isDisplayable() returns true when a component is in the *displayable state* (the component is connected to a native screen resource [defined shortly], typically by being added to a container).
- boolean isVisible() returns true when a component is in the *visible state* (the component appears on the screen). The companion void setVisible(boolean b) method lets you show (b is true) or hide (b is false) a component.
- boolean isShowingQ returns true when a component is in the *showing state* (the component is visible and is contained in a container that is also visible and showing). This method is useful for determining whether or not a component has been obscured by another component. It returns false when obscured, whereas isVisible() would continue to return true.

MenuComponent's repertoire of methods is much shorter. However, it shares some commonality with Component. For example, both classes declare a method for specifying the component's font.

Some of Component's and MenuComponent's methods have been deprecated and should not be used. For example, Component declares Java.awt.peer.ComponentPeer getPeer( ) and MenuComponent declares java.awt.peer.MenuComponentPeer getPeer( ). Both deprecated methods hint at how AWT implements its predefined components.

AWT leverages the platform's windowing system to create various components. When you add a component to a container, AWT creates a peer object whose class implements a ComponentPeer or MenuComponentPeer subinterface. For example, AWT creates a Java. awt. peer. ButtonPeer instance when you add a Button component class instance to a container.

Behind the scenes, the component object communicates with the peer object, which communicates with native code in a JDK library. This code communicates with the platform's windowing system, which manages the *native screen resource* (a native window) that appears on the screen.

For example, when you add a Button instance to a container, AWT calls Component's void addNotify() method, which obtains the current toolkit and calls its ButtonPeer createButton(Button target) method to create this toolkit's Button peer.

Ultimately, the windowing system is asked to create a button native screen resource. For example, on a 32-bit Windows operating system, the native screen resource could be obtained via a call to the Createwindow( ) or CreateWindowEx( ) Win32 API function.

AWT components except for those created from nonpredefined classes that directly extend Component or Container are known as *heavyweight components* because of their corresponding peer interfaces and native screen resources. Components created from custom Component and Container subclasses are known as *lightweight components* because they do not have peer interfaces and native screen resources (they reuse their closest ancestor's peer, which is how Swing works). You can call Component's boolean is Lightweight () method to determine if a component is lightweight.

As you explore the JDK documentation for the various component classes, you'll discover many useful constructors and methods. For example, Button declares a Button(String label) constructor for initializing a button to the specified label text. Alternatively, you could call the Button( ) constructor to create a

Button with no label. Regardless of which constructor you use, you can always call Button's void setLabel(String label) and String getLabel( ) methods to specify and retrieve the label text that is displayed on the button. (Changing a button's displayed text invalidates the button; AWT then performs validation, which causes the component hierarchy to be re-laid out.)

Components are easy to create, as demonstrated by the following example, which creates a Yes button:

```
Button btnYes = new Button("Yes");
```

Containers Overview

Buttons, labels, textfields, and other components cannot be.placed directly on the screen; they need to be placed in a container window that is placed directly on the screen.

AWT provides several container classes in the Java. awt package. AWT's Container class is the root class for all AWT containers. Directly beneath Container are Panel, ScrollPane, and Window:

- Panel is the simplest container. It provides space in which an application can attach any other component, including other panels.
- ScrollPane implements automatic horizontal and/or vertical scrolling for a single *child* (contained) component. A container that contains a component is referred to as that component's *parent*.
- Window is a top-level window with no borders. Its Dialog subclass describes a *dialog box* (a window for soliciting input from the user) and its Frame subclass describes *a frame window* (a top-level window with borders, including a titlebar). Dialog's FileDialog subclass describes a dialog box for selecting a file.

Container declares many container-oriented methods. For example, Component add (Component comp) appends component comp to the container, Component[ ] getComponents( ) returns an array of the container's components, and int getComponentCount( ) returns the number of components in the container.

Window declares a void pack() method for making a top-level window just large enough to display all its components at their *preferred* (natural) sizes. Also, pack( ) makes the window (and any owner of the window—dialog boxes are typically owned by other windows) displayable when not already displayable.

Window also declares a void setSize(int width, int height) method that lets you size a window to a specific size (in pixels).

Continuing from the previous example, suppose you want to add the Yes button to a panel (which might also contain a No button). The following example shows you how to accomplish this task:

```
Panel pnl = new PanelQ; pnl.add(btnYes);
```

Layout Managers Overview

Containers can contain components but cannot lay them out on the screen (e.g., in rows, in a grid, or in some other arrangement). Layout managers handle this task. A layout manager is typically associated with a container to lay out the container's components. AWT provides several layout managers in the Java. awt package: BorderLayout (lay out no more than five components in a container's north, south, east, west, and center areas), CardLayout (treat each contained component as a card; only one card is visible at a time, and the container acts as a stack of cards), FlowLayout (arrange components in a horizontal row), GridBagLayout (lay out components vertically, horizontally, or along their *baseline* [line serving as an origin for the purpose of layout] without requiring that the components be of the same size), and GridLayout (lay out the components in a rectangular grid).

Layout manager classes implement the Java. awt. LayoutManager interface, which declares methods that AWT calls when a container's components need to be laid out. You don't need to be aware of these methods unless you're planning to create your own layout manager. If so, you'll also want to be aware of Java.awt. LayoutManager2, a LayoutManager subinterface.

Layout managers learn about a component's/container's preferred, maximum, and minimum sizes by calling Component's Dimension getPreferredSizeQ, Dimension getMaximumSizeQ, and Dimension getMinimumSizeQ methods. (The aforementioned layout manager classes don't take maximum size into account because these classes were introduced in JDK 1.0, and support for maximum size was not introduced [via LayoutManager2] until JDK 1.1.)

Each container has a default layout manager. For example, Frame's default layout manager is BorderLayout, whereas Panel's default layout manager is FlowLayout. You can replace this default by calling Container's void setLayout(LayoutManager mgr) method to install your own layout manager, as demonstrated here:

```
Panel pnl = new PanelQ;
pnl.setLayout(new GridLayout(3, 2));
```

The first line creates a Panel that defaults to FlowLayout. The second line replaces this layout manager with a Grid Layout that lays out a maximum of six components in a three-row-by-two-column grid.

Events Overview

Users press keys, click buttons, move the mouse, select menuitems, and perform other GUI interactions. Each interaction is known as an *event,* and is described by a concrete Java. awt. event subclass of the abstract Java. awt.AWTEvent class.

AWTEvent is subclassed by several event classes: ActionEvent, AdjustmentEvent, AncestorEvent, ComponentEvent, HierarchyEvent, InputMethodEvent, InternalFrameEvent, InvocationEvent, ItemEvent, andTextEvent.

ComponentEvent is the superclass for ContainerEvent, FocusEvent, InputEvent, PaintEvent, and WindowEvent. InputEvent is the abstract superclass for KeyEvent, which is subclassed by MenuKeyEvent, • and MouseEvent, which is subclassed by MenuDragMouseEvent and MouseWheelEvent.

Components that generate events are known as *event sources.* As events occur, AWTEvent subclass instances are created to describe them. Each instance is posted to an *event queue* and subsequently *dispatched* (sent) to the appropriate event listeners that were previously registered with the event source. Event listeners respond to these events in some way, which typically involves updating the GUI.

An event listener is registered with a component by calling the component class's appropriate addxListenerQ method on die component instance, where x is replaced with an event class name without the Event suffix. For example, you would register an action listener with a button by calling Button's void addActionListener(ActionListener al) method.

ActionListener is an interface in the Java. awt. event package. AWT calls its void actionPerf ormed(ActionEvent ae) method with the ActionEvent object when an action event occurs.

The following example registers an action listener with the previously created Yes button:

```
btnYes.addActionListener(new ActionListener()
    {
        public void actionPerformed(ActionEvent ae)
        {
            System.out.println("Yes was clicked");
        }
    };
```

When the user clicks the Yes button, AWT calls actionPerformedQ with an ActionEvent object as this method's argument. The listener responds by outputting a message on the standard output device.

Button also declares a void removeActionListener(ActionListener al) method for unregistering the previously registered action listener identified as al. Other component classes also declare their own removexListener(xListener) methods.

ActionListener declares a single method, but some listeners declare multiple methods. For example, WindowListener declares seven methods. Because it can be tedious to override each method wherever you need to implement the interface, AWT also provides the concept of an *adapter,* which is a convenience class that implements a multimethod interface by providing an empty version of each method. For example, the Java. awt. event package includes a WindowAdapter class, which you'll see demonstrated shortly.

Demonstrating Components, Containers, Layout Managers, and Events

Now that you've learned some basics of components, containers, layout managers, and events (and event listeners), let's find out how to combine them into a useful AWT-based GUI. I've created a simple temperature-conversion application that presents a GUI for obtaining degree input, displaying degree output, and triggering conversions to degrees Celsius/Fahrenheit. The following listing presents the source code.

A simple GUI consisting of two labels, two textflelds, and two buttons

```
import Java.awt.Button;
import Java.awt.EventOueue;
import Java.awt.Frame;
import Java.awt.GridLayout;
import Java.awt.Label;
import Java.awt.Panel;
import Java.awt.TextField;
import Java.awt.Window;

import Java.awt.event.ActionEvent;
import Java.awt.event.ActionListener;
import Java.awt.event.WindowAdapter; import Java.awt.event.WindowEvent;

class TempVerter extends Frame
{
    TempVerter()
    {
        super("TempVerter");
        addWindowListener(new WindowAdapter()
            {
                @Override
                public void windowClosing(WindowEvent we)
                {
                    System.out.println("window closing");
                    disposeQ;
                @Override
                public void windowClosed(WindowEvent we)
                {
                    System. out. println( "window closed");
                }
            }};
  Panel pnlLayout = new PanelQ;
  pnlLayout.setLayout(new GridLayout(3,
  pnlLayout . add (new Label( "Degrees" ) ) ;
```

CHAPTER 4

```
final TextField txtDegrees = new TextField(lO);
pnlLayout . add (txtDegrees );
pnlLayout . add (new Label (" Result "));
final TextField txtResult = new TextField(30);
pnlLayout . add (txtResult) ;
ActionListener al;
al = new ActionListener ()
  {
      @Override
      public void actionPerformed(ActionEvent ae)
      {
         try
         {
             double value = Double.parseDouble(txtDegrees.getTextQ);
             double result = (value-32.0)*5. 0/9.0;
             txtResult. set Text ("Celsius = "+result);
         }
         catch (NumberFormatException nfe)
         {
         {
             System . err . println ( " bad input " ) ;
         }
      }
  }
Button btnConvertToCelsius = new Button ("Convert to Celsius");
btnConvertToCelsius . addAction Listener (al) ;
pullLayout . add(btnConvertToCelsius) ;
al = new ActionListenerQ
  {
      @Override
      public void actionPerformed(ActionEvent ae)
      {
         try
         {
             double value = Double. parseDouble(txtDegrees.getTextQ);
             double result = value*9. 0/5. 0+32.0;
             txtResult. setText("Fahrenheit = "+result);
         }
         catch (NumberFormatException nfe)
         {
             System . err . println ( " bad input " ) ;
         }
      }
  }
  Button btnConvertToFahrenheit = new Button ("Con vert to Fahrenheit");
  btnConvertToFahrenheit.addActionListener(al);
  pullLayout.add(btnConvertToFahrenheit);
  add(pnlLayout);
  pack();
```

```
    setResizable(false);
    setVisible(true);
  }
  public static void main(String[] args)
  {
    Runnable r = new RunnableQ
        {
            @Override
            public void run()
            {
                new TempVerterQ;
            }
        };
    EventOueue . invokeLater (r);
  }
}
```

Following several import statements, the above listing presents the temperature-conversion application's TempVerter class, which extends the Frame class to describe a frame window that displays the GUI.

TempVerter declares a noargument constructor for constructing the GUI. Its main () method instantiates TempVerter and invokes its noargument constructor to create the GUI.

main() does not directly execute new TempVerter( ); . Doing so would construct the GUI on the main thread. Instead, main( ) defers GUI creation to a special AWT thread known as the *event-dispatch thread (EOT)*. It does so by creating a Java. lang. Runnable instance whose run( ) method executes new TempVerter ();, and by passing this runnable to the Java . awt . EventOueue class's void invokeLater(Runnable runnable) class method, which executes the runnable on the EDT.

main() defers GUI creation to the EDT to avoid potential thread-synchronization problems. Because it's beyond this chapter's scope to discuss these problems, check out *The Java Tutorial* (http : //download .oracle . com/ javase/tutorial/uiswing/concurrency/dispatch . html) and the "Swing threading and the event-dispatch thread" article (http: //www.javaworld.com/ javaworld/ jw-08-2007/jw-08-swingthreading. html) for more information. (Although these sources discuss this topic in a Swing context, other sources also include AWT. Therefore, you should create AWT-based as well as Swing-based GUIs on the EDT.)

TempVerter( ) first invokes the Frame(String title) constructor via super("TempVerter"); so that TempVerter will appear on the frame window's titlebar. It then registers a window listener with the frame window so mat this window will close (and the application will end) when the user closes the window (by clicking the X button on the window's titlebar, for example).

The listener is an instance of a WindowAdapter anonymous subclass, which overrides WindowListener's void windowClosing(WindowEvent we) and void windowClosed(WindowEvent we) methods. Clicking X or selecting Close from the window's system menu triggers a call to windowClosing(). You would typically override this method to save changes (e.g., a text editor's unsaved edits).

To properly terminate the application, windowClosing() must invoke Window's void disposeQ method, which releases all the native screen resources used by the window and posts a window-closed event to the application's event queue. AWT subsequently dispatches this event by invoking windowClosed () to signify that the window has closed. Any final cleanup can be performed in this method.

Continuing, the constructor instantiates Panel to contain the GUI's components. It then assigns a three-row-by-two-column CridLayout layout manager to this container to manage its components.

Each of the first two grid rows presents Label and Text Field instances. The label tells the user what to enter or indicates that the textfield is displaying a result. The textfield solicits input or presents output. The value passed to each TextField constructor specifies the textfield's width in terms of displayable columns, where a *column* is defined as an approximate average character width (and is platform-dependent).

The final grid row presents a pair of Button instances for performing conversions. Each instance is assigned an action listener that responds to a button click by obtaining the top textfield's text (via TextField's String getText() method, which is inherited from TextField's TextComponent superclass), converting it to a number, and assigning it to the bottom textfield by calling TextField's overriding void set Text (String t) method.

After populating the panel, the constructor adds the panel to the frame window. It then invokes pack() to ensure that the frame window is made large enough to display its components at their preferred sizes, invokes Frame's void setResizable(boolean resizable) method with a false argument to prevent the user from resizing the frame window (and making it look ugly), and invokes setVisible() with a true argument to display the frame and its components.

After the constructor returns to main (), this class method exits. However, the frame window remains on the screen because it's connected to a native screen resource and because the running EDT is a nondaemon thread. Compile the above listing (javac TempVerter. Java) and run this application (Java Tempverter).

When you enter nonnumeric text or leave the Degrees textfield empty, TempVerter outputs a "bad input" message to the standard output device. Also, when you close the window, this application outputs "window closing" followed by "window closed" messages on separate lines.

The resulting GUI doesn't look professional, but we can improve the GUI's appearance with a little bit of effort, as demonstrated in the following listing.

Improving TempVerter's GUI

```
import java.awt.Button;
import Java.awt.EventOueue;
import Java.awt.Frame;
import Java.awt.GridLayout;
import Java.awt.Label;
import Java.awt.Panel;
import Java.awt.TextField;

import Java.awt.event.ActionEvent;
import Java.awt.event.ActionListener;
import Java.awt.event.WindowAdapter;
import Java.awt.event.WindowEvent;

class TempVerter
{
    static Panel createGUl()
    {
        Panel pnlLayout = new Panel();
        pullLayout.setLayout(new GridLayout(3, 1));
        Panel pnlTemp = new Panel();
        pnlTemp.add(new Label("Degrees"));
final TextField txtOegrees = new TextField(lO);
pnlTemp.add (txtDegrees ) ;
pnlLayout.add(pnlTemp) ;
pnlTemp=new Panel();
```

```
pnlTemp.add(new Label( "Result"));
final TextField txtResult = new TextField(30);
pnlTemp. add(txtResult);
pnlLayout. add(pnlTemp);
pnlTemp = new Panel();
ActionListener al;
al = new ActionListener ()
    {
        @Override
        public void actionPerformed(ActionEvent ae)
        {
            try
            {
                double value = Double. parseDouble(txtDegrees.getTextQ);
                double result = (value-32.o)*5. 0/9.0;
                txtResult. set Text ("Celsius = "+result);
            }
            catch (NumberFormatException nfe)
            {
                System.err.println( "bad input" );
            }
        }
    };
Button btnConvertToCelsius = new Button ("Con vert to Celsius");
btnConvertToCelsius.addActionListener(al);
pnlTemp. add(btnConvertToCelsius);
al = new ActionListenerQ
    {
    @Override
    public void actionPerformed(ActionEvent ae)
    {
        try
        {
            double value = Double. parseDouble (txtDegrees. get TextQ);
            double result = value*9. 0/5. 0+32.0;
            txtResult. set Text ("Fahrenheit = "+result);
        }
        catch (NumberFormatException nfe)
        {
            System . err . println ( " bad input " ) ;
        }
    }
}
Button btnConvertToFahrenheit = new Button("Convert to Fahrenheit");
btnConvertToFahrenheit.addActionListener(al);
pnlTemp.add (btnConvertToFahrenheit ) ;
pnlLayout.add(pnlTemp) ;
return pnlLayout;
}
```

```
public static void main(String[] args)
{
    Runnable r = new RunnableQ
        {
            @Override
            public void run()
            {
                final Frame f = new Frame ("TempVerter");
                f.addWindowListener (new WindowAdapter ( )
                {
                    @Override
                    public void windowClosing(WindowEvent we)
                    {
                        f.dispose();
                    }
                };
                f.add(createGUI());
                f.pack();
                f.setResizable(f alse) ;
                f.setVisible(true);
            }
        }
    EventOueue . invokeLater (r) ;
    }
}
```

The above listing presents an alternative architecture for creating a GUI. Instead of subclassing Frame, this class is instantiated directly and various methods are called to configure and display the frame window. (It's convenient to create a class method such as createGUI( ) that returns a Panel object containing the entire GUI. The returned Panel instance is passed to Frame's add() method to install the GUI.)

The labels are left-aligned by executing ((FlowLayout)

pnlTemp.getLayout()) .setAlignment(FlowLayout.LEFT); on each of the two pnlTemp variables that stores a label and a textfield. This method call obtains pnlTemp's default flow layout manager and calls FlowLayout's void setAlignment(int alignment) method on this instance to align the panel's components to the left edge of the container (thanks to FlowLayout's LEFT constant)—FlowLayout leaves a default 5-pixel gap on each side of the panel that serves as a margin.

However, the textfields are not left aligned. To align diem, we need to set the preferred size of the wider Degrees label to the preferred size of the narrower Result label. Similarly, we need to set the preferred size of the Convert to Celsius button to the preferred size of the Convert to Fahrenheit button so that they have equal widths.

These tasks can be accomplished in part by introducing the following void fixGUI (Frame) class method into the TempVerter class:

```
static void fixGUI(Frame f)
{
    Panel pnl = (Panel) f.getComponents()[o]; // 1
    Panel pnlRow = (Panel) pnl.getComponents()[o]; // 2
    Label l1 = (Label) pnlRow.getComponentsQfo]; // 3
```

```
        pnlRow = (Panel) pnl.getComponents()[1]; // 4
        Label 12 = (Label) pnlRow.getComponents()[o]; // 5
        11.setPreferredSize(12.getPreferredSize()); // 6
        pnlRow = (Panel) pnl.getComponents()[2]; // 7
        Button btnToC = (Button) pnlRow.getComponents()[o]; // 8
        Button btnToF = (Button) pnlRow.getComponents()[1]; // 9
        otnToC.setPreferredSize(btnToF.getPreferredSizeQ); // 10
    }
```

fixCUI(Frame) is invoked with a reference to the TempVerter frame window (TempVerter.this provides that reference). It first invokes f .getComponentsQ [0] to obtain the panel that was added to the frame window.

pnl/pnlLayout contains three Panel instances (recall pnlTemp). The second line fetches die first of these instances and assigns its reference to pnlRow. The third line extracts the Degrees label component, which is the first component (at position 0) within this panel.

The fourth line fetches the second Panel instance that contains the Result label and its associated textfield. The fifth line extracts this label.

The sixth line invokes getPref erredSize() on the Result label, and then invokes Component's void setPref erredSize(Dimension pref erredSize) method with this preferred size to shrink the width of the Degrees label so that both textfields are left-aligned.

The seventh line fetches the third Panel instance, which contains the two buttons, the eighth and ninth lines extract these buttons, and the tenth line sets the preferred size of the Convert to Celsius button to that of the wider Convert to Fahrenheit button.

Introducing fixGUI (Frame) into TempVerter is only part of the solution. We must also call this method, and the appropriate place to do so is between the frame window's pack( ) and setVisible( ) method calls.

fixGUI( ) must be called after pack() because the preferred sizes are not known until after pack() has been called. This method must be called before setVisible( ) because it changes preferred sizes. setVisible() can accommodate these changes when they are made before this method is called. However, when they are made after calling setVisible( ), pack( ) will have to be called a second time.

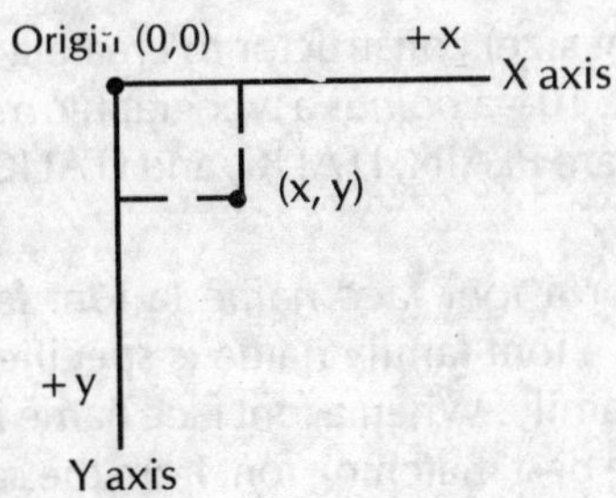

Graphics declares various methods for drawing on the surface and setting context state. Its drawing methods include the following:

- void drawLine(int xl, int yl, int x2, int y2) draws a line in the current color from (xl, yl) to (x2, y2).
- void drawOval(int x, int y, int width, int height) draws the outline of an oval in the current color such that the oval fits within the *bounding box* (smallest enclosing rectangle) whose upper-left corner is at (x, y) and whose extents are (width, height). The oval covers an area that is width + i pixels wide and height + l pixels tall.
- void drawRect(int x, int y, int width, int height) draws the outline of a rectangle in the current

color whose upper-left corner is at (x, y) and whose extents are (width, height), such that the right edge is located at x + width and the bottom edge is located at y + height.

- void drawString(String str, int x, int y) draws the characters specified by str in the current color and using the current font. The baseline of the leftmost character is at (x, y). '
- void fillOval(int x, int y, int width, int height) draws a filled oval in the current color such that the oval fits within the bounding box whose upper-left corner is at (x, y) and whose extents are (width, height).
- void fillRect(int x, int y, int width, int height) draws a rilled rectangle in the current color whose upper-left corner is at (x, y) and whose extents are (width, height), such that the right edge is located at x + width-l and the bottom edge is located at y + height-l.

State methods include the following:

- void setColor(Color c) sets the current color to the Java.awt.Color instance passed to c. Color declares several uppercase/lowercase Color constants for common colors (e.g., RED/red, GREEN/green, and BLUE/blue) and constructors for describing arbitrary colors—it's conventional to use the uppercase color constants. A companion Color getColor () method returns the current color.
- void setFont(Font f) sets the current font to the Java. awt. Font instance passed to f. A companion Font get Font () method returns the current font.

The following example demonstrates various drawing and state methods: public void paint(Graphics g)

```
{
    g.setColor(Color.RED);
    g.drawLine(lO, 10, 20, 20);
    g.setFont(new Font("Arial", Font.BOLD, 10));
    g.drawString("Hello", 35, 35);
}
```

The first statement sets the current color to Color .RED and the second statement draws a line in this color from starting point (10,10) to ending point (20, 20). (When you don't specify a color before drawing, the color defaults to the component's background color, which is returned from Component's Color getBackgroundQ method.)

The third statement calls Font's Font(String name, int style, int size) constructor to create a Font object that describes a font named Arial with style BOLD and point size 10—a *pointis* a typographic measurement that's approximately 1/72 of an inch. (Other supported styles are PLAIN, ITALIC, and ITALIC combined with BOLD.) This object is then installed as the current font.

The font name can be *a font family name* (such as Arial) or *a font face name* (a font family name combined with style information, such as Arial Bold). When a font family name is specified, the style argument is used to select the most appropriate face from the family. When a font face name is specified, the face's style and the style argument are merged to locate the best matching font from the same family. For example, when face name "Arial Bold" is specified with style Font .ITALIC, AWT looks for a face in the "Arial" family that is bold and italic, and may associate the font instance with the physical font face "Arial Bold Italic". The style argument is merged with the specified face's style, not added or subtracted. This means, specifying a bold face and a bold style does not double-embolden the font, and specifying a bold face and a plain style does not lighten the font.

Java supports logical fonts and physical fonts. A *logicalfontis* a font that's guaranteed to be supported on all platforms; pass one of Font's predefined DIALOG, DIALOG_INPUT, MONOSPACED, SANS_S£RIF, and SERIF String constants to FontQ to select a logical font. A *physical font is* a nonlogical font that may or may not be supported on all platforms. Arial is an example of a widely supported physical font—it's probably available on all the platforms where Java runs.

Finally, the fourth statement draws Hello in the current color and font with baseline at (35, 35). I previously defined *baseline as* the line serving as an origin for the purpose of layout. This term is also defined as the line separating a font's ascent from its descent, as the following figure illustrates.

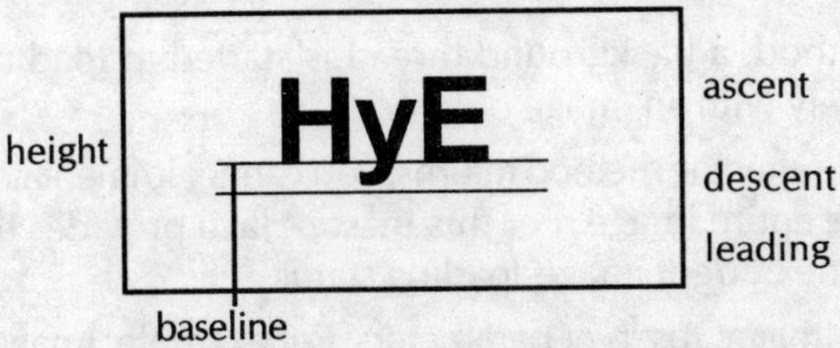

Every font is associated with various measurements. The *ascent* is that portion of the font's characters above the baseline; the *descent is* that portion of these characters below the baseline. Extra space added between lines of text is known as *leading.* When added together, ascent, descent, and leading form the font's *height.* Lastly, the *advance* roughly specifies the baseline location where the next character should appear.

AWT's Java. awt. FontMetrics class encapsulates this measurement information. You can obtain an instance of this class by calling the Graphics class's FontMetrics getFontMetrics() method, which returns the font metrics for the current font. Among its various methods, you will find the int stringWidth (String str) method (which returns the total advance width for showing str's characters in the current font) useful for centering a string horizontally.

Although you can paint on any component (including a container) by subclassing the component class and overriding pa int (), you should try to avoid doing so, to avoid confusing the user or someone who's reviewing your code. Instead, you should take advantage of AWT's Canvas class, which is intended for this purpose.

To use Canvas, you must extend this class and override paint(). You also need to specify its preferred size so that you can view the canvas on the screen. Accomplish this task'by overriding getPref erredSize() to return a Dimension object containing the canvas's extents, or by invoking setPreferredSize() with a Dimension object containing the preferred size (as demonstrated in fixGUI()).

Images

AWT supports GIF, JPEG, and PNG images via Java. awt. Image, Toolkit, and other classes. Because Java 2D largely obviates the need to work with these classes, I won't discuss AWT's support for images in great detail. However, you should know something about this support because various JFC classes (such as javax. swing. ImageIcon) work with Image, and even provide constructors and/or methods that take Image arguments and (in regard to methods) return Image instances.

The Toolkit class declares several createImage() methods for creating and returning Image objects from various sources. For example, Image create!mage(String filename) returns an Image object that represents the image defined in the file identified by filename.

Toolkit also declares two getImage() methods that create and return Image objects. Unlike their createImage() counterparts, the getImageQ methods cache Image objects and can return the same object to different callers. This sharing mechanism helps AWT save heap space, especially when large images are loaded. In contrast, the createImageQ methods always return new Image objects that are not shared among callers.

Image objects represent images but do not contain them: a loaded image is associated with an Image object. This dichotomy exists because Java was originally used mainly in a web browser context.

At that time, computers and network connections were much slower than they are today, and loading large images over the wire was a time-consuming process. Rather than force an *applet* (a browser-based application) to wait until an image had completely loaded (and annoy the user), it was decided that methods for loading images would load them asynchronously via background threads while occupying the user's attention elsewhere.

When you invoke a createImage () or getImage () method, a background thread is started to load the image, and createImage()/getImage() returns immediately with an Image object.

Because the image may not be fully loaded until sometime after the method returns, you cannot immediately obtain the image's width and height, or even draw the entire image. For this reason, Java provides the Java. awt. image. ImageObserver interface to provide the current image-loading status.

Various Image and Graphics methods are declared with ImageObserver parameters. For example, Image's int getWidth(ImageObserver observer) and int getHeight(ImageObserver observer) methods are called with an image observer that helps these methods determine that the image has been loaded to the point where they can return its width or height, or that the width/height is still not available, in which case they return -1.

Similarly, the Graphics class's boolean drawImage(Image img, int x, int y, ImageObserver observer) method is called with an image observer that helps it determine what part of the image to draw—the image's upper-left corner is located at (x, y). When an image is not completely loaded, the, image observer calls one of Component's repaint() methods, to reinvoke paint() so that a subsequent call can be made to drawImage () to draw the newly-loaded pixels.

Data Transfer

GUI-based applications often need to transfer data between or within themselves. For example, a text editor's user may want to cut selected text to the system clipboard and subsequently paste the clipboard's text to another location within the document being edited.

AWT supports transferring arbitrary objects between applications via the *system clipboard,* and transferring objects within an application via a *private clipboard.* This support consists of the Java, awt.datatransfer package with its ClipboardOwner, Flavor Listener, FlavorMap, FlavorTable, and Transferable interfaces; and Clipboard, DataFlavor, FlavorEvent, StringSelection, SystemFlavorMap, MimeTypeParseException, and UnsupportedFlavorException classes.

Clipboard provides a mechanism for transferring data to a clipboard by using cut/copy/paste operations. You can obtain a *singleton* (single instance) Clipboard object that provides access to the native clipboard facilities offered by the platform's windowing system by calling Toolkit's Clipboard getSystemClipboardQ method; for example, Clipboard clipboard = Toolkit. getDefault Toolkit. getSystemClipboard ();. Alternatively, you can obtain a private clipboard by instantiating Clipboard.

Clipboard declares a void setContents(Transferable contents, ClipboardOwner owner) method that sets the current contents of the clipboard to the specified transferable object and registers the' specified clipboard owner as the owner of the new contents. This method throws java.lang.IllegalStateException when the clipboard is currently unavailable. The transferable object that's passed to contents is created from a class that implements the Transferable interface in terms of the following three methods:

- Object getTransferData(DataFlavor flavor) returns an object containing the data being transferred. The Data Flavor argument identifies the *flavor* (format) of this data (e.g., a string or a JPEG image) by encapsulating the data's Multipurpose Internet Mail Extensions (MIME) type—http: / /en. wikipedia.org/wiki/MIME and http: //en .wikipedia.org/wiki/Internet_media_type discuss MIME—and a human-presentable name describing this data format. This method throws Java. io. IOException when the data is no longer available in the requested flavor, and UnsupportedFlavorException when the requested data flavor isn't supported.

- DataFlavor[] getTransferDataFlavors( ) returns an array of DataFlavor objects that indicate the flavors of the data that this transferable object can provide.
- boolean isDataFlavorSupported(DataFlavor flavor) indicates whether or not the specified flavor is supported; true returns when flavor is supported.

Each time that you invoke setContents( ), the object passed to owner is the owner of the clipboard content. If you call this method with a different owner, AWT notifies the previous owner that it's no longer the owner (some other content is on the clipboard) by calling ClipboardOwner's void lostOwnership(Clipboard clipboard, Transferable contents) method.

Because users typically want to copy, cut, and paste text, Java. awt. datatransf er provides StringSelection as an implementation of Transferable and ClipboardOwner (lostOwnership() is left empty; you must subclass StringSelection and override lostOwnership() when you need this notification). You would use StringSelection to transfer strings to and from a clipboard.

The following example presents copy(), cut(), and pasteQ methods that showyou how to perform copy, cut, and paste operations in the context of the TextArea class. The example specifies a ta variable that references a TextArea instance, and a clipboard variable that references a Clipboard instance:

```
void copy()
{
    StringSelection ss = new StringSelection(ta.getSelectedTextQ);
    clipboard.setContents(ss, ss);
}
void cut()
{
    copy();
    ta.replaceRange("", ta.getSelectionStart(), ta.getSelectionEnd());
}
void pasteQ
{
    Transferable clipData = clipboard.getContents(this);
    if (clipData != null)
        try
        {
        if (clipData.isDataFlavorSupported(DataFlavor.stringFlavor))
        }
        String text = (String)
            clipData.getTransferData(DataFlavor.stringFlavor);
        ta.replaceRange(text, ta.getSelectionStartQ,
            ta.getSelectionEnd( ) ) ;
        }
    }
    catch (UnsupportedFlavorException ufe)
    {
        ta.setText(" Flavor not supported");
    }
    catch (lOException ioe)
    {
        ta. set Text ("No data to paste");
    }
}
```

copy ( ) 's first task is to extract the selected text from the textarea by calling TextComponent's. String getSelectedText( ) method. It then passes this text to the StringSelection(String data) constructor to create a transferable object that contains this text.

Continuing, copy( ) passes this object to the clipboard by invoking clipboard. setContents(ss, ss). The same StringSelection object (ss) is passed as the transferable object and the clipboard owner because StringSelection implements Transferable and ClipboardOwner.

cut( ) is much simpler. This method first invokes copy( ) to copy the selected text to the clipboard. It then invokes TextArea's void replaceRange(String str, int start, int end) method to remove the selected text (delimited by the integer values returned from TextComponent's int getSelectionStart( ) and int getSelectionEnd( ) methods) by replacing it with the empty string.

paste( ) is the most complex of the three methods. It first invokes Clipboard's Transferable getContents(Object requestor) method to return a transferable object representing the current contents of the clipboard (or null when the clipboard is empty). The requestor parameter is currently not used; it may be implemented in a future release of the Java.awt.datatransf er package.

If the returned transferable isn't null, paste( ) invokes isDataFlavorSupported( ) on this object with DataFlavor . stringFlavor as the argument. This method returns true when the requested flavor is supported. In other words, isDataFlavorSupported ( ) returns true when the clipboard contains text; it would return false when the clipboard contained an image (for example).

If isDataFlavorSupported() returns true, paste () calls getTransferData( ) to return the string and then replaces the selected string with this content.

TextArea contains built-in support for performing copy, cut, and paste operations by pressing the Ctrl-C, Ctrl-X, and Ctrl-Vkey combinations. However, neither TextArea nor its TextComponent superclass provides methods for performing these tasks. As a result, you would have to supply your own copyQ, cut ( ), and paste( ) methods (such as those shown previously) when you wanted to programmatically perform these operations (perhaps in response to the user selecting Copy, Cut, or Paste from an Edit menu).

CHAPTER 5

Interacting with Filesystems

In this chapter you will read about:

- RandomAccessFile.
- Streams.
- OutputStreamd and InputStream.
- Externalization.
- PrintStream.

Introduction

Applications often interact with the filesystem to output data to and/or input data from files. Java's standard class library supports filesystem access via its classic File, RandomAccessFile, stream, and writer/reader APIs. Chapter 8 introduces you to File, RandomAccessFile, and various stream and writer/reader APIs.

File

Applications often interact with a *filesystem,* which is usually expressed as a hierarchy of files and directories starting from a *root directory.*

Windows and other platforms on which a Java Virtual Machine (JVM) runs typically support at least one filesystem. For example, a Unix or Linux platform combines all *mounted* (attached and prepared) disks into one virtual filesystem. In contrast, Windows associates a separate filesystem with each active disk drive.

Java offers access to the platform's available filesystem(s) via its concrete Java. io. File class. File declares the File [ ] listRoots () class method to return the root directories (roots) of available filesystems as an array of File objects.

The following listing presents a DumpRoots application that uses listRoots() to obtain an array of available filesystem roots and then outputs the array's contents.

Dumping available filesystem roots to the standard output device

```
import Java. io. File;
class DumpRoots
{
public static void main(String[] args)     ,
File[] roots = File.listRootsQ; for (File root: roots)
System. out. println(root);
```

When I run this application on my Windows XP platform, I receive the following output, which reveals four available roots:

```
A:\
C:\
D:\
E:\
```

If I ran DumpRoots on a Unix or Linux platform, I would receive one output line consisting of the. virtual filesystem root (/).

Apart from using listRootsQ, you can obtain a File instance by calling a File constructor such as File(String pathname), which creates a File instance that stores the pathname string. The following assignment statements demonstrate this constructor:

```
File filel = new File("/x/y");
File file2 = new File("C:\\temp\\x.dat");
```

The first statement assumes a Unix or Linux platform, starts the pathname with root directory symbol /, and continues with directory name x, separator character /, and file or directory name y. (It also works on Windows, which assumes this path begins at the root directory on the current drive.)

The second statement assumes a Windows platform, starts the pathname with drive specifier C:, and continues with root directory symbol \, directory name temp, separator character \, and filename x.dat (although x.dat might refer to a directory).

Each statement's pathname is an *absolute pathname,* which is a pathname that starts with the root directory symbol; no other information is required to locate the file/directory that it denotes. In contrast, a *relative pathname* doesn't start with the root directory symbol; it's interpreted via information taken from some other pathname.

File instances contain abstract representations of file and directory pathnames (these files or directories may or may not exist in their filesystems) by storing *abstract pathnames,* which offer platform-independent views of hierarchical pathnames. In contrast, user interfaces and operating systems use platform-dependent *pathname strings to* name files and directories.

An abstract pathname consists of an optional platform-dependent prefix string, such as a disk-drive specifier, "/" for the Unix root directory, or "\\" for a Windows Universal Naming Convention (UNO pathname; and a sequence of zero or more string names. The first name in an abstract pathname may be a directory name or, in the case of Windows UNC pathnames, a hostname. Each subsequent name denotes a directory; the last name may denote a directory or a file. The *empty abstract pathname* has no prefix and an empty name sequence.

The conversion of a pathname string to or from an abstract pathname is inherently platform-dependent. When a pathname string is converted to an abstract pathname, the names within it are separated by the default name-separator character or by any other name-separator character that is supported by the underlying platform. For example, File(String pathname) converts pathname string /x/y to abstract pathname /x/y on a Unix or Linux platform, and this same pathname string to abstract pathname \x\y on a Windows platform.

When an abstract pathname is converted into a pathname string, each name is separated from the next by a single copy of the default name-separator character.

File offers additional constructors for instantiating this class. For example, the following constructors merge parent and child pathnames into combined pathnames that are stored in File objects:

- File(String parent, String child) creates a new File instance from a parent pathname string and a child pathname string.
- File(File parent, String child) creates a new File instance from a parent pathname File instance and a child pathname string.

Each constructor's parent parameter is passed a *parent pathname,* a string that consists of all pathname components except for the last name, which is specified by child. The following statement demonstrates this concept via File(String, String):

```
File files = new File("prj/books/", "bj?");
```

The constructor merges relative parent pathname pr j/books/ with child pathname bj7 into relative pathname prj/books/bj7.

After obtaining a File object, you can interrogate it to learn about its stored abstract pathname by calling the methods that are described in the following table.

Table File Methods for Learning About a Stored Abstract Pathname

Method	Description
File getAbsoluteFileQ	Return the absolute form of this File object's abstract pathname. This method is equivalent to new File(this.getAbsolutePath()).
String getAbsolutePathQ	Return the absolute pathname string of this File object's abstract pathname. If it's already absolute, the pathname string is returned as if by calling getPath (). If it's the empty abstract pathname, the pathname string of the current user directory (identified via user.dir) is returned. Otherwise, the abstract pathname is resolved in a platform-dependent

	manner. On Unix platforms, a relative pathname is made absolute by resolving it against the current user directory. On Windows platforms, the pathname is made absolute by resolving it against the current directory of the drive named by the pathname, or the current user directory when there's no drive.
File getCanonicalFile()	Return the *canonical* (simplest possible, absolute and unique) form of this File object's abstract pathname. This method throws java.io.IOException when an I/O error occurs (creating the canonical pathname may require filesystem queries); it equates to new File(this.getCanonicalPath()).
String getCanonicalPath()	Return the canonical pathname string of this File object's abstract pathname. This method first converts this pathname to absolute form when necessary, as if by invoking getAbsolutePath(), and then maps it to its unique form in a platform-dependent way. Doing so typically involves removing redundant names such as "." and".." from the pathname, resolving symbolic links (on Unix platforms), and converting drive letters to a standard case (on Windows platforms). This method throws IOException when an I/O error occurs (creating the canonical pathname may require filesystem queries).
String getName()	Return the filename or directory name denoted by this File object's abstract pathname. This name is the last in a pathname's name sequence. The empty string is returned when the pathname's name sequence is empty.
String getParent()	Return the parent pathname string of this File object's abstract pathname, or return null when this pathname doesn't name a parent directory.
File getParentFile()	Return a File object storing this File object's abstract pathname's parent abstract pathname; return null when the parent pathname isn't a directory.
String getPath()	Convert this File object's abstract pathname into a pathname string where the names in the sequence are separated by the character stored in File's separator field. Return the resulting pathname string.
boolean isAbsolute()	Return true when this File object's abstract pathname is absolute; otherwise, return false when it's relative. The definition of absolute pathname is system dependent. On Unix platforms, a pathname is absolute when its prefix is"/". On Windows platforms, a pathname is absolute when its prefix is a drive specifier followed by "\", or when its prefix is "\\".
String toString()	A synonym for getPath().

The above table refers to IOException, which is the common exception superclass for those exception classes that describe various kinds of I/O errors, such as Java. io. FileNotFoundException.

You can interrogate the filesystem to learn about the file or directory represented by a File object's abstract pathname by calling the methods that are described in next table.

Table File Methods for Learning About a File or Directory

Method	Description
boolean canExecute()	Return true when this File object's abstract pathname represents an existing file that the application is allowed to execute.
boolean canRead()	Return true when this File object's abstract pathname represents an existing readable file.
boolean canWrite()	Return true when this File object's abstract pathname represents an existing file that can be modified.
boolean exists()	Return true if and only if the file or directory that's denoted by this File object's abstract pathname exists.
boolean isDirectory()	Return true when this File object's abstract pathname refers to an existing directory.
boolean isFile()	Return true when this File object's abstract pathname refers to an existing normal file. A file is *normal* when it's not a directory and satisfies other platform-dependent criteria: it's not a symbolic link or a named pipe, for example. Any nondirectory file created by a Java application is guaranteed to be a normal file.
boolean isHidden ()	Return true when the file denoted by this File object's abstract pathname is hidden. The exact definition of *hidden* is platform dependent. On Unix/Linux platforms, a file is hidden when its name begins with a period character. On Windows platforms, a file is hidden when it has been marked as such in the filesystem.
long lastModif led ()	Return the time that the file denoted by this File object's abstract pathname was last modified, or 0 when the file doesn't exist or an I/O error occurred during this method call. The returned value is measured in milliseconds since the *Unix epoch* (00:00:00 GMT, January 1,1970).
long length ()	Return the length of the file denoted by this File object's abstract pathname. The return value is unspecified when the pathname denotes a directory, and will be 0 when the file doesn't exist.

The following listing instantiates File with its pathname command-line argument, and calls all the File methods described in above table to learn about the pathname's file/directory.

Obtaining file/directory information

```
import Java.io.File;
import java.io.IOException;

import Java.util.Date;

class FileDirectorylnfo
{
   public static void main(final String[] args) throws lOException
   {
      if (args.length != l)
      {
```

```
            System.err.println("usage: Java FileDirectorylnfo pathname");
            return;
        }
        File file = new File(args[o]);
        System.out.println("About "+file+":");
        System.out.println("Can execute = "+file.canExecute());
        System.out.println("Can read = "+file.canRead());
        System.out.println("Can write = "+file.canWrite());
        System.out.println("Exists = "+file.exists());
        System.out.println("Is directory = "+file.isDirectory());
        System.out.println("Is file = "+file.isFile());
        System.out.println("Is hidden = "+file.isHidden());
        System.out.println("Last modified = "+new Date(file.lastModified()));
        System.out.println("Length = "+file.length());
```

For example, suppose I have a three-byte read-only file named x.dat. When I specify Java FileDirectoryInf o x. dat, I observe the following output:

```
About x.dat:
Can execute = true
Can read = true
Can write = true
Exists = true j
Is directory = false
Is file = true
Is hidden = false
Last modified = Wed Aug 24 18:45:07 CDT 2011
Length = 3
```

File declares five methods that return the names of files and directories located in the directory identified by a File object's abstract pathname. Table 8-3 describes these methods.

Table File Methods for Obtaining Directory Content

Method	Description
String[] list()	Return a potentially empty array of strings naming the files and directories in the directory denoted by this File object's abstract pathname. If the pathname doesn't denote a directory, or if an I/O error occurs, this method returns null. Otherwise, it returns an array of strings, one string for each file or subdirectory in the directory. Names denoting the directory itself and the directory's parent directory are not included in the result. Each string is a filename rather than a complete path. Also, there's no guarantee that the name strings in the resulting array will appear in alphabetical or any other order.
String[] list(FilenameFilter filter)	A convenience method for calling list() and returning only those Strings that satisfy filter.
File[] listFiles()	A convenience method for calling list (), converting its array of Strings to an array of Files, and returning the Files array.
File[] listFiles(FileFilter filter)	A convenience method for calling list(), converting its array of Strings to an array of F iles, but only for those Strings that satisfy filter, and returning the Files array.

Filef] listFiles(FilenameFilter	A convenience method for calling list (), converting its filter) array of Strings to an array of Files, but only for those Strings that satisfy filter, and returning the Files array.

The overloaded list () methods return arrays of Strings denoting file and directory names. The second method lets you return only those names of interest (such as only names ending with extension . txt) via a Java. io. FilenameFilter-based filter object.

The FilenameFilter interface declares a single boolean accept(File dir, String name) method that's called for each file/directory located in the directory identified by the File object's abstract padiname:

- dir identifies the parent portion of the pathname (the directory path).
- name identifies the final directory name or me filename portion of the pathname.

The accept () method uses these arguments to determine whether or not the file or directory satisfies its criteria for what is acceptable. It returns true when the file/directory name should be included in the returned array; otherwise, this method returns false.

The following listing presents a Dir(ectory) application that uses list (FilenameFilter) to obtain only those names that end with a specific extension.

Listing specific names

```
import Java.io.File;
import Java.io.FilenameFilter;

class Dir
{
   public static void main(final String[] args)
   {
      if (args.length != 2)
      {
         System.err.println("usage: Java Dir dirpath ext"); return;
      }
      File file = new File(args[o]);
      FilenameFilter fnf = new FilenameFilter()
         {
            public boolean accept(File dir, String name)
            {
               return name.endsWith(args[l]);
            }
         };
      String[] names = file.list(fnf);
      for (String name: names)
      System. out . println (name) ;
   }
}
```

When I, for example, specify Java Dir c:\windows bmp on my XP platform, Dir outputs only those \windows directory filenames that have the bmp (bitmap) extension:

```
Blue Lace I6.bmp i
Coffee Bean. bmp
FeatherTexture . bmp
Gone Fishing.bmp
```

```
Creenstone.bmp
Prairie Wind. bmp
Rhododendron.bmp
River Sumida.bmp
Santa Fe Stucco.bmp
Soap Bubbles.bmp
winnt.bmp
winnt256.bmp
Zapotec.bmp
```

The overloaded listFiles ( ) methods return arrays of Files. For the most part, they're symmetrical with their list() counterparts. However, listFiles(FileFilter) introduces an asymmetry.

The Java. io.FileFilter interface declares a single boolean accept (String pathname) method that's called for each file/directory located in the directory identified by the File object's abstract pathname. The argument passed to pathname identifies the complete path of the file or directory.

The accept () method uses this argument to determine whether or not the file or directory satisfies its criteria for what is acceptable. It returns true when the file/directory name should be included in the returned array; otherwise, this method returns false.

File also declares several methods for creating files and manipulating existing files. The followng table describes these methods.

Table File Methods for Creating Files and Manipulating Existing Files

Method	Description
boolean createNewFile ()	Atomically create a new, empty file named by this File object's abstract pathname if and only if a file with this name does not yet exist. The check for file existence and the creation of the file when it doesn't exist are a single operation that's atomic with respect to all other filesystem activities that might affect the file. This method returns true when the named file doesn't exist and was successfully created, and returns false when the named file already exists. It throws IOException when an I/O error occurs.
static File createTempFile(String prefix, String suffix)	Create an qmpty file in the default temporary file directory using the given prefix and suffix to generate its name. This overloaded class method calls its three-parameter variant, passing prefix, suffix, and null to this other method, and returning this other method's return value.
static File createTempFile(String prefix, String suffix, File directory)	Create an empty file in the specified directory using the given prefix and suffix to generate its name. The name begins with the character sequence specified by prefix and ends with the character sequence specified by suffix; " .tmp" is used as the suffix when suffix is null. This method returns the created file's pathname when successful. It throws java.lang.IllegalArgumentException when prefix contains fewer than three characters, and IOException when the file couldn't be created.
boolean delete()	Delete the file or directory denoted by this File object's abstract pathname. Return true when successful; otherwise, return false. If the

	pathname denotes a directory, the directory must be empty in order to be deleted.
void deleteOnExit()	Request that the file or directory denoted by this File object's abstract pathname be deleted when the JVM terminates. Reinvoking this method on the same File object has no effect. Once deletion has been requested, it's not possible to cancel the request. Therefore, this method should be used with care.
boolean mkdir()	Create the directory named by this File object's abstract pathname. Return true when successful; otherwise, return false.
boolean mkdirs()	Create the directory and any necessary intermediate directories named by this File object's abstract pathname. Return true when successful; otherwise, return false.
boolean renameTo(File dest)	Rename the file denoted by this File object's abstract pathname to dest. Return true when successful; otherwise, return false. This method throws NullPointerException when dest is null. Many aspects of this method's behavior are platform dependent. For example, the rename operation might not be able to move a file from one filesystem to another, the operation might not be atomic, or it might not succeed when a file with the destination pathnariie already exists. The return value should always be checked to make sure that the rename operation was successful.
boolean setLastModified(long time)	Set the last-modified time of the file or directory named by this File object's abstract pathname. Return true when successful; otherwise, return false. This method throws IllegalArgumentException when time is negative. All platforms support file-modification times to the nearest second, but some provide more precision. The time value will be truncated to fit the supported precision. If the operation succeeds and no intervening operations on the file take place, the next call to lastModif ied() will return the (possibly truncated) time value passed to this method.
boolean setReadOnly()	Mark the file or directory denoted by this File object's abstract pathname so that only read operations are allowed. After calling this method, the file or directory is guaranteed not to change until it's deleted or marked to allow write access. Whether or not a read-only file or directory can be deleted depends upon the filesystem.

Suppose you're designing a text-editor application that a user will use to open a text file and make changes to its content. Until the user explicitly saves these changes to the file, you want the text file to remain unchanged.

Because the user doesn't want to lose these changes when the application crashes or the computer loses power, you design the application to save these changes to a temporary file every few minutes. This way, the user has a backup of the changes.

You can use the overloaded createTempFileQ methods to create the temporary file. If you don't specify a directory in which to store this file, it's created in the directory identified by the Java. io. tmpdir system property.

You probably want to remove the temporary file after the user tells the application to save or discard the changes. The deleteOnExit () method lets you register a temporary file for deletion; it's deleted when the JVM ends without a crash/power loss.

Finally, File implements the Java.lang.Comparable interface's compareTo() method, and overrides equals() and hashCode(). The following table describes these miscellaneous methods.

Table File's Miscellaneous Methods

Method	Description
int compareTo(File pathname)	Compare two pathnames lexicographically. The ordering defined by this method depends upon the underlying platform. On Unix/Linux platforms, alphabetic case is significant when comparing pathnames; on Windows platforms, alphabetic case is insignificant. Return zero when pathname's abstract pathname equals this File object's abstract pathname, a negative value when this File object's pathname is less than pathname, and a positive value otherwise. To accurately compare two File objects, call getCanonicalFile() on each File object and then compare the returned File objects.
boolean equals(Object obj)	Compare this File object with obj for equality. Abstract pathname equality depends upon the underlying platform. On Unix/Linux platforms, alphabetic case is significant when comparing pathnames; on Windows platforms, alphabetic case is not significant. Return true if and only if obj is not null and is a File object whose abstract pathname denotes the same file/directory as this File object's abstract pathname.
int hashCode()	Calculate and return a hash code for this abstract pathname. This calculation depends upon the underlying platform. On Unix/Linux platforms, a pathname's hash code is the exclusive OR of its pathname string's hash code and decimal value 1234321. On Windows platforms, the hash code is the exclusive OR of the lowercased pathname string's hash code and decimal value 1234321. The current locale (discussed in Appendix C) is not taken into account when lowercasing the pathname string.

RandomAccessFile

Files can be created and/or opened for *random access* in which write and read operations can occur until the file is closed. Java supports this random access via its concrete Java. io. RandomAccessFile class. RandomAccessFile declares the following constructors:

- RandomAccessFile(File file, String mode) creates and opens a new file if it doesn't exist, or opens an existing file. The file is identified by file's abstract pathname and is created and/or opened according to mode.
- RandomAccessFile(String pathname. String mode) creates and opens a new file if it doesn't exist, or opens an existing file. The file is identified by pathname and is created and/or opened according to mode.

Either constructor's mode argument must be one of "r", "rw", "rws", or "rwd"; otherwise, the constructor throws IllegalArgumentException. These string literals have the following meanings:

- " r" informs the constructor to open an existing file for reading only. Any attempt to write to the file results in a thrown instance of the IOException class.

- " rw" informs the constructor to create and open a new file when it doesn't exist for reading and writing, or open an existing file for reading and writing.
- "rwd" informs the constructor to create and open a new file when it doesn't exist for reading and writing, or open an existing file for reading and writing. Furthermore, each update to the file's content must be written synchronously to the underlying storage device.
- "rws" informs the constructor to create and open a new file when it doesn't exist for reading and writing, or open an existing file for reading and writing. Furthermore, each update to the file's content or metadata must be written synchronously to the underlying storage device.

The "rwd" and "rws" modes ensure than any writes to a file located on a local storage device are written to the device, which guarantees that critical data isn't lost when the operating system crashes. No guarantee is made when the file doesn't reside on a local device. These constructors throw FileNotFoundException when mode is "r" and the file identified by pathname cannot be opened (it might not exist or it might be a directory), or when mode is "rw" and pathname is read-only or a directory.

The following example demonstrates the second constructor by attempting to open an existing random access file via the "r" mode string:

```
RandomAccessFile raf = new RandomAccessFile("employee.dat", "r");
```

A random access file is associated with a *file pointer,* a cursor that identifies the location of the next byte to write or read. When an existing file is opened, the file pointer is set to its first byte, at offset 0. The file pointer is also set to 0 when the file is created.

Write and read operations start at the file pointer and advance it past the number of bytes written or read. Operations that write past the current end of the file cause the file to be extended. These operations continue until the file is closed.

RandomAccessFile declares a wide variety of methods. I present a representative sample of these methods in the following table.

Table RandomAccessFile Methods

Method	Description
void close ()	Close the file and release any associated platform resources. Subsequent writes or reads result in IOException. Also, the file cannot be reopened with this RandomAccessFile object. This method throws IOException when an I/O error occurs.
FileDescriptor getFD()	Return the file's associated file descriptor object. This method throws IOException when an I/O error occurs.
long getFilePointer()	Return the file pointer's current zero-based byte offset into the file. This method throws IOException when an I/O error occurs.
long length()	Return the length (measured in bytes) of the file. This method throws IOException when an I/O error occurs.
int read()	Read and return (as an int in the range 0 to 255) the next byte from the file, or return -1 when the end of the file is reached. This method blocks when no input is available, and throws IOException when an I/O error occurs.
int read(byte[] b)	Read up to b. length bytes of data from the file into byte array b. This method blocks until at least one byte of input is available. It returns the number of bytes read into the array, or returns -1 when the end of

the file is reached. It throws NullPointerException when b is null, and IOException when an I/O error occurs.

char readChar()	Read and return a character from the file. This method reads two bytes from the file starting at the current file pointer. If the bytes read, in order, are bl and b2, where 0 < = bl, b2 < = 255, the result is equal to (char) ((bl«8) | b2). This method blocks until the two bytes are read, the end of the file is detected, or an exception is thrown. It throws Java. io. EOFException (a subclass of IOException) when the end of the file is reached before reading both bytes, and IOException when an I/O error occurs.
int readInt()	Read and return a signed 32-bit integer from the file. This method reads four bytes from the file starting at the current file pointer. If the bytes read, in order, are bl, b2, b3, and b4, where 0 < = bl, b2, b3, b4 < = 255, the result is equal to (bi«24) | (b2«l6) + (b3«8) + b4. This method blocks until the four bytes are read, the end of the file is detected, or an exception is thrown. It throws EOFException when the end of the file is reached before reading all four bytes, and IOException when an I/O error occurs.
void seek(long pos)	Set the file pointer's current offset to pos (which is measured in bytes from the beginning of the file). When the offset is set beyond the end of the file, the file's length doesn't change. The file length will only change by writing after the offset has been set beyond the end of the file. This method throws IOException when the value in pos is negative, or when an I/O error occurs.
void setLength(long newLength)	Set the file's length. If the present length as returned by length () is greater than newLength, the file is truncated. In this case, if the file offset as returned by getFilePointerQ is greater than newLength, the offset will be equal to newLength after set Length () returns. If the present length is smaller than newLength, the file is extended. In this case, the contents of the extended portion of the file are not defined. This method throws IOException when an I/O error occurs.
int skipBytes(int n)	Attempt to skip over n bytes. This method skips over a smaller number of bytes (possibly zero) when the end of file is reached before n bytes have been skipped. It doesn't throw EOFException in this situation. When n is negative, no bytes are skipped. The actual number of bytes skipped is returned. This method throws IOException when an I/O error occurs.
void write(byte[] b)	Write b. length bytes from byte array b to the file starting at the current file pointer position. This method throws IOException when an I/O error occurs.
void write(int b)	Write the lower eight bits of b to the file at the current file pointer position. This method throws IOException when an I/O error occurs.
void writeChars(String s)	Write string s to the file as a sequence of characters starting at the current file pointer position. This method throws IOException when an I/O error occurs.

void writeInt(int i)	Write 32-bit integer i to the file starting at the current file pointer position. The four bytes are written with the high byte first. This method throws IOException when an I/O error occurs.

Most of the above table's methods are fairly self-explanatory. However, the getFDQ method requires further enlightenment.

When a file is opened, the underlying platform creates a platform-dependent structure to represent the file. A handle to this structure is stored in an instance of the Java. io. FileDescriptor class, which getFDQ returns.

FileDescriptor is a small class that declares three FileDescriptor constants named in, out, and err. These constants let System.in, System.out, and System.err provide access to the standard input, standard output, and standard error streams.

FileDescriptor also declares a pair of methods:

- void sync() tells the underlying platform to *flush* (empty) the contents of the open file's output buffers to their associated local disk device. syncQ returns after all modified data and attributes have been written to the relevant device. It throws Java.io. SyncFailedException when the buffers cannot be flushed, or because the platform cannot guarantee that all the buffers have been synchronized with physical media.
- boolean valid () determines whether or not this file descriptor object is valid. It returns true when the file descriptor object represents an open file or other active I/O connection; otherwise, it returns false.

Data that is written to an open file ends up being stored in the underlying platform's output buffers. When the buffers fill to capacity, the platform empties them to the disk. Buffers improve performance because disk access is slow.

However, when you write data to a random access file that's been opened via mode "rwd" or "rws", each write operation's data is written straight to the disk. As a result, write operations are slower than when the random access file was opened in "rw" mode.

Suppose you have a situation that combines writing data through the output buffers and writing data directly to the disk. The following example addresses this hybrid scenario by opening the file in mode "rw" and selectively calling FileDescriptor's syncQ method:

```
RandomAccessFile raf = nc,.¹ RandomAccessFile("employee.dat", "rw");
FileDescriptor fd = raf.getFDQ;
// Perform a critical write operation.
raf.write(...);
// Synchronize with underlying disk by flushing platform's output buffers to
disk.
fd.syncQ;
// Perform non-critical write operation where synchronization is not
necessary.
raf.write(...);
// Do other work.
// Close file, emptying output buffers to disk.
raf.close();
```

RandomAccessFile is useful for creating *a flat file database,* a single file organized into records and fields. A record stores a single entry (e.g., a part in a parts database) and *afield* stores a single attribute of the entry (e.g., a part number).

A flat file database typically organizes its content into a sequence of fixed-length records. Each record is further organized into one or more fixed-length fields.

Streams

Along with File and RandomAccessFile, Java uses streams to perform I/O operations. A *stream* is an ordered sequence of bytes of arbitrary length. Bytes flow over *an output stream* from an application to a destination, and flow over an *input stream* from a source to an application.

Java recognizes various stream destinations; for example, byte arrays, files, screens, and *sockets* (network endpoints). Java also recognizes various stream sources. Examples include byte arrays, files, keyboards, and sockets. (I discuss sockets in Chapter 9.)

Stream Classes Overview

The Java. io package provides several output stream and input stream classes that are descendents of the abstract OutputStream and InputStream classes.

Other Java packages provide additional output stream and input stream classes. For example, Java. util. zip provides five output stream classes that compress uncompressed data into various formats, and five matching input stream classes that uncompress compressed data from the same formats:

- CheckedOutputStream
- CheckedInputStream
- DeflaterOutputStream
- DeflaterInputStream
- CZIPOutputStream
- CZIPInputStream
- InflaterOutputStream
- InflaterInputStream
- ZipOutputStream
- ZipInputStream

Outputstream and Inputstream

Java provides the Outputstream and Inputstream classes for performing stream I/O. Outputstream is the superclass of all output stream subclasses. The following table describes OutputStream's methods.

Table Outputstream Methods

Method	Description
void close ()	Close this output stream and release any system resources associated with the stream. This method throws IOException when an I/O error occurs. (Because Outputstream implements Closeable, you can use output streams with the try-with-resources statement.)
void flush ()	Flush this output stream by writing any buffered output bytes to the destination. If the intended destination of this output stream is an abstraction provided by the underlying platform (for example, a file), flushing the stream only guarantees that bytes previously written to the stream are passed to the underlying platform for writing; it doesn't guarantee that they're actually written to a physical device such as a disk drive. This method throws IOException when an I/O error occurs.

void write(byte[] b)	Write b. length bytes from byte array b to this output stream. In general, write(b) behaves as if you specified write(b, 0, b.length). This method throws NullPointerException when b is null, and IOException when an I/O error occurs.
void write(byte[] b, int off, int len)	Write len bytes from byte array b starting at offset off to this output stream. This method throws NullPointerException when b is null; java.lang.IndexOutOfBoundsException when off is negative, len is negative, or off + len is greater than b. length; and IOException when an I/O error occurs.
void write(int b)	Write byte b to this output stream. Only the eight low-order bits are written; the 24 high-order bits are ignored. This method throws IOException when an I/O error occurs.

The flush() method is useful in a long-running application where you need to save changes every so often; for example, the previously mentioned text-editor application that saves changes to a temporary file every few minutes. Remember that f lush () only flushes bytes to the platform; doing so doesn't necessarily result in the platform flushing these bytes to the disk.

InputStream is the superclass of all input stream subclasses. The following table describes InputStream's methods.

Table InputStream Methods

Method	Description
int available()	Return an estimate of the number of bytes that can be read from this input stream via the next read () method call (or skipped over via skip()) without blocking the calling thread. This method throws IOException when an I/O error occurs. It's never correct to use this method's return value to allocate a buffer for holding all the stream's data because a subclass might not return the total size of the stream.
void close()	Close this input stream and release any system resources associated with the stream. This method throws IOException when an I/O error occurs. (Because InputStream implements Closeable, you can use input streams with the try-with-resources statement.)
void mark(int readlimit)	Mark the current position in this input stream. A subsequent call to reset () repositions this stream to the last marked position so that subsequent read operations reread the same bytes. The readlimit argument tells this input stream to allow that many bytes to be read before invalidating this mark (so that the stream cannot be reset to the marked position).
boolean markSupported()	Return true when this input stream supports mark() and reset(); otherwise, return false.
int read()	Read and return (as an int in the range 0 to 255) the next byte from this input stream, or return -1 when the end of the stream is reached. This method blocks until input is available, the end of the stream is detected, or an exception is thrown. It throws IOException when an I/O error occurs.

int read(byte[] b)	Read some number of bytes from this input stream and store them in byte array b. Return the number of bytes actually read (which might be less than b's length but is never more than this length), or return -1 when the end of the stream is reached (no byte is available to read). This method blocks until input is available, the end of the stream is detected, or an exception is thrown. It throws NullPointerException when b is null, and IOException when an I/O error occurs.
int read(byte[] b, int off, int len)	Read no more than len bytes from this input stream and store them in byte array b, starting at the offset specified by off. Return the number of bytes actually read (which might be less than len but is never more than len), or return -1 when the end of the stream is reached (no byte is available to read). This method blocks until input is available, the end of the stream is detected, or an exception is thrown. It throws NullPointerException when b is null; IndexOutOfBoundsException when off is negative, len is negative, or len is greater than b. length-of f; and IOException when an I/O error occurs.
void reset()	Reposition this input stream to the position at the time markQ was last called. This method throws IOException when this input stream has not been marked or the mark has been invalidated.
long skip (long n)	Skip over and discard n bytes of data from this input stream. This method might skip over some smaller number of bytes (possibly zero); for example, when the end of the file is reached before n bytes have been skipped. The actual number of bytes skipped is returned. When n is negative, no bytes are skipped. This method throws IOException when this input strearn'doesn't support skipping or when some other I/O error occurs.

InputStream subclasses such as ByteArrayInputStream support marking the current read position in the input stream via the mark () method, and later return to that position via the reset () method.

FileOutputStream and FileInputStream

Files are common stream destinations and sources. The concrete FileOutputStream class lets you write a stream of bytes to a file; the concrete FileInputStream class lets you read a stream of bytes from a file.

FileOutputStream subclasses OutputStream and declares five constructors for creating file output streams. For example, FileOutputStream(String name) creates a file output stream to the existing file identified by name. This constructor throws FileNotFoundException when the file doesn't exist and cannot be created, it is a directory rather than a normal file, or the file cannot be otherwise opened for output.

The following example uses FileOutputStream(String name) to create a file output stream with employee. dat as its destination:

```
FileOutputStream fos = new FileOutputStream("employee.dat");
```

FileInputStream subclasses InputStream and declares three constructors for creating file input streams. For example, FileInputStream(String name) creates a file input stream from the existing file identified by name. This constructor throws FileNotFoundException when the file doesn't exist, it is a directory rather than a normal file, or there is some other reason for why the file cannot be opened for input.

The following example uses FileInputStream(String name) to create a file input stream with employee.dat as its source:

```
FileInputStream fis = new FileInputStream("employee.dat");
```

FilterOutputStream and FilterInputStream

File streams pass bytes unchanged to their destinations. Java also supports *filter streams* that buffer, compress/uncompress, encrypt/decrypt, or otherwise manipulate an input stream's byte sequence before it reaches its destination.

A *filter output stream* takes the data passed to its write () methods (the input stream), niters it, and writes the filtered data to an underlying output stream, which might be another filter output stream or a destination output stream such as a file output stream.

Filter output streams are created from subclasses of the concrete FilterOutputStream class, an OutputStream subclass. FilterOutputStream declares a single FilterOutputStream(OutputStream out) constructor that creates a filter output stream built on top of out, the underlying output stream.

BufferedOutputStream and BufferedInputStream

FileOutputStream and FileInputStream have a performance problem. Each file output stream write() method call and file input stream read() method call results in a call to one of the underlying platform's native methods, and these native method calls slow down I/O.

The concrete BufferedOutputStream and BufferedInputStream filter stream classes improve performance by minimizing underlying output stream write() and underlying input stream read() method calls. Instead, calls to BufferedOutputStream's write() and BufferedInputStream's read() methods take Java buffers into account:

- When a write buffer is full, write () calls the underlying output stream write () method to empty the buffer. Subsequent calls to BufferedOutputStream's write () methods store bytes in this buffer until it's once again full.
- When the read buffer is empty, read () calls the underlying input stream read () method to fill the buffer. Subsequent calls to BufferedInputStream's read() methods return bytes from this buffer until it's once again empty.

BufferedOutputStream declares the following constructors:

- BufferedOutputStream(OutputStream out) creates a buffered output stream that streams its output to out. An internal buffer is created to store bytes written to out.
- BufferedOutputStream(OutputStream out, int size) creates a buffered output stream that streams its output to out. An internal buffer of length size is created to store bytes written to out.

The following example chains a BufferedOutputStream instance to a FileOutputStream instance. Subsequent write () method calls on the Buf f eredOutputStream instance buffer bytes and occasionally result in internal writeQ method calls on the encapsulated FileOutputStream instance:

```
FileOutputStream fos = new FileOutputStream("employee.dat");
BufferedOutputStream bos = new BufferedOutputStream(fos); // Chain bos to
fos.
bos.write(o);  // Write to employee.dat through the buffer.
// Additional writeQ method calls.    i
bos.closeQ; // This method call internally calls fos's close() method.
```

BufferedInputStream declares the following constructors:

- BufferedInputStream(InputStream in) creates a buffered input stream that streams its input from in. An internal buffer is created to store bytes read from in.
- BufferedInputStream(InputStream in, int size) creates a buffered input stream that streams its input from in. An internal buffer of length size is created to store bytes read from in.

The following example chains a Buff eredInputStream instance to a FileInputStream instance. Subsequent read() method calls on the Buff eredInputStream instance unbuffer bytes and occasionally result in internal read() method calls on the encapsulated FileInputStream instance:

```
FileInputStream fis = new FileInputStream("employee.dat");
BufferedInputStream bis = new BufferedInputStream(fis); // Chain bis to fis.
int ch = bis.readQ;  // Read employee.dat through the buffer.
// Additional read() method calls.
bis.close(); // This method call internally calls fis's closeQ method.
```


DataOutputStream and DataInputStream

FileOutputStream and FileInputStream are useful for writing and reading bytes and arrays of bytes. However, they provide no support for writing and reading primitive type values (such as integers) and strings.

For this reason, Java provides the concrete DataOutputStream and DataInputStream filter stream classes. Each class overcomes this limitation by providing methods to write or read primitive type values and strings in a platform-independent way:

- Integer values are written and read in *big-endian format* (the most significant byte comes first). Check out Wikipedia's "Endianness" entry (http://en.wikipedia.org/wiki/Endianness) to learn about the concept of *endianness*.
- Floating-point and double precision floating-point values are written and read according to the IEEE 754 standard, which specifies four bytes per floating-point value and eight bytes per double precision floating-point value.
- Strings are written and read according to a modified version of *UTF-8,* a variable-length encoding standard for efficiently storing two-byte Unicode characters. Checkout Wikipedia's "UTF-8" entry (http://en.wikipedia.org/wiki/Utf-8) to learn more about UTF-8.

DataOutputStream declares a single DataOutputStream(OutputStream out) constructor. Because this class implements the DataOutput interface, DataOutputStream also provides access to the same-named write methods as provided by RandomAccessFile.

DataInputStream declares a single DataInputStream(InputStream in) constructor. Because this class implements the DataInput interface, DataInputStream also provides access to the same-named read methods as provided by RandomAccessFile.

Object Serialization and Deserialization

Java provides the DataOutputstream and DataInputStream classes to stream primitive type values and String objects. However, you cannot use these classes to stream non-String objects. Instead, you must use object serialization and deserialization to stream objects of arbitrary types.

Object serialization is a JVM mechanism for serializing object state into a stream of bytes. Its deserialization counterpart is a JVM mechanism for deserializing this state from a byte stream.

Java supports three forms of serialization and deserialization: default serialization and deserialization, custom serialization and deserialization, and externalization.

Default Serialization and Deserialization

Default serialization and deserialization is the easiest form to use but offers little control over how objects are serialized and deserialized. Although Java handles most of the work on your behalf, there are a couple of tasks that you must perform.

Your first task is to have the class of the object that's to be serialized implement the java.io.Serializable interface (directly, or indirectly via the class's superclass). The rationale for implementing Serializable is to avoid unlimited serialization.

Unlimited serialization is the process of serializing an entire *object graph* (all objects that are reachable from a starting object). Java doesn't support unlimited serialization for the following reasons:

- *Security.* If Java automatically serialized an object containing sensitive information (such as a password or a credit card number), it would be easy for a hacker to discover this information and wreak havoc. It's better to give the developer a choice to prevent this from happening.
- *Performance.* Serialization leverages the Reflection API. Earlier, you learned that reflection slows down application performance. Unlimited serialization could really hurt an application's performance.
- *Objects not amenable to serialization:* Some objects exist only in the context of a running application and it's meaningless to serialize them. For example, a file stream object that's deserialized no longer represents a connection to a file.

The following listing declares an Employee class that implements the Serializable interface to tell the JVM that it's okay to serialize Employee objects.

Implementing Serializable

```
class Employee implements Java.io.Serializable
{
    private String name;
    private int age;
    Employee(String name, int age)
    {
        this.name = name;
        this.age = age;
    }
    String getName() { return name; }
    int getAgeQ { return age;
}
```

Because Employee implements Serializable, the serialization mechanism will not throw NotSerializableException when serializing an Employee object. Not only does Employee implement Serializable, the String class also implements this interface.

Your second task is to work with the ObjectOutputStream class and its void writeObject (Object obj) method to serialize an object, and the OutputInputstream class and its Object readObject () method to deserialize the object.

Java provides the concrete ObjectOutputStream class to initiate the serialization of an object's state to an object output stream. This class declares an ObjectOutputStream(OutputStream out) constructor that chains the object output stream to the output stream specified by out.

When you pass an output stream reference to out, this constructor attempts to write a serialization header to that output stream. It throws NullPointerException when out is null, and IOException when an I/O error prevents it from writing this header.

ObjectOutputStream serializes an object via its writeObject() method. This method attempts to write information about obj's class followed by the values of obj's instance fields to the underlying output stream.

writeObject() doesn't serialize the contents of static fields. In contrast, it serializes the contents of all instance fields that are not explicitly prefixed with the transient reserved word. For example, consider the following field declaration:

```
public transient char[] password;
```

This declaration specifies transient to avoid serializing a password for some hacker to encounter. The JVM's serialization mechanism ignores any instance field that's marked transient.

writeObjectQ throws IOException or an instance of an IOException subclass when something goes wrong. For example, this method throws NotSerializableException when it encounters an object whose class doesn't implement Serializable.

Java provides the concrete Objectinputstream class to initiate the deserialization of an object's state from an object input stream. This class declares an ObjectInputStream(InputStream in) constructor that chains the object input stream to the input stream specified by in.

When you pass an input stream reference to in, this constructor attempts to read a serialization header from that input stream. It throws NullPointerException when in is null, IOException when an I/O error prevents it from reading this header, and Java. io. StreamCorruptedException (an indirect subclass of IOException) when the stream header is incorrect.

Objectinputstream deserializes an object via its readObjectQ method. This method attempts to read information about ob j 's class followed by the values of ob j 's instance fields from the underlying input stream.

readObjectQ throws java.lang.ClassNotFoundException, IOException, or an instance of an IOException subclass when something goes wrong. For example, this method throws java.io.OptionalDataException when it encounters primitive values instead of objects.

Custom Serialization and Deserialization

My previous discussion focused on default serialization and deserialization (with the exception of marking an instance field transient to prevent it from being included during serialization). However, situations arise Where you need to customize these tasks.

For example, suppose you want to serialize instances of a class that doesn't implement Serializable. As a workaround, you subclass this other class, have the subclass implement Serializable, and forward subclass constructor calls to the superclass.

Although this workaround lets you serialize subclass objects, you cannot deserialize these serialized objects when the superclass doesn't declare a noargument constructor, which is required by the deserialization mechanism.

Externalization

Along with default serialization/deserialization and custom serialization/deserialization, Java supports externalization. Unlike default/custom serialization/deserialization, *externalization* offers complete control over the serialization and deserialization tasks.

Java supports externalization via its Java. io. Externalizable interface. This interface declares the following pair of public methods:

- void writeExternal(ObjectOutput out) saves the calling object's contents by calling various methods on the out object. This method throws IOException when an I/O error occurs. (java.io.ObjectOutput is a subinterface of DataOutput and is implemented by Ob jectOutputStream.)
- void readExternal(Object!nput in) restores the calling object's contents by calling various methods on the in object. This method throws IOException when an I/O error occurs, and ClassNotFoundException when the class of the object being restored cannot be found. (Java. io .Ob jectInput is a subinterface of DataInput and is implemented by ObjectInputStream.)

If a class implements Externalizable, its writeExternal() method is responsible for saving all field values that are to be saved. Also, its readExternal() method is responsible for restoring all saved field values and in the order they were saved.

RefactoringListing of Employee class to support externalization

```
import Java.io.Externalizable;
import Java.io.lOException;
import java.io.Objectlnput;
import java.io.ObjectOutput;

class Employee implements Externalizable
{
    private String name;
    private int age;
    public Employee()
    {
        System.out.printIn("Employee() called");
    }
    Employee(String name, int age)
    {
        this.name = name;
        this. age = age;
    }
    String getNameQ { return name; }
    int getAgeQ { return age; }
    @Override
    public void readExternal(Object!nput in)
        throws lOException, ClassNotFoundException
    {
        System. out. println("readExternal() called");
        name = in.readUTF();
        age = in.readlnt();
    }
    @Override
    public void writeExternal(ObjectOutput out) throws lOException
    {
        System . out . println ( "writeExternal ( ) called" ) ;
        out.writeUTF(name);
        out.writelnt(age);
    }
}
```

Employee declares a public Employee () constructor because each class that participates in externalization must declare a public noargument constructor. The deserialization mechanism calls this constructor to instantiate the object.

Initiate externalization by instantiating ObjectOutputStream and calling its writeObjectQ method, or by instantiating ObjectlnputStream and calling its readObjectQ method.

Suppose you compiled the above listing SerializationDemo. Java source code and the listing's Employee. Java source code in the same directory. Now suppose you executed Java SerializationDemo. In response, you would observe the following output:

```
writeExternalQ called
Employee() called
readExternalQ called
John Doe
36
```

Before serializing an object, the serialization mechanism checks the object's class to see if it implements Externalizable. If so, the mechanism calls writeExternal(). Otherwise, it looks for a private writeObject(ObjectOutputStream) method, and calls this method if present. If this method isn't present, the mechanism performs default serialization, which includes only non-transient instance fields.

Before deserializing an object, the deserialization mechanism checks the object's class to see if it implements Externalizable. If so, the mechanism attempts to instantiate the class via the public noargument constructor. Assuming success, it calls readExternal().

If the object's class doesn't implement Externalizable, the deserialization mechanism looks for a private readObject(ObjectInputStream) method. If this method isn't present, the mechanism performs default deserialization, which includes only non-transient instance fields.

PrintStream

Of all the stream classes, PrintStream is an oddball: it should have been named PrintOutputStream for consistency with the naming convention. This filter output stream class writes string representations of input data items to the underlying output stream.

PrintStream instances are print streams whose various print() and println() methods print string representations of integers, floating-point values, and other data items to the underlying output stream. Unlike the print () methods, println () methods append a line terminator to their output.

The pr intln () methods call their corresponding pr int () methods followed by the equivalent of the void println() method, which eventually results in line, separator's value being output. For example, void println(int x) outputs x's string representation and calls this method to output the line separator.

PrintStream offers two other features that you'll find useful:

- Unlike other output streams, a print stream never rethrows an IOException instance thrown from the underlying output stream. Instead, exceptional situations set an internal flag that can be tested by calling PrintStream's boolean checkError() method, which returns true to indicate a problem.
- PrintStream objects can be created to automatically flush their output to the underlying output stream. In other words, the f lush () method is automatically called after a byte array is written, one of the println() methods is called, or a newline is written. The PrintStream instances assigned to System.out and System, err automatically flush their output to the underlying output stream.

Writers and Readers

Java's stream classes are good for streaming sequences of bytes, but they're not good for streaming sequences of characters because bytes and characters are two different things: a byte represents an 8-bit data item and a character represents a 16-bit data item. Also, Java's char and String types naturally handle characters instead of bytes.

More importantly, byte streams have no knowledge of *character sets* (sets of mappings between integer values [known as *code points]* and symbols, such as Unicode) and their *character encodings* (mappings between the members of a character set and sequences of bytes that encode these characters for efficiency, such as UTF-8).

If you need to stream characters, you should take advantage of Java's writer and reader classes, which were designed to support character I/O (they work with char instead of byte). Furthermore, the writer and reader classes take character encodings into account.

Java provides the Writer and Reader classes for performing character I/O. Writer is the superclass of all writer subclasses. The following list identifies differences between Writer and OutputStream:

- Writer declares several append () methods for appending characters to this writer. These methods exist because Writer implements the java.lang.Appendable interface, which is used in partnership with the Formatter class to output formatted strings.
- Writer declares additional write () methods, including a convenient void write(String str) method for writing a String object's characters to this writer.

Reader is the superclass of all reader subclasses. The following list identifies differences between Reader and InputStream:

- Reader declares read(char[]) andread(char[], int, int) methods instead of read(byte[]) and read(bytef], int, int) methods.
- Reader doesn't declare an available() method.
- Reader declares a boolean ready() method that returns true when the next read() call is guaranteed not to block for input.
- Reader declares an int read(CharBuffer target) method for reading characters from a character buffer.

OutputStreamWriter and InputStreamReader

The concrete OutputStreamWriter class (a Writer subclass) is a bridge between an incoming sequence of characters and an outgoing stream of bytes. Characters written to this writer are encoded into bytes according to the default or specified character encoding.

Each call to an OutputStreamWriter write() method causes an encoder to be called on the given character(s). The resulting bytes are accumulated pi a buffer before being written to the underlying output stream. The characters passed to the write () methods are not buffered.

OutputStreamWriter declares four constructors, including the following:

- OutputStreamWriter(OutputStream out) creates a bridge between an incoming sequence of characters (passed to OutputStreamWriter via its append() and write() methods) and underlying output stream out. The default character encoding is used to encode characters into bytes.
- OutputStreamWriter(OutputStream out, String charsetName) creates a bridge between an incoming sequence of characters (passed to OutputStreamWriter via itsappend() andwrite() methods) and underlying output stream out. charsetName identifies the character encoding used to encode characters into bytes. This constructor throws java.io.UnsupportedEncodingException when the named character encoding isn't supported.

The following example uses the second constructor to create a bridge to an underlying file output stream so that Polish text can be written to an ISO/IEC 8859-2-encoded file.

```
FileOutputStream fos = new FileOutputStream("polish.txt");
OutputStreamWriter osw = new OutputStreamWriter(fos,  "8859_2");
char ch =  '\u0323¹; // Accented N.
osw.write(ch);
```

The concrete InputStreamReader class (a Reader subclass) is a bridge between an incoming stream of bytes and an outgoing sequence of characters. Characters read from this reader are decoded from bytes according to the default or specified character encoding.

Each call to an InputStreamReader read() method may cause one or more bytes to be read from the underlying input stream. To enable the efficient conversion of bytes to characters, more bytes may be read ahead from the underlying stream than are necessary to satisfy the current read operation.

InputStreamReader declares four constructors, including the following:

- InputStreamReader (InputStream in) creates a bridge between underlying input stream in and an outgoing sequence of characters (returned from InputStreamReader via its readQ methods). The default character encoding is used to decode bytes into characters.
- InputStreamReader(InputStream in, String charsetName) creates a bridge between underlying input stream in and an outgoing sequence of characters (returned from InputStreamReader via its read() methods). charsetName identifies the character encoding used to decode bytes into characters. This constructor throws UnsupportedEncodingException when the named character encoding isn't supported.

The following example uses the second constructor to create a bridge to an underlying file input stream so that Polish text can be read from an ISO/IEC 8859-2-encoded file.

```
FilelnputStream fis = new FileInputStream("polish.txt");
InputStreamReader isr = new InputStreamReader(fis,  "8859_2");
char ch = isr.read(ch);
```

FileWriter and FileReader

FileWriter is a convenience class for writing characters to files. It subclasses OutputStreamWriter, and its constructors call OutputStreamWriter(OutputStream). An instance of this class is equivalent to the following code fragment:

```
FileOutputStream fos = new FileOutputStream(pathname);
OutputStreamWriter osw;
osw = new OutputStreamWriter(fos, System.getProperty("file.encoding"));
```

CHAPTER 6

JAVA & and Web Services

In this chapter you will read about:

- Web Services.
- SOAP-Based Web Services.
- RESTful Web Services.
- Java and Web Serrvices.
- Google's Charts Web Services.

Introduction

This chapter first introduces you to the topic of web services, emphasizing the SOAP-based and RESTful categories. This chapter then reveals Java's support for web service development in terms of its web service-oriented APIs, annotations, and tools. You also learn about Java's lightweight HTTP server for deploying your web services to a simple web server and testing them in this environment. Armed with a basic understanding of web services and Java's support for their development, you next learn how to develop SOAP-based and RESTful web services. For each web service category, you learn how to create and access your own web service, and then learn how to access an external web service.

This chapter also closes by presenting five advanced web service topics: accessing SOAP-based web services via the SAAJ API, installing a JAX-WS handler to log the flow of SOAP messages, installing a customized lightweight HTTP server to perform authentication, sending attachments to clients from a RESTful web service, and using dispatch clients with providers.

What Are Web Services?

No standard definition for web service has yet been devised because this term means different things to different people. For example, some people define web service as a web application; others define web service in terms of a protocol (e.g., SOAP) that's used by applications to communicate across the Web. Perhaps the best way to define web service is to first define this term's parts:

- *Web:* A huge interconnected network of resources, where a *resource* is a Uniform Resource Identifier (URI)-named data source such as a spreadsheet document, a digitized video, a web page, or even an application. These resources can be accessed via standard Internet protocols (e.g., HTTP or SMTP).
- *Service: A* server-based application or software component that exposes a resource to clients via an exchange of messages according to a *message exchange pattern* (MEP) —see http://en.wikipedia.org/wiki/Message_Exchange_Pattern. The *request-responseMEP* is typical.

Given these definitions, we can define *web service* as a server-based application/software component that exposes a Web-based resource to clients via an exchange of messages. These messages may or may not be based on XML, and can be thought of as invoking web service functions and receiving invocation results.

Web services can be classified as simple or complex. Simple web services don't interact with other web services; for example, a standalone server-based application with a single function that returns the current time for a specified timezone. In contrast, complex web services often interact with other web services. For example, a generalized social network web service might interact with Twitter and Facebook web services to obtain and return to its client all Twitter and all Facebook information for a specific individual. Complex web services are also known as *mashups* because they *mash* (combine) data from multiple web services.

SOAP-Based Web Services

A *SOAP-based web service* is a widely used category of web service based on SOAP, an XML language for defining *Messages* (abstract function invocations or their responses) that can be understood by both ends of a network connection. An exchange of SOAP messages is called an *operation,* which corresponds to a function call and its response. Related operations are often grouped into an *interface,* which is conceptually similar to a Java interface. A binding provides concrete details on how an interface is bound to a messaging protocol (particularly SOAP) to communicate commands, error codes, and other items over the wire.

Although SOAP can be used by itself, as demonstrated later in this chapter's discussion of the SAAJ API, SOAP is typically used with *Web Services Description Language* (WSDL, pronounced whiz-dull), an XML language for defining the operations provided by the service. Unlike WSDL, SOAP, which once stood for Simple Object Access Protocol, is no longer considered to be an acronym. (SOAP is neither simple nor does it relate to objects.)

A WSDL *document is* a formal contract between a SOAP-based web service and its clients, providing all the details needed to interact with the web service. This document lets you group messages into operations and operations into interfaces. It also lets you define a binding for each interface as well as the endpoint address. You will explore WSDL document architecture while learning how to create a SOAP-based web service later in this chapter.

As well as supporting WSDL documents, SOAP-based web services have the following properties:

- *The ability to address complex nonfunctional requirements such as security and transactions:* These requirements are made available via a wide variety of specifications. To promote interoperability among these specifications, an industry consortium known as the *Web Services Interoperability Organization* (WS-I) was formed. WS-I has established a set of profiles, where a *profile is* a set of named web service specifications at specific revision levels, together with a set of implementation and interoperability guidelines recommending how the specifications may be used to develop interoperable web services. For example, the very first profile, WS-I Basic Profile 1.0, consists of the following set of nonproprietary web service specifications: SOAP 1.1, WSDL 1.1, UDDI 2.0, XML 1.0 (Second Edition), XML Schema Part 1: Structures, XML Schema Part 2: Datatypes, RFC2246: The Transport Layer Security Protocol Version 1.0, RFC2459: Internet X.509 Public Key Infrastructure Certificate and CRL Profile, RFC2616: HyperText Transfer Protocol 1.1, RFC2818: HTTP over TLS, RFC2965: HTTP State Management Mechanism, and The Secure Sockets Layer Protocol Version 3.0. Additional profile examples include WS-I Basic Security Profile and Simple SOAP Binding Profile. For more information on these and other profiles, visit the WS-I website at http://www.ws-i.org/. Java 7 supports the WS-I Basic Profile.
- *The ability to interact with a web service asynchronously.* Web service clients should be able to interact with a web service in a nonblocking, asynchronous manner. Client-side asynchronous invocation support of web service operations is provided in Java 7.

SOAP-based web services execute in an environment that includes a service requester (the client), a service provider, and a service broker.

The service requester, typically a client application (e.g., a web browser), or perhaps another web service, first locates the service provider in some manner. For example, the service requester might send a WSDL document to a service broker, which responds with another WSDL document identifying the service provider's location. The service requester then communicates with the service provider via SOAP messages.

Service providers need to be published so that others can locate and use them. In August 2000, an open industry initiative known as *Universal Description, Discovery, and Integration* (UDDI) was launched to let businesses publish service listings, discover each other, and define how the services or software applications interact over the Internet. However, this platform-independent, XML-based' registry was not widely adopted and currendy isn't used. Many developers found UDDI to be overly complicated and lacking in functionality, and opted for alternatives such as publishing the information on a website. For example, Google makes its public; web services (e.g., Google Maps) available through its http: //code .google. com/more/ website.

The SOAP messages that flow between service requesters and service providers are often unseen, being passed as requests and responses between the SOAP libraries of their *web service protocol stacks* (see http://en.wikipedia.org/wiki/Web_services_protocol_stack). However, it's possible to access these messages directly.

RESTful Web Services

SOAP-based web services can be delivered over various protocols such as HTTP, SMTP, FTP, and the more recent Blocks Extensible Exchange Protocol —see http: //www. rf c-editor.org/rf c/rf C3080.txt. Delivering SOAP messages over HTTP can be thought of as a special case of a RESTful web service.

Representational State Transfer (REST) is a software architecture style for distributed *hypermedia systems* (systems in which images, text, and other resources are located around networks and are accessible via hyperlinks). The hypermedia system of interest in a web services context is the World Wide Web.

The central part of REST is the URI-identifiable resource. REST identifies resources by their Multipurpose Internet Mail Extensions (MIME) types (such as text/xml). Also, resources have states that are captured by their representations. When a client requests a resource from a RESTful web service, the service sends a MIME-typed representation of the resource to die client.

Clients use HTTP's POST, GET, PUT, and DELETE verbs to retrieve representations of resources and to manipulate resources —REST views these verbs as an API and maps them onto the database Create, Read, Update, and Delete (CRUD) operations (see http: //en.wikipedia.org/wiki/Create,_read,_update_and_delete for an introduction to CRUD). The following table reveals this mapping.

Table HTTP Verbs and Their CRUD Counterparts

HTTP Verb	CRUD Operation
POST	Create new resource based on request data.
GET	Read existing resource without producing side effects (don't modify the resource).
PUT	Update existing resource with request data.
DELETE	Delete existing resource.

Each verb is followed by a URI that identifies the resource. (This immensely simple approach is fundamentally incompatible with SOAP's approach of sending encoded messages to a single resource.) The URI might refer to a collection, such as http://tutortutor.ca/library, or to an element of the collection, such as http://tutortutor.ca/library/978l430234135 —these URIs are only illustrations. For POST and PUT requests, XML-based resource data is passed as the body of the request. For example, you could interpret POST http://tutortutor.ca/library HTTP/ l.l (where HTTP/ l.l describes the requester's HTTP version) as a request to insert POST'S XML data into the http://tutortutor.ca/library collection resource.

For GET and DELETE requests, the data is typically passed as query strings, where a *query string is* that portion of a URI beginning with a" ?" character. For example, where GET http: //tutortutor. ca/library might return a list of identifiers for all books in a library resource, GET http: //tutortutor. ca/library?isbn = 978l430234135 would probably return a representation of the book resource whose query string identifies International Standard Book Number (ISBN) 9781430234135. As well as relying on HTTP verbs and MIME types when making requests, REST relies on HTTP's standard response codes, such as 404 (requested resource not found) and 200 (resource operation successful), along with MIME types (when resource representations are being retrieved) for obtaining responses.

Java and Web Services

Prior to Java 6, Java-based web services were developed exclusively with the Java EE SDK. Although Java EE is the preferred approach for developing web services from a production perspective, because Java EE-based servers provide a very high degree of scalability, a security infrastructure, monitoring facilities, and so on, the repeated deployment of a web service to a Java EE container is time consuming and slows down development.

Java 6 simplified and accelerated web services development by incorporating APIs, annotations, tools, and a lightweight HTTP server (for deploying your web services to a simple web server and testing them in this environment) into its core. Java 7 also supports these components.

Web Service APIs

Java provides several APIs that support web services. In addition to the various JAXP APIs that were discussed earlier, Java provides the JAX-WS, JAXB, and SAAJ APIs:

- *Java APIforXML Web Services (JAX-WS):* The main API for building web services and clients (in Java) that communicateivia XML. JAX-WS replaces the older Java API for Remote Procedure Call Web Services (JAX-RPC) API, and is assigned package javax.xml.ws and various subpackages. Java 7 supports JAX-WS 2.2.4.
- *Java Architecture for XML Binding (JAXB):* The API for mapping XML Schema-based data types to Java objects and vice versa —see Chapter 10 to learn about XML Schema. JAX-WS delegates data-binding tasks to JAXB. This API is assigned package javax. xml. bind and various subpackages. Java 7 supports JAXB 2.2.4.
- *Soap with Attachments API for Java (SAAJ):* The API for creating, sending, and receiving SOAP messages with/without attachments. According to Jitendra Kotamraju's "No SAAJ RI dependency in JAX-WS RI" blog post at http://weblogs.Java.net/blog/jitu/archive/2007/09/no_saaj_ri_depe_l.html, JAX-WS's dependency on SAAJ for SOAP messages was removed in the reference implementation of JAX-WS 2.1.3 (known as *Metro,* see http://jax-ws.java.net/). This API is assigned the javax.xml. soap package. Java 7 supports SAAJ 1.3.

Web Service Annotations

Java 6 introduced several web service annotation types that facilitate web service development, by letting you describe web services declaratively via metadata. You can still develop web services without these annotation types, but you'll soon appreciate their convenience if you decide not to use them.

Most web service annotation types are either part of the Web Services MetaData API (see http://jcp.org/en/jsr/detail?id=181), which is assigned packages javax. jws and javax. jws.soap, or belong to the javax.xml.ws package. The javax. jws package provides the following annotation types:

- HandlerChain associates the web service with an externally defined handler chain.
- Oneway indicates that a given @WebMethod annotation has only an input message and no output message.
- WebMethod customizes a method that is exposed as a web service operation.
- WebParam customizes the mapping of an individual parameter to a WSDL message element's part element.
- WebResult customizes the mapping of the return value to a WSDL message element's part element.
- WebService marks a Java class as implementing a web service, or a Java interface as defining a service endpoint interface.

The following annotation types (three of which are deprecated in favor of using the HandlerChai,n annotation type) belong to the javax. jws. soap package:

- InitParam describes an initialization parameter (a name/value pair passed to the handler during initialization). This annotation type is deprecated.
- SOAPBinding specifies the mapping of the web service onto the SOAP protocol.
- SOAPMessageHandler specifies a single SOAP message handler that runs before and after the web service's business methods. This handler is called in response to SOAP messages targeting the service. This annotation type is deprecated.
- SOAPMessageHandlers specifies a list of SOAP protocol handlers that run before and after the web service's business methods. These handlers are called in response to SOAP messages targeting the service. This annotation type is deprecated.

Finally, javax.xml.ws's most important annotation types from a RESTful webservice perspective are WebServiceProvider and Binding.

Web Service Tools

Java provides four command-line-based tools that facilitate web service development. Two of these tools are used to convert between XML Schema-based schemas and Java classes, and the other pair of tools is used in the context of WSDL documents:

- schemagen: WSDL documents use XML Schema data types to describe web service function return and parameter types. This tool generates a schema (often stored in a file with a .xsd extension) from Java classes —one schema file is created for each referenced namespace. After the schema has been created, *XML instance documents* (XML documents that adhere to their schemas) can be converted to and from Java objects via JAXB. The classes contain all the information needed by JAXB to parse the XML for *marshaling* (converting Java objects to XML) and *unmarshaling* (converting XML to Java objects) —the application doesn't perform XML parsing.
- wsgen: This tool reads a compiled web service endpoint interface and generates JAX-WS portable artifacts for web service deployment and invocation. It can alternatively generate a WSDL file and corresponding XML Schema document (when its -wsdl option is specified). This tool isn't required when publishing a web service via Endpoint. publish(), which automatically generates the artifacts and WSDL/schema. You'll learn about Endpoint. publish() later in this chapter.
- wsimport: This tool generates client-support Java classes (artifacts) from a given WSDL document. These classes facilitate writing a client against the service.
- xjc: This tool generates Java classes from a schema. The generated classes contain properties mapped to the XML elements and attributes defined in the schema.

Lightweight HTTP Server

The Java 7 reference implementation includes a lightweight HTTP server for deploying and testing web services. The server implementation supports the HTTP and HTTPS protocols, and its associated API can be used to create a customized web server to enhance your web service testing or for other purposes.

The server's API is not a formal part of Java, which means that it's not guaranteed to be part of nonreference Java implementations. As a result, the lightweight HTTP server API is stored in the following packages instead of being distributed in packages such as Java. net. httpserver and Java.net.httpserver.spi:

- com. sun. net. httpserver: This package provides a high-level HTTP server API for building embedded HTTP servers.

- com.sun.net.httpserver.spi: This package provides a pluggable service provider API for installing HTTP server replacement implementations.

The com. sun. net. httpserver package contains an HttpHandler interface, which you must implement to handle HTTP request-response exchanges when creating your own HTTP server. This package also contains seventeen classes; the four most important classes are described in the following table.

Table Important Classes in com. sun. net. httpserver

Class	Description
HttpServer	Implements a simple HTTP server bound to an IP address/port number, and listens for incoming TCP connections from clients. One or more associated HttpHandlers process requests and create responses.
HttpsServer	An HttpServer subclass that provides support for HTTPS. It must be associated with an HttpsConf igurator object to configure the HTTPS parameters for each incoming Secure Sockets Layer (SSL) connection.
HttpContext	Describes a mapping between a root URI path and an HttpHandler implementation that is invoked to handle those requests targeting the path.
HttpExchange	Encapsulates an HTTP request and its response. An instance of this class is passed to HttpHandler's void handle(HttpExchange exchange) method to handle the request and generate a response.

Implementing your own lightweight HTTP server consists of three tasks:

1. Create the server. The abstract HttpServer class provides an HttpServer creatednetSocketAddress addr, int backlog) class method for creating a server that handles the HTTP protocol. This method's addr argument specifies a java.net.InetSocketAddress object containing an IP address and port number for the server's listening socket. The backlog argument specifies the maximum number of TCP connections that can be queued while waiting for acceptance by the server; a value less than or equal to zero causes a system default value to be used. Alternatively, you can pass null to addr or invoke HttpServer's HttpServer create 0 class method to create a server not bound to an address/port. If you choose this alternative, you will need to invoke HttpServer's void bind(InetSocketAddress addr, int backlog) method before you can use the server.
2. Create a context. After creating the server, you need to create at least one context (an instance of a subclass of the abstract HttpContext class) that maps a root URI path to an implementation of HTTPHandler. Contexts help you organize the applications run by the server (via HTTP handlers). (The HttpServer Java documentation shows how incoming request URIs are mapped to HttpContext paths.) You create a context by invoking HttpServer's HttpContext createContext(String path, HttpHandler handler) method, where path specifies the root URI path, and handler specifies the HttpHandler implementation that handles all requests that target this path. If you prefer, you can invoke HttpContext createContext(String path) without specifying an initial handler. You would later specify the handler by calling HttpContext's void setHandler(HttpHandler h) method.
3. Start the server. After you have created the server and at least one context (including a suitable handler), the final task is to start the server. Accomplish this task by calling HttpServer's void startO method.

Working with SOAP-Based Web Services

JAX-WS supports SOAP-based web services. This section first shows you how to create and access your own SOAP-based temperature-conversion web service, publish this web service locally via the default lightweight HTTP server, and access the service via a simple client. It then shows you how to access the Sloan Digital Sky Survey's SOAP-based image cutout web service to obtain astronomy images.

Creating and Accessing a Temperature-Conversion Web Service

The temperature-conversion web service, which I've named Temp Verier, consists of a pair of functions for converting degrees Fahrenheit to degrees Celsius and vice versa. Although this example could be architected as a single Java class, I've chosen to follow best practices by architecting it as a Java interface and a Java class. The following listing presents the web service's TempVerter interface.

TempVerter's Service Endpoint Interface

```
package ca.tutortutor.tv;
import javax.jws.WebMethod;
import javax.jws.WebService;

@WebService
public interface TempVerter
{
    @WebMethod double c2f(double degrees);
    @WebMethod double f2c(double degrees);
}
```

TempVerter describes a *Service Endpoint Interface (SEI),* which is a Java interface that exposes a web service interface's operations in terms of abstract Java methods. Clients communicate with SOAP-based web services via their SEIs.

Accessing the Image Cutout Web Service

Although you can create and access your own SOAP-based web services, you might want to access SOAP-based web services created by others. For example, the Sloan Digital Sky Survey (http: //www. sdss. org) makes available astronomical images from its image archive via its Image Cutout web service.

Image Cutout's operations are described by its WSDL document at http: //casjobs. sdss .org/ImgCutoutDR5/ ImgCutout. asmx?wsdl. For example, this WSDL document identifies an operation named GetDpeg for returning a JPEG image of an area of the night sky located in terms of right accension (see http:// en.wikipedia.org/wiki/Right_ascension) and declination (see http: //en. wikipedia. org/wiki/Declination) degree values.

Before you can write a Java application that lets you access this web service to obtain (and then display) arbitrary images, you need to create artifacts (in the form of Java classes) that let this application interact with the web service. You can generate these artifacts by executing the following wsimport command line:

```
wsimport -keep http://casjobs.sdss.org/ImgCutoutDR5/ImgCutout.asmx7wsdl
```

wsimport creates an org directory within the current directory, org contains an sdss subdirectory, which contains a skyserver subdirectory, which stores the generated classfiles. Furthermore, skyserver stores their source files (thanks to the -keep option).

The generated ImgCutout .Java source file reveals a noargument ImgCutout constructor along with an

ImgCutoutSoap getImgCutoutSoapQ method. Furthermore, ImgCutoutSoap declares a public byte[] getDpeg(double ra, double dec, double scale, int width, int height, String opt) method that corresponds to the GetDpeg operation. Your application interacts with Image Cutout via this constructor and these methods.

The getJpeg() method's parameters are described here:

- ra and dec specify the center coordinates of the image in terms of right ascension and declination values, where each value is expressed in degrees.
- scale specifies a scaling value in terms of arcseconds per pixel. One arcsecond equals 1/1296000 of a circle.
- width and height identify the dimensions of the returned image.
- opt identifies a sequence of character codes for drawing over the image; for example, C (draw a grid over the image), L (label the image), and I (invert the image).

The get]peg() method returns the image as an array of bytes. It never returns a null reference. When an error occurs, the method returns an image that presents the error message.

Given this information, you next need to figure out how to invoke get]peg(). The following steps accomplish this task:

1. Import ImgCutout and ImgCutoutSoap from the org.sdss.skyserver package.
2. Instantiate ImgCutout.
3. Invoke getImgCutoutSoapO on the ImgCutout instance.
4. Invoke getJpegO on the returned ImgCutoutSoap instance.

Working with RESTful Web Services

JAX-WS also supports RESTrul web services. This section first shows you how to create and access your own RESTful library web service, publish this web service locally via the default lightweight HTTP server, and access the service via a simple client. It then shows you how to access Google's RESTful Charts web service to obtain chart images corresponding to entered data values.

Accessing Google's Charts Web Service

Accessing someone else's RESTful web service is easier than creating your own because you can forget about JAX-WS and deal only with HttpURLConnection to make a request and retrieve the necessary data. Furthermore, you aren't restricted to retrieving XML data. For example, Google's RESTful Charts web service (http: //code. google. com/apis/chart/image/docs/making_charts. html), which is also known as the Chart API, lets you dynamically create and return images of bar, pie, and other kinds of charts.

Google Charts is accessed via the https: //chart. googleapis. com/chart URI. You append a query string to this URI that identifies the chart type, size, data, labels, and any other needed information. For example, query string "?cht=p3&chs=450x200&chd=t:60,40&chl=01%20(60%) |02%20(40%)" describes the following chart type, size, data, and label parameters:

- cht=p3 specifies the chart type as a three-dimensional pie chart.
- chs=450x200 specifies the chart size as 450 pixels wide by 200 pixels high —a chart should be at least twb-and-one-half times as wide as it is tall so that all labels are fully visible.
- chd=t:60,40 specifies the chart data in a simple text format —this format consists of a single series of comma-separated values; multiple series are specified by using a vertical bar to separate one series from the next —where the first data item (for the first pie chart slice) is 60 and the second data item (for the second slice) is 40.

- chl=0l%20(60%) 102%20(40%) specifies the chart labels for the pie chart slices as Ql (60%) and Q2 (40%) —labels are separated by vertical bars and must be URL-encoded (which is why each space character is replaced with %20).

Google Charts defaults to returning the chart as a PNG image. You can return a GIF image instead by including the chof=gif parameter in the query string, or even return a JavaScript Object Notation (JSON)-formatted document (see http: //en .wikipedia .org/wiki/JSON) by including the chof=j son parameter.

Advanced Web Service Topics

Now that the basics of creating and accessing SOAP-based and RESTful web services are out of the way, you're probably ready for more advanced material. This section introduces five advanced web service topics.

You first receive an introduction to the SAAJ API for working with SOAP-based web services at a lower level. You then learn how to create a JAX-WS handler to log the flow of SOAP messages. Next, you learn how to create and install a custom lightweight HTTP server to perform authentication, and also learn how to create a RESTful web service that returns attachments (e.g., a JPEG image) to its clients. Finally, you dig deeper into JAX-WS by exploring the interplay between providers and dispatch clients, and learn how to create a dispatch client that accesses the Source instance returned from a web service provider's invokeQ method via a different Source instance in an alternate Library client application.

Working with SAAJ

Soap with Attachments API for Java (SAAJ) is the Java API for creating, sending, and receiving SOAP messages that may or may not have MIME-typed attachments. SAAJ is a lower-level alternative to JAX-WS for sending and receiving SOAP messages.

Although header blocks are defined by the application, their start tags may contain the following SOAP-defined attributes to indicate how SOAP nodes should process them:

- encodingStyle identifies the rules used tojserialize parts of a SOAP message
- role identifies the SOAP node (via a URI) to which the header block is targeted — this SOAP 1.2-introduced attribute replaces the SOAP 1.1 actor attribute, which performs the same function
- mustllnderstand indicates whether processing of the header block is mandatory (value 1 in SOAP 1.1; true in SOAP 1.2) or optional (value 0 in SOAP 1.1; false in SOAP 1.2)
- relay indicates whether the header block targeted at a SOAP receiver must be relayed to another node if not processed —this attribute was introduced in SOAP 1.2

The Body element contains information that targets the ultimate receiver node. This information is known as the *payload,* and consists of a SOAP-defined Fault child element describing *& fault* (an error being reported by the web service), or child elements that are specific to the web service.

The Fault element contains error and status information that a web service returns to a client. SOAP 1.1 specifies the following child elements of Fault:

- faultcode: This mandatory element provides information about the fault in a form that can be processed by software. SOAP defines a small set of SOAP fault codes that cover basic faults; this set can be extended by applications.
- faultstring: This mandatory element provides information about the fault in a human-readable format.
- faultactor: This element contains the URI of the SOAP node that generated the fault. A SOAP node that is not the ultimate SOAP receiver must include faultactor when creating a fault; an ultimate SOAP receiver doesn't have to include this element, but might choose to do so.

- detail: This element carries application-specific error information related to the Body element. It must be present when Body's contents couldn't be processed successfully. The detail element must not be used to carry error information belonging to header blocks; detailed error information belonging to header blocks is carried within these blocks.

SOAP 1.2 specifies the following child elements of Fault:

- Code: This mandatory element provides information about the fault in a form that can be processed by software. It contains a Value element and an optional Subcode element.
- Reason: This mandatory element provides information about the fault in a human-readable format. Reason contains one or more Text elements, each of which contains information about the fault in a different language.
- Node: This element contains the URI of the SOAP node that generated the fault. A SOAP node that is not the ultimate SOAP receiver must include Node when creating a fault; an ultimate SOAP receiver doesn't have to include this element, but might choose to do so.
- Role: This element contains a URI that identifies the role the node was operating in when the fault occurred.
- Detail: This optional element contains application-specific error information related to the SOAP fault codes describing the fault. Its presence has no significance as to which parts of the faulty SOAP message were processed.

The following listing presents an example SOAP message.

A SOAP message for calling a SOAP-based library web service's getTitle() function to retrieve a book's title when given its ISBN

```
<SOAP-ENV:Envelope xmlns:SOAP-ENV="http://schemas.xmlsoap.org/soap/envelope/"
      xmlns: xsd=" http: //www. w3. org/2001/XMLSchema"
      xmlns:xsi="http://www.w3.org/2001/XMLSchema-instance">
   <SOAP-ENV:Header />
   <SOAP-ENV:Body>
      <lns:getTitle xmlns:lns="http://tutortutor.ca/library">
         <isbn xsi:type="xsd:string">9781430234135</isbn>
      </lns:getTitle>
   </SOAP-ENV:Body>
</SOAP-ENV:Envelope>
```

This SOAP message describes a request to a library web service to execute its getTitle () function. Furthermore, it describes the type and value of the ISBN argument passed to this function's isbn parameter.

The message begins with the SOAP-ENV-prefrxed <Envelope> tag, which describes the SOAP message's envelope. The commonly used SOAP-ENV prefix corresponds to the SOAP 1.1 namespace that provides the schema for SOAP envelopes. The xsd and xsi prefixes correspond to the XML Schema structures and XML Schema Instance namespaces, and are used to denote the XML Schema type that describes the kind of data being passed to getTitleQ (a string) via the isbn element.

The empty Header element signifies that there is no SOAP header. In contrast, the Body element identifies a single getTitle operation request.

The getTitle element is namespace-qualified, as recommended by the SOAP 1.1 and 1.2 specifications. In contrast, the isbn child element of getTitle is not namespace-qualified because it inherits getTitle's namespace—the SOAP 1.1 and 1.2 specifications do not mandate that such child elements be namespace-qualified.

SAAJ API Overview

SAAJ is a small API that lets you perform the following tasks:

- Create an endpoint-to-endpoint connection
- Create a SOAP message
- Create an XML fragment
- Add content to the header of a SOAP message
- Add content to the body of a SOAP message
- Create attachment parts and add content to them
- Access/add/modify parts of a SOAP message
- Create/add/modify SOAP fault information
- Extract content from a SOAP message
- Send a SOAP request-response message

SAAJ is associated with the javax. xml. soap package, which contains 14 interfaces and 13 classes. Various interfaces and classes extend their counterparts in the org. w3c. dom package, implying that part of a SOAP message is organized as a tree of nodes.

The following classes and interfaces are used to specify the structure of a SOAP message:

- SOAPMessage represents the entire SOAP message. It contains a single SOAPPart instance and zero or more AttachmentPart instances.
- SOAPPart contains a SOAPEnvelope instance, which represents the actual SOAP Envelope element.
- SOAPEnvelope optionally contains a SOAPHeader instance and also contains a mandatory SOAPBody instance.
- SOAPHeader represents the SOAP message's header block(s).
- SOAPBody contains either a SOAPFault object or a SOAPBodyElement object containing the actual SOAP payload XML content.
- SOAPFault stores a SOAP fault message.

Working with SAAJ involves creating a SOAP connection, creating SOAP messages, populating each message with content and optional attachments, sending the messages to an endpoint, and retrieving replies.

You create a connection by working with the SOAPConnectionFactory and SOAPConnection classes. As its name implies, SOAPConnectionFactory is a factory class for retrieving SOAPConnection instances (actually, instances of subclasses of the abstract SOAPConnection class). A SOAPConnection instance represents an endpoint-to-endpoint connection to the web service; the client and web service exchange messages over this connection. The following example shows you how to instantiate the factory and obtain a SOAP connection:

```
SOAPConnectionFactory soapcf = SOAPConnectionFactory.newInstance();
SOAPConnection soapc = soapcf.createConnection();
```

Instantiate the factory by calling SOAPConnectionFactory's SOAPConnectionFactory newInstanceQ method. This method throws SOAPException when a SOAPConnectionFactory instance cannot be created. If a nonOracle Java implementation doesn't support the SAAJ communication infrastructure, this method throws an instance of the java.lang.UnsupportedOperationException class.

After instantiating SOAPConnectionFactory, call this instance's SOAPConnection createConnectionQ method to create and return a new SOAPConnection object. This method throws SOAPException when it's unable to create this object.

Create a SOAP message by working with the MessageFactory and SOAPMessage classes. MessageFactory provides a pair of methods for returning a MessageFactory instance:

- MessageFactory newInstanceQ creates a MessageFactory object based on the default SOAP 1.1 implementation. This method follows an ordered lookup procedure to locate the MessageFactory implementation class. This procedure first examines the javax.xml.soap.MessageFactory system property, and lastly calls an instance of the SAAJMeta Factory class's MessageFactory newMessageFactory (String protocol) method to return that factory. This method throws SOAPException when it's unable to create the factory.
- MessageFactory new!nstance(String protocol) creates a MessageFactory object that is based on the SOAP implementation specified by the protocol argument, which is one of the SOAPConstants interface's DEFAULT_SOAP_PROTOCOL, DYNAMIC_SOAP_PROTOCOL, SOAP_1_1_PROTOCOL, or SOAP_1_2_PROTOCOL constants. This method throws SOAPException when it's unable to create the factory.

After instantiating MessageFactory, call one of the following methods to create a SOAPMessage instance:

- SOAPMessage createMessageQ creates and returns a new SOAPMessage object (actually, an instance of a concrete subclass of this abstract class) with default SOAPPart, SOAPEnvelope, SOAPBody (initially empty) and SOAPHeader objects. This method throws SOAPException when a SOAPMessage instance cannot be created, and UnsupportedOperationException when the MessageFactory instance's protocol is DYNAMIC_SOAP_PROTOCOL.
- SOAPMessage createMessage(MimeHeaders headers, InputStream in)internalizes the contents of the given Java. io. InputStream object into a new SOAPMessage object and returns this object. The MimeHeaders instance specifies transport-specific headers that describe the various attachments to the SOAP message. This method throws SOAPException when a SOAPMessage instance cannot be created, IOException when there's a problem reading data from the input stream, and IllegalArgumentException when the MessageFactory instance requires one or more MIME headers to be present in the argument passed to headers and these headers are missing.

The following example shows you how to instantiate the factory and create a SOAPMessage object that is ready to be populated:

```
MessageFactory mi = MessageFactory.newInstance();
SOAPMessage soapm = mi.createMessage();
```

SOAPMessage describes a SOAP message optionally followed by MIME-typed attachments. The SOAP message part of this object is defined by an instance of a concrete subclass of the abstract SOAPPart class. SOAPPart encapsulates an instance of a class that implements the SOAPEnvelope interface, and the SOAPEnvelope instance encapsulates instances of classes that implement the SOAPHeader and SOAPBody interfaces. Call SOAPMessage's SOAPPart getSOAPPart() method to return the SOAPPart instance. You can then call SOAPPart's SOAPEnvelope getEnvelope() method to return the SOAPEnvelope instance, and call SOAPEnvelope's SOAPBody getBody() and SOAPHeader getHeader() methods to return the SOAPEnvelope instance's SOAPBody and SOAPHeader instances.

The following example shows you how to obtain the SOAPPart, SOAPEnvelope, and SOAPBody instances from the SOAPMessage instance, and also how to detach the SOAPHeader instance:

```
SOAPPart soapp = soapm.getSOAPPart();
SOAPEnvelope soape = soapp.getEnvelope();
SOAPBody soapb = soape.getBodyQ;
```

```
soape.getHeader().detachNode();
```


SOAPEnvelope and various other interfaces extend SOAPElement, which provides methods that are applicable to different kinds of element implementation instances. For example, the SOAPElement addNamespaceDeclaration(String prefix. String uri) method is useful for adding a namespace declaration with the specified prefix and uri values to a SOAPEnvelope instance. The following example shows how to add declarations for the xsd and xsi namespaces shown in Listing 11-16 to its Envelope element:

```
soape.addNamespaceDeclaration("xsd", "http://www.w3.org/2001/XMLSchema");
soape.addNamespaceDeclaration("xsi", "http: //www.w3.org/2001/XMLSchema-
instance");
```

The SOAPBody instance contains either content or a fault. Adding content to the body first requires that you create SOAPBodyElement objects (to store this content) and add these objects to the SOAPBody instance. This task is accomplished by calling either of SOAPBody's two addBody Element () methods, which create the SOAPBodyElement object, add it to the SOAPBody object, and return a reference to the created object so that you can create method call chains.

When a new subelement of the SOAP Body element is created, you must specify a fully qualified name in the form of a Name instance or a OName instance. Because the Java documentation for the Name interface states that it may be deprecated in favor of OName, you should get into the habit of using OName instead of Name. As a result, you should use SOAPBody's SOAPBodyElement addBodyElement (OName qname) method instead of using this interface's SOAPBodyElement addBodyElement(Name name) method, as demonstrated here:

```
OName name = new OName("http://tutortutor.ca/library", "getTitle", "Ins");
SOAPElement soapel = soapb.addBodyElement(name);
```

SOAPBodyElement instances store subelement instances. You create these subelements and add them to the SOAPBodyElement instance by calling SOAPElement's various addChildElement() methods, such as SOAPElement addChildElement(String localName), which creates a subelement object having the specified localName, adds this subelement object to the SOAPBodyElement object on which this method is called, and returns a reference to the created SOAPElement object for chaining together method calls.

You can then attach a text node to a body element or a subelement by calling SOAPElement's SOAPElement addTextNode(String text) method. You can also call SOAPElement's void setAttribute(String name, String value) methdd (inherited from SOAPElement's org.w3c.dom.Element ancestor interface) to add attributes to the subelement as appropriate. The following example demonstrates:

```
soapel.addChildElement("isbn").addTextNode("9781430234135").setAttribute("xsi:type",
"xsd:string");
```

Attachments are instances of concrete subclasses of the abstract AttachmentPart class. If you need to include an attachment with the SOAP message, call one of SOAPMessage'screateAttachment?art() methods to create and return an AttachmentPart object. After configuring this object, call SOAPMessage's void addAttachmentPart(AttachmentPart attachmentPart) method to add the given attachmentPart -referenced object to this SOAPMessage object.

To send the SOAP message and receive a reply, invoke SOAPConnection's SOAPMessage call(SOAPMessage request, Object to) method. The specified request message is sent to the endpoint identified by to, which may be a String or URL instance. This method throws SOAPException when a SOAP problem occurs, and blocks until it receives a SOAP message, which it returns as a SOAPMessage object. The following example provides a demonstration:

```
String endpoint = "http://tutortutor.ca/library/GetTitle";
// Send the request message identified by soapm to the web service at the
specified
// endpoint and return the response message.
SOAPMessage response = soapc.call(soapm, endpoint);
```

Alternatively, you can call SOAPConnection's SOAPMessage get(Object to) method to request a SOAP message. As with call(), let() blocks until there is a reply, and throws SOAPException when a SOAP problem occurs.

After finishing your call() and/or get () invocations, call SOAPConnection's void closeQ method to close the connection to the endpoint. If this method has already been called, a subsequent attempt to close the connection results in a thrown SOAPException instance.

Logging SOAP Messages with a JAX-WS Handler

The RomanNumerals application used SOAPMessage's void writeTo(OutputStream out) method to dump SOAP messages to the standard output stream. If you want to accomplish this task in the context of TempVerterClient application, you need to install a JAX-WS handler. JAX-WS lets you install a chain of handlers on a web service class, a client class, or both to perform custom processing of request and response messages. For example, you might use a handler to add security information to the message or to log message details.

A *handler is* an instance of a class that ultimately implements the javax.xml.ws. handler. Handler<C extends MessageContext> interface in terms of the following methods:

- void close(MessageContext context) is called at the conclusion of a MEP just before the JAX-WS runtime dispatches a message, fault or exception. This method lets a handler clean up any resources used for processing request-only or request-response message exchanges.
- boolean handleFault(C context) is invoked for fault message processing. This method returns true when the handler wants to continue handling fault messages; otherwise, it returns false. It may throw javax.xml.ws. ProtocolException (a subclass of WebServiceException) or RuntimeException to cause the JAX-WS 'runtime to cease the handler's fault processing and dispatch the fault.
- boolean handleMessage(C context) is invoked for normal processing of inbound and outbound messages. This method returns true when the handler wants to continue handling such messages; otherwise, it returns false. It may throw ProtocolException or RuntimeException to cause the JAX-WS runtime to cease the handler's normal message processing and generate a fault.

Each method is called with a MessageContext or subinterface argument that stores a map of properties for handlers to use to communicate withjeach other and for other purposes. For example, MessageContext. MESSAGE_OUTBOUND_PROPERTY stores a Boolean object that identifies a message's direction. During a request (from client to web service), this property's value is Boolean .TRUE from a client handler's perspective and Boolean .FALSE from a web service handler's perspective.

RESTful Web Services and Attachments

RESTful web services that implement Provider<Source> cannot return arbitrary MIME-typed data (e.g., a JPEG image). They can only return XML messages with no attachments. If you want to return an attachment (such as an image file), your web service class must implement the Provider<DataSource>

interface; the javax.activation.DataSource interface provides the JavaBeans Activation Framework with an abstraction of an arbitrary collection of data.

Providers and Dispatch Clients

This chapter presents high-level and low-level approaches to working with JAX-WS. The high-level approach requires you to work with SEIs and SIBs; it simplifies and hides the details of converting between Java method invocations and their corresponding SOAP-based XML messages. The low-level approach lets you work directly with XML messages, and must be followed to implement a RESTful web service.

While discussing how to implement a RESTful web service with JAX-WS. Behind the scenes, the JAX-WS runtime takes the information received from the URL connection and creates the proper object to pass to invoke(). It also takes the object returned from invoke () and makes its contents available to the client via the URL connection's output stream.

CHAPTER 7

JAVA 7 and Android

In this chapter you will read about:

- Android Architecture.
- Application Architecture.
- Broadcast Receivers.
- Java7MeetsAndroid.

Introduction

Developing apps for Android devices is popular these days. Perhaps you would like to learn how to develop your own Android apps with Java 7 (although you cannot use APIs and language features newer than Java 5). This chapter presents a rapid introduction to app development. You first learn about Android architecture and the architecture of an Android app. You then learn how to install the Android SDK and a platform so that you have the tools and an environment to begin app development. Because the SDK provides an emulator to emulate Android devices, you next learn how to create and start an Android Virtual Device (AVD), which you can use to test your apps in lieu of an actual Android device. Finally, you're introduced to a simple app, learn how to create this app via the SDK, and learn how to install and run the app on an AVD.

Exploring Android and Android App Architectures

The *Android Developer's Guide* (http: //developer. android. com/guide/index. html) defines *Android* as a *software stack* (a set of software subsystems needed to deliver a fully functional solution) for mobile devices. This stack includes an operating system (a modified version of the Linux kernel), *middleware* (software that connects the low-level operating system to high-level apps), and key apps (written in Java) such as a web browser (known as Browser) and a contact manager (known as Contacts). Android offers the following features:

- Application framework enabling reuse and replacement of app components
- Bluetooth, EDGE, 3G, and WiFi support (hardware dependent)
- Camera, GPS, compass, and accelerometer support (hardware dependent)
- Dalvik virtual machine optimized for mobile devices
- GSM Telephony support (hardware dependent)
- Integrated browser based on the open source WebKit engine
- Media support for common audio, video, and still image formats (MPEG4, H.264, MP3, AAC, AMR, JPG, PNG, GIF)
- Optimized graphics powered by a custom 2D graphics library; 3D graphics based on the OpenGL ES 1.0 specification (hardware acceleration optional)
- SQLite for structured data storage

Android apps are written in Java and can access only the Java APIs described in the API reference at http: //developer. android. com/reference/packages. html (as well as Android-oriented third-party APIs). They cannot access Java APIs beyond Java 5. This restriction affects Java 7's try-with-resources statement, which is based on the new Java. lang. AutoCloseable interface and API support for suppressed exceptions. You cannot use try-with-resources in your Android source code.

Android Architecture

The Android software stack consists of apps at the top, middleware (consisting of an application framework, libraries, and the Android runtime) in the middle, and a Linux kernel with various drivers at the bottom. Users care about apps, and Android ships with a variety of useful core apps, which include Browser, Contacts, and Phone. All apps are written in Java. Apps form the top layer of Android's architecture. Directly beneath the app layer is the *application framework*, a set of high-level building blocks for creating apps. The application framework is preinstalled on Android devices and consists of the following components:

- *Activity Manager.* This component provides an app's *lifecycle* and maintains a shared activity stack for navigating within and among apps. (I discuss both concepts later in this chapter when I present activities.)
- *Content Providers:* These components encapsulate data (e.g., the Browser app's bookmarks) that can be shared among apps.
- *Location Manager.* This component makes it possible for an Android device to be aware of its physical location.
- *Notification Manager.* This component lets an app notify the user of a significant event (e.g., a message's arrival) without interrupting what the user is currently doing.
- *Package Manager.* This component lets an app learn about other app packages that are currently installed on the device. (App packages are discussed later in this chapter.)
- *Resource Manager* This component lets an app access its application resources, a topic that I discuss later in this chapter.
- *Telephony Manager.* This component lets an app learn about a device's telephony services. It also handles making and receiving phone calls.
- *View System:* This component manages user interface elements and user interface-oriented event generation. (I briefly discuss these topics later in this chapter.)
- *Window Manager.* This component organizes the screen's real estate into windows, allocates drawing surfaces, and performs other window-related jobs.

The components of the application framework rely on a set of C/C++ libraries to perform their jobs. Developers interact with the following libraries by way of framework APIs:

- *FreeType.* This library supports bitmap and vector font rendering.
- *libc.* This library is a BSD-derived implementation of the standard C system library, tuned for embedded Linux-based devices.
- *LibWebCore:* This library offers a modern and fast web browser engine that powers the Android browser and an embeddable web view. It's based on WebKit (http: //en. wikipedia. org/wiki/ WebKit) and is also used by the Google Chrome and Apple Safari browsers.
- *Media Framework:* These libraries, which are based on PacketVideo's OpenCORE, support the playback and recording of many popular audio and video formats, as well as working with static image files. Supported formats include MPEG4, H.264, MP3, AAC, AMR, JPEG, and PNG.
- *OpenGL IES:* These 3D graphics libraries provide an OpenGL implementation based on OpenGL ES 1.0 APIs. They use hardware 3D acceleration (where available) or the included (and highly optimized) 3D software rasterizer.
- *SGL:* This library provides the underlying 2D graphics engine.
- *SQLite.* This library provides a powerful and lightweight relational database engine that's available to all apps, and that's also used by Mozilla Firefox and Apple's iPhone for persistent storage.
- SSL: This library provides secure sockets layer-based security for network communication.
- *Surface Manager.* This library manages access to the display subsystem, and seamlessly composites 2D and 3D graphic layers from multiple apps.

Android provides a runtime environment that consists of core libraries (implementing a subset of the Apache Harmony Java 5 implementation) and the Dalvik virtual machine (a non-Java virtual machine that's based on processor registers instead of being stack-based).

Each Android app defaults to running in its own Linux process, which hosts an instance of Dalvik. This virtual machine has been designed so that devices can run multiple virtual machines efficiently. This efficiency is largely due to Dalvik executing Dalvik Executable (DEX)-based files—DEX is a format that's optimized for a minimal memory footprint.

Perhaps you're wondering how it's possible to have a non-Java virtual machine run Java code. The answer is that Dalvik doesn't run Java code. Instead, Android transforms compiled Java classfiles into the DEX format, and it's this resulting code that gets executed by Dalvik.

Finally, the libraries and Android runtime rely on the Linux kernel (version *2.6.x)* for underlying core services, such as threading, low-level memory management, a network stack, process management, and a driver model. Furthermore, the kernel acts as an abstraction layer between the hardware and the rest of the software stack.

App Architecture

The architecture of an Android app differs from that of an application running on the desktop. App architecture is based upon components that communicate with each other via intents, are described by a manifest, and may use application resources. Collectively, these items are stored in an app package.

Components

An *Android app* is a collection of *components* (activities, broadcast receivers, content providers, and services) that run in a Linux process and that are managed by Android. These components share a set of environmental resources, including databases, preferences, a filesystem, and the Linux process.

This component-oriented architecture lets an app reuse the components of other apps, provided that those other apps permit reuse of their components. Component reuse reduces overall memory footprint, which is very important for devices with limited memory.

For example, suppose you're creating a drawing app that lets users choose a color from a palette, and suppose that another app has developed a suitable color chooser and permits this component to be reused. In this scenario, the drawing app can call upon that other app's color chooser to have the user select a color rather than provide its own color chooser. The drawing app doesn't contain the other app's color chooser or even link to this other app. Instead, it starts up the other app's color chooser component when needed.

Android starts a process when any part of the app (e.g., the aforementioned color chooser) is needed, and instantiates the Java objects for that part. This is why Android's apps don't have a single entry point (noC-stylemain() function, for example). Instead, apps use components that are instantiated and run as needed. Activities, broadcast receivers, and services communicate with each other via *intents,* which are messages that describe operations to perform (e.g., send an email or choose a photo), or (in the case of broadcasts) provide descriptions of external events that have occurred (a device's camera being activated, for example) and are being announced.

Because nearly everything in Android involves intents, there are many opportunities to replace existing components with your own components. For example, Android provides the intent for sending an email. Your app can send that intent to activate the standard mail app, or it can register an activity (discussed shortly) that responds to the "send an email" intent, effectively replacing the standard mail app with its own activity.

These messages are implemented as instances of the android, content, intent class. An intent object describes a message in terms of some combination of the following items:

- *Action:* A string naming the action to be performed or, in the case of broadcast intents, the action that took place and is being reported. Actions are described by intent constants such as ACTION_CALL (initiate a phone call), ACTION_EDIT (display data for the user to edit), and ACTION_MAIN (start up as the initial activity). You can also define your own action stririgs for activating the components in your app. These strings should include the app package as a prefix ("com. example. project. SELECT_COLOR", for example).
- *Category.* A string that provides additional information about the kind of component that should handle the intent. For example, CATEGORY_LAUNCHER means that the calling activity should appear in the device's app launcher as a top-level app. (The app launcher is briefly discussed later in this chapter.)
- *Component name:* A string that specifies the fully qualified name (package plus name) of a component class to use for the intent. The component name is optional. When set, the intent object is delivered to an instance of the designated class. When not set, Android uses other information in the intent object to locate a suitable target.
- *Data:* The uniform resource identifier (URI) of the data on which to operate (e.g., a person record in a contacts database).
- *Extras:* A set of key-value pairs providing additional information that should be delivered to the component handling the intent. For example, given an action for sending an e-mail message, this information could include the message's subject, body, and so on.
- *Flags:* Bit values that instruct Android on how to launch an activity (e.g., which task the activity should belong to—tasks are discussed later in this chapter) and how to treat the activity after launch (e.g., whether the activity can be considered a recent activity). Hags are represented by constants in the intent class; for example, FLAG_ACTIVITY_NEW_TASK specifies that this activity will become the start of a new task on this history stack—the history stack is discussed later in this chapter.
- *Type:* The Multipurpose Internet Mail Extensions (MIME) type of the intent data. Normally, Android infers a type from the data. By specifying a type, you disable that inference.

Intents can be classified as explicit or implicit. An *explicit intent* designates the target component by its name (the previously mentioned component name item is assigned a value). Because component names are usually unknown to the developers of other apps, explicit intents are typically used for app-internal messages (e.g., an activity that launches another activity located within the same app). Android delivers an explicit intent to an instance of the designated target class. Only the intent object's component name matters for determining which component should get the intent.

An *implicit intent doesn't* name a target (the component name isn't assigned a value). Implicit intents are often used to start components in other apps. Android searches for the best component (a single activity or service to perform the requested action) or components (a set of broadcast receivers to respond to the broadcast announcement) to handle the implicit intent. During the search, Android compares the contents of the intent object to *intent filters,* manifest information associated with components that can potentially receive intents.

Filters advertise a component's capabilities and identify only those intents that the component can handle. They open up the component to the possibility of receiving implicit intents of the advertised type. When a component has no intent filters, it can receive only explicit intents. In contrast, a component with filters can receive explicit and implicit intents. Android consults an Intent object's action, category, data, and type when comparing the intent against an intent filter. It doesn't take extras and flags into consideration.

Activities

An *activity is* a component that presents a user interface so that the user can interact with the app. For example, Android's Contacts app includes an activity for entering a new contact, its Phone app includes an activity for dialing a phone number, and its Calculator app includes an activity for performing basic calculations.

Although an app can include a single activity, it's more typical for apps to include multiple activities. For example, Calculator also includes an "advanced panel" activity that lets the user calculate square roots, perform trigonometry, and carry out other advanced mathematical operations. Activities are described by subclasses of the android, app. Activity class, which is an indirect subclass of the abstract android. content. Context class. Activity subclasses override various Activity *lifecycle callback methods* that Android calls during the life of an activity.

Broadcast Receivers

A *broadcast receiver is* a component that receives and reacts to broadcasts! Many broadcasts originate in system code; for example, an announcement that the timezone has been changed or the battery power is low.

Apps can also initiate broadcasts. For example, an app may want to let other apps know that some data has finished downloading from the network to the device and is now available for them to use.

Content Providers

A *content provider* is a component that makes a specific set of an app's data available to other apps. The data can be stored in the Android filesystem, in an SQLite database, or in any other manner that makes sense.

Content providers are preferable to directly accessing raw data because they decouple component code from raw data formats. This decoupling prevents code breakage when formats change.

Services

A *service* is a component that runs in the background for an indefinite period of time, and which doesn't provide a user interface. As with an activity, a service runs on the process's main thread; it must spawn another thread to perform a time-consuming operation. Services are classified as local or remote:

- A *local service* runs in the same process as the rest of the app. Such services make it easy to implement background tasks.
- A *remote service* runs in a separate process. Such services let you perform interprocess communication.

Consider a service that plays music in response to a user's music choice via an activity. The user selects the song to play via this activity, and a service is started in response to the selection. The rationale for using a service to play the music is that the user expects the music to keep playing even after the activity that initiated the music leaves the screen.

Manifest

Android learns about an app's various components (and more) by examining the app's XML-structured manifest file, AndroidManif est. xml. For example, the following listing shows how this file might declare activity component.

SimpleApp 's manifest file

```
<?xml version="1.0" encoding="utf-8"?>
<manifest xmlns:android="http://schemas.android.com/apk/res/android"
      package="ca.tutortutor.simpleapp">
    <application android:label="@string/app_name" android:icon="@drawable/
icon">
      <activity android:name=".SimpleActivity" android:label="@string/
app_name">
        <intent-filter>
          <action android:name="android.intent.action.MAIN" />
          <category android:name="android.intent.category.LAUNCHER" />
        </intent-filter>
      </activity> <!— ... —>
    </application>"
</manifest>
```

The listing begins with the <?xml version="1.0" encoding="utf-8" ?> prolog, which identifies this file as an XML version 1.0 file whose content is encoded according to the TJTF-8 encoding standard.

The listing next presents the manifest element, which is this XML document's root element: android identifies the Android namespace, and package identifies the app's Java package—each app must have its own Java package, which is ca. tutortutor. simpleapp in this example. Additional attributes can be specified. For example, you can specify versionCode and versionName attributes when you want to identify version information.

Nested within manifest is application, which is the parent of app component elements. Its label and icon attributes refer to label and icon application resources that Android devices display to represent the app, and which serve as defaults for individual components whose start tags don't specify these attributes.

Nested within application is an activity element that describes an activity component. The name attribute identifies a class (SimpleActivity) that implements the activity. This name begins with a period character to imply that it's relative to ca .tutortutor. simpleapp. The activity element can override application's label and icon attributes with its own component-specific label and icon attributes. When either attribute isn't present, activity inherits application's label or icon attribute value.

Nested within activity is intent-filter. This element declares the capabilities of the component described by the enclosing element. For example, it declares the capabilities of the SimpleActivity component via its nested action and category elements:

- action identifies the action to perform. For example, this element's name attribute can be assigned "android.intent.action.MAIN" to identify the activity as the app's entry point (the first activity to run when the user launches the app).
- category identifies a component category. This tag's name attribute is assigned "android. intent. category. LAUNCHER" to identify the activity as needing to be displayed in the app launcher (discussed later).

The <!-- ... -- > comment tag indicates that a manifest can define multiple components. For example, I referred to a SimpleActivity2 class while discussing activities. Before you could start this activity (explicitly or implicitly), you would need to introduce an activity element into the manifest.

Consider the following activity element:

```
<activity android:name=".SimpleActivity2" ...>
```

```
    <intent-filter>
        <action android:name="android.intent.action.VIEW" />
        <data android:mimeType="image/jpeg" />
        <category android:name="android.intent.category.DEFAULT" />
    </intent-filter>
</activity>
```

SimpleActivity2's intent-filter element helps Android determine that this activity is to be launched when the Intent object's values match the following tag attribute values:

- <action>'s name attribute is assigned "android.intent.action.VIEW".
- <data>'s mimeType attribute is assigned the "image/jpeg" MIME type.
- <category>'s name attribute is assigned "android. intent. category .DEFAULT" to allow the activity to be launched without explicitly specifying its component.

AndroidManif est. xml may contain additional information, such as naming any libraries that the app needs to be linked against (besides the default Android library), and identifying all app-enforced permissions (via permission elements) to other apps, such as controlling who can start the app's activities.

Also, the manifest may contain uses-permission elements to identify permissions that the app needs. For example, an app that needs to use the camera would specify the following element: <uses-permission android:name="android.permission.CAMERA"/>.

At app install time, permissions requested by the app (via uses-permission) are granted to it by Android's package installer, based on checks against the digital signatures of the apps declaring those permissions and/or interaction with the user.

No checks with the user are done while an app is running. It was granted a specific permission when installed and can use that feature as desired, or the permission wasn't granted and any attempt to use the feature will fail without prompting the user.

Application Resources

As well as having a set of *environmental resources* (e.g., databases, preferences, a filesystem, threads, and the Linux process) for its components to share, an app can have its own *application resources:* property animations, tween animations, state lists of colors, drawables, layouts, menus, raw files, simple values (e.g., strings), and arbitrary XML files.

Android requires that an app store its application resources files in the following table's subdirectories (and their subdirectories, where appropriate) of the app's res directory.

Table Application Resource Subdirectories

Directory	Description
anim	Contains XML files that describe tween animations—see http: // developer. android. com/guide/topics/graphics/view-animation. html#tween-animation to learn about tween animations.
animator	Contains XML files that describe Android 3.0+ property animations—see http://developer.android.com/guide/topics/graphics/animation.html to learn about property animations.
color	Contains XML files that describe state lists of colors.

drawable	Contains bitmap files (.png, .9.png, .jpg, .gif) or XML files that are compiled into bitmap files, *nine-patches* (resizable bitmaps), state lists, shapes, animation drawables, and other drawables.

Installing the Android SDK and an Android Platform

Now that you have a basic understanding of the Android and Android app architectures, you'll probably want to create an app. However, you cannot do so until you've installed the Android SDK and have also installed an Android platform. This section shows you how to accomplish these tasks.

Accessing System Requirements

Google provides an Android SDK distribution file for each of the Windows, Intel-based Mac OS X, and Linux (i386) operating systems. Before downloading and installing this file, you must be aware of SDK requirements. You cannot use the SDK when your development platform doesn't meet these requirements.

The Android SDK supports the following operating systems:

- Windows XP (32-bit), Vista (32- or 64-bit), or Windows 7 (32- or 64-bit)
- Mac OS X 10.5.8 or later (x86 only)
- Linux (tested on Ubuntu Linux, Lucid Lynx): GNU C Library (glibc) 2.11 or later is required. 64-bit distributions must be able to run 32-bit applications. To learn how to add support for 32-bit applications, see the Ubuntu Linux installation notes at http://developer.android.com/sdk/installing.html#troubleshooting.

You'll quickly discover that the Android SDK is organized into various components: SDK tools, SDK platform tools, different versions of the *Android platform* (also known as the Android software stack), SDK add-ons, USB driver for Windows, samples, and offline documentation. Each component requires a minimum amount of disk storage space; the total required amount of space depends on which components you choose to install:

- *SDK Tools:* The SDK's tools require approximately 35MB of disk storage space and must be installed.
- *SDK Platform Tools:* The SDK's platform tools require approximately 6MB of disk storage space and must be installed.
- *Android platform:* Each Android platform corresponds to a specific version of Android and requires approximately 150MB of disk storage space. At least one Android platform must be installed.
- *SDKAdd-on:* Each optional SDK add-on (e.g., Google APIs or a third-party vendor's API libraries) requires approximately 100MB of disk storage space.
- *USB Driver for Windows:* The optional USB driver for the Windows platform requires approximately 10MB of disk stbrage space. When you're developing on Mac OS X or Linux, you don't need to install the USB driver.
- *Samples:* Each Android platform's optional app examples require approximately 10MB of disk storage space.
- *Offline documentation:* Instead of having to be online to access the Android documentation, you can choose to download the documentation so that you can view it even when not connected to the Internet. The offline documentation requires approximately 250MB of disk storage space.

Finally, you should ensure that the following additional software is installed:

- *JDKS, JDK6, orJDK 7:* You need to install one of these Java Development Kits (JDKs) to compile Java code. It's not sufficient to have only a Java Runtime Environment ORE) installed. Also, you cannot use Java 7 language features that rely on APIs newer than Java 5; the try-with-resources statement is unusable.
- *Apache Ant.* You need to install Ant 1.8 or later so that you can build Android projects.

Installing the Android SDK

Point your browser to http: //developer. android. com/sdk/index. html and download the current release of the Android SDK for your platform. For example, you would download one of android-sdk_r12-windows.zip (Windows), android-sdk_rl2-mac_x86.zip (Mac OSX [Intel]), andandroid-sdk_r!2-linux_x86.tgz (Linux [i386]) to install Android SDK Release 12.

For example, if you run Windows, download android-sdk_rl2-windows.zip. After unarchiving this file, move the unarchived android-sdk-windows home directory to a convenient location in your filesystem; for example, you might move the unarchived C:\unzipped\android-sdk_rl2-windows\android-sdk-windows home directory to the root directory on your C: drive, resulting in C:\android-sdk-windows.

A subsequent examination of android-sdk-windows shows that this home directory contains the following subdirectories and files:

- *add-ons:* This initially empty directory stores add-ons from Google and other vendors; for example, the Google APIs add-on is stored here.
- *platforms:* This initially empty directory stores Android platforms in separate subdirectories. For example, Android 2.3 would be stored in one platforms subdirectory, whereas Android 2.2 would be stored in another platforms subdirectory.
- tools: This directory contains a set of platform-independent development and profiling tools. The tools in this directory may be updated at any time, independent of Android platform releases.
- *SDK Manager,* exe: *A* special tool that launches the Android SDK and AVD Manager tool, which you use to add components to your SDK.
- *SDK Readme. txt:* This text file welcomes you to the Android SDK and discusses installing an Android platform.

The tools directory contains a variety of useful tools, including the following:

- *android:* Creates and updates Android projects; updates the Android SDK with new platforms, add-ons, and documentation; and creates, deletes, and views *AVDs* (descriptors that describe virtual devices).
- *emulator.* Runs a full Android software stack down to the kernel level, and includes a set of preinstalled apps (e.g., Browser) that you can access. The emulator tool launches an *AVD.*
- *sqlite3:* Manages SQLite databases created by Android apps.
- *zipalign:* Performs archive alignment optimization on APKs.

Installing an Android Platform

Installing the Android SDK is insufficient for developing Android apps; you must also install at least one Android platform. You can accomplish this task via the SDK Manager tool.

Run SDK Manager. This tool presents the Android SDK and AVD Manager dialog box, followed by the Refresh Sources and Choose Packages to Install dialog boxes.

The Android SDK and AVD Manager dialog box identifies virtual devices, installed packages, and available packages. It also lets you configure proxy server and other settings.

When this dialog box appears for the first time, the Virtual devices entry in the list appearing on the right side of the dialog box is highlighted, and the pane to the right of that list identifies all AVDs that have been created (this list will probably be empty).

After presenting this dialog box, SDK Manager scans Google's servers for available component packages to install. The Refresh Sources dialog box reveals its progress.

After SDK Manager finishes its scan (which may take a few minutes), it presents the Choose Packages to Install dialog box to let you choose SDK components to install. (If you've installed Android SDK Release 12, and haven't previously installed Android, the only installed component is Android SDK Tools, revision 12.)

The Choose Packages to Install dialog box shows a Packages list that identifies those packages that can be installed. It displays checkmarks beside packages that have been accepted for installation, and displays question marks beside those packages that have yet to be accepted.

For the highlighted package, Package Description & License presents a package description, a list of other packages that are dependent on this package being installed, information about the archive that houses the package, and additional information. Also, you can select a radio button to accept or reject the package. If you reject the highlighted package, an X icon will replace the checkmark or question mark icon.

Android Platform versions 3.0 and higher refer to tablet-oriented Android. Versions less than 3.0 refer to smartphone-oriented Android. Because this chapter focuses on Android 2.3.3, the only packages that you need to install are Android SDK Platform-tools, revision 6 and SDK Platform Android 2.3.3, API 10, revision 2. All other checked package entries can be unchecked by clicking the Reject option radio button on their respective panes (or by double-clicking list entries).

Installing Archives might present an "'adb kill-server' failed—run manually if necessary" message. This message refers to a platform tool named adb, which stands for Android Debug Bridge (ADB).

ADB manages the state of an emulator instance or an Android-powered device. It includes a server that runs as a background process on the development machine. The installer must kill this process before installing platform tools. When this process isn't running, you'll see the aforementioned message.

You'll probably encounter the ADB Restart dialog box, which tells you that a package dependent on Android Debug Bridge (ADB) has been updated, and asking you whether you want to restart ADB now. At this point, it doesn't matter which button you click—you would probably click Yes when the ADB server process had been running before you started to install a package and you want to resume this process following the installation.

Click Close on the Installing Archives dialog box to finish installation.

You should now observe the Android SDK and AVD Manager's Installed packages pane displaying Android SDK Platform-tools, revision 6 and SDK Platform Android 2.3.3, API 10, revision 2 in addition to Android SDK Tools, revision 12. You should also observe the following new subdirectories:

- platform-tools (in android-sdk-windows)
- android-10 (inandroid-sdk-windows/platforms)

platform-tools contains development tools that may be updated with each platform release. Its tools include aapt (Android Asset Packaging Tool—view, create, and update Zip-compatible archives (.zip, .jar, .apk); and compile resources into binary assets), the aforementioned adb tool, anddx (Dalvik

Executable—generate Dalvik DEX code from Java". class" files), android-10 stores Android 2.3.3 data and user interface-oriented files.

Creating, Installing, and Running an App

Now that you've installed the Android SDK, installed an Android platform, and created and started an AVD, you're readyto create an app, and install and run this app on the AVD. This section introduces you to an app named Dava7MeetsAndroid. After presenting and discussing the app's source code and related files, it shows you how to create this app, and install and run it on the previously started AVD.

Introducing JavaTMeetsAndroid

Java7MeetsAndroid is a single-activity app that presents an image and a button. The image shows Duke, the Java mascot, over a glowing 7. The button, labeled Wave, starts an animation of Duke waving when clicked.

The following listing presents the Java7MeetsAndroid class.

An activity for making Duke wave

```
package ca.tutortutor.j7ma;
import android.app.Activity;
import android.graphics.drawable.AnimationDrawable;
import android.os.Bundle;
import android.view.View;
import android.widget.Button;
import android.widget.ImageView;

public class Dava7MeetsAndroid extends Activity
{
    AnimationDrawable dukeAnimation;
    ("Override
    public void onCreate(Bundle savedlnstanceState)
    {
        super.onCreate(savedlnstanceState);
        setContentView(R.layout.main);
        ImageView dukelmage = (ImageView) findViewByld(R.id.duke);

        dukelmage. setBackgroundResource (R. drawable. duke_wave);
        dukeAnimation = (AnimationDrawable) dukelmage.getBackgroundQ;
        final Button btnWave = (Button) findViewByld(R.id.wave);
        View.OnClickListener ocl;
        ocl = new View.OnClickListenerQ
        {
            @Override
            public void ondick(View v)
            {
                dukeAnimation.stop();
                dukeAnimation.start();
            }
        };
```

```
        btnWave.setOnClickListener(ocl);
    }
}
```

The above listing begins with a package statement that names the package (ca.tutortutor. J7ma) in which its]ava7MeetsAndroid class is stored, followed by a series of import statements that import various Android API types. This listing next describes the Java7MeetsAndroid class, which extends Activity.

Java7MeetsAndroid first declares a dukeAnimation instance field of type android. graphics. drawable. AniitiationDrawable. Objects of type AnitnationDrawable describe frame-by-frame animations, in which the current drawable is replaced with the next drawable in the animation sequence.

All the app's work takes place in 3ava7MeetsAndroid's overriding onCreate(Bundle) method: no other methods are required, which helps to keep this app simple. onCreate(Bundle) first invokes its same-named superclass method, a rule that must be followed by all overriding activity methods.

This method then executes setContentView(R.layout.main) to establish the app's user interface. R.layout.main is an identifier (ID) for an application resource, which resides in a separate file. You interpret this ID as follows:

- R is the name of a class that's generated (by the aapt tool) when the app is being built. This class is named R because its content identifies various kinds of application resources (e.g., layouts, images, strings, and colors).
- layout is the name of a class that's nested within R. All application resources whose IDs are stored in this class describe specific layout resources. Each kind of application resource is associated with a nested class that's named in a similar fashion. For example, string identifies string resources.
- main is the name of an int constant declared within layout. This resource ID identifies the main layout resource. Specifically, main refers to a main. xml file that stores the main activity's layout information, main is Dava7MeetsAndroid's only layout resource.

R. layout .main is passed to Activity's void setContentView(int layoutResID) method to tell Android to create a user interface screen using the layout information stored in main. xml. Behind the scenes, Android creates the user interface components described in main.xml and positions them on the screen as specified by main.xml's layout data.

The screen is based on *views* (abstractions of user interface components) and *view groups* (views that group related user interface components). Views are instances of classes that subclass the android, view. View class and are analogous to AWT/Swing components. View groups are instances of classes that subclass the abstract android. view. ViewGroup class and are analogous to AWT/Swing containers. Android refers to specific views (e.g., buttons or spinners) as *widgets*.

Continuing, onCreate(Bundle) executes ImageView dukelmage = (ImageView) findViewByld(R.id.duke);. This statement first calls View's View findViewBy!d(int id) method to find the android. widget. ImageView element declared in main. xml and identified as duke, and instantiate ImageView and initialize it to its declarative information. The statement then saves this object's reference in local variable dukelmage.

The subsequent dukelmage. setBackgroundResource(R. drawable. duke_wave); statement invokes ImageView's inherited (from View) void setBackgroundResourceMethod(int resID) method to set the view's background to the resource identified by resID. The R.drawable.duke_wave argument identifies an XML file named duke_wave. xml (presented later), which stores information on the animation, and which is stored in res's drawable subdirectory. The setBackgroundResource() call links the dukelmage view to ' the sequence of images described by duke_wave. xml and that will be drawn on this view; the initial image is drawn as a result of this method call.

ImageView lets an app animate a sequence of drawables by calling AnimationDrawable methods. Before the app can do this, it must obtain ImageView's AnimationDrawable. The dukeAnimation = (AnimationDrawable) dukelrnage.getBackgroundQ; assignment statement that follows accomplishes this task by invoking ImageView's inherited (from View) Drawable getBackground () method to return the AnimationDrawable for this ImageView, which is subsequently assigned to the dukeAnimation field. The AnimationDrawable instance is used to start and stop an animation (discussed shortly).

onCreate(Bundle) now turns its attention to creating the Wave button. It invokes f indByViewld(int) to obtain the button information from main. xml, and then instantiate the android. widget. Button class.

The View class's nested onClickListener interface is then employed to create a listener object whose void onClick(View v) method is invoked whenever the user clicks the button. The listener is registered with its Button object by calling View's void setOnClickListener (AdapterView.OnClickListener listener) method.

Wave's click listener invokes dukeAnimation. stop(); followed bydukeAnimation.start(); to stop and then start the animation. The stop() method is called before start () to ensure that a subsequent click of the Wave button causes a new animation to begin.

Along with Listing 12-3's Java7MeetsAndroid. Java source file, DavayMeetsAndroid relies on three XML resource files and several PNG images.

The following listing presents main.xml, which describes screen layout.

The main. xml file storing layout information that includes a pair of widgets

```
<?xml version="1.o" encoding="utf-8"?>
<LinearLayout xmlns:android="http://schemas.android.com/apk/res/android"
    android:orientation="vertical"
    android:layout_width="fill_parent"
    android:layout_height="fill_parent"
    android:gravity="center" android:background^"#ffffff">
<ImageView android:id="@+id/duke"
    android:layout_width="wrap_content"
    android:layout_height="wrap_content"
    android:layout_marginBottom="10dip"/>
<Button android :id="|«>+id/wave"
    android:layout_width="wrap_content"
    android:layout_height="wrap_content"
    android:text="@string/wave"/>
</LinearLayout>
```

Following the XML declaration, the listing declares a LinearLayout element that specifies a *layout* (a view group that arranges contained views on an Android device's screen in some manner) for arranging contained widgets (including nested layouts) either horizontally or vertically across the screen.

The < Linear Layout> tag specifies several attributes for controlling this linear layout. These attributes include the following:

- orientation identifies the linear layout as horizontal or vertical - contained widgets are laid out horizontally or vertically. The default orientation is horizontal, "horizontal" and "vertical" are the only legal values that can be assigned to this attribute.
- layout_width identifies the width of the layout. Legal values include "f ill_parent" (be as wide as

the parent) and "wrap_content" (be wide enough to enclose content), f ill_parent was renamed to match_parent in Android 2.2, but is still supported and widely used.

- layout_height identifies the height of the layout. Legal values include "f ill_parent" (be as tall as the parent) and "wrap_content" (be tall enough to enclose content).
- gravity identifies how the layout is positioned relative to the screen. For example, "center" specifies that the layout should be centered horizontally and vertically on the screen.
- background identifies a background image, a gradient, or a solid color. For simplicity, I've hardcoded a hexadecimal color identifier to signify a solid white background (#ffffff).

The LinearLayout element encapsulates ImageView and Button elements. Each of these elements specifies an id attribute that identifies the element so that it can be referenced from code. The *resource identifier* (special syntax that begins with @) assigned to this attribute begins with the @+id prefix. For example, @+id/duke identifies the ImageView element as duke; this element is referenced from code by specifying R. id. duke.

These elements also specify layout_width and layout_height attributes for determining how their content is laid out. Each attribute is assigned wrap_content so that the element will appear at its natural size.

ImageView specifies a layoutjnarginBottom attribute to identify a space separator between itself and the button that follows vertically. The space is specified as 10 dips, or *density-independent pixels* (virtual pixels that apps can use to express layout dimensions/positions in a screen density-independent way).

The Button element's text attribute is assigned @string/wave, which references a string resource named wave. This string resource is stored in an XML file named strings .xml, which is stored in the values subdirectory of res.

Nested inside the animation-list element is a sequence of item elements. Each item element identifies one drawable in the animation sequence via its drawable attribute. The @drawable/dukex resource reference (where x ranges from 0 through 9) identifies an image file whose name starts with duke in res's drawable directory. The duration attribute identifies the number of milliseconds that must elapse before the next item element's drawable is displayed.

The following listing presents Java7MeetsAndroid's AndroidManif est.xml file.

Describing the Java7MeetAndroid app

```
<?xml version="1.0" encoding="utf-8"?>
<manifest xmlns:android="http://schemas.android.com/apk/res/android"
          package="ca.tutortutor.j7ma"
          android:versionCode="1"
          android:versionName="1.0">
    <application  android:label="@string/app_name" android:icon="@drawable/
icon">
        <activity android:name="Java7MeetsAndroid"
                  android:label="@string/app_name">
          <intent-filter>
              <action android:name="android.intent.action.MAIN" />
              <category android:name="android.intent.category.LAUNCHER" />
          </intent-filter>
        </activity>
    </application>
</manifest>
```

Creating Java7MeetsAndroid

Several steps must be followed to create Java?MeetsAndroid. The first step is to use the android tool to create a project. When used in this way, android requires you to adhere to the following syntax (which is spread across multiple lines for readability):

android create project —target *target_ID*
—name *your_project_name*
—path */path/to/your/project/project_name*
—activity *your_activity_name*
—package *your_package_namespace*

Except for —name (or -n), which specifies the project's name (when provided, this name will be used for the resulting . apk filename when you build your app), all the following options are required:

- The --target (or -t) option specifies the app's build target. The *target_ID* value is an integer value that identifies an Android platform. You can obtain this value by invoking android list targets. If you've only installed the Android 2.3.3 platform, this command should output'a single Android 2.3.3 platform target identified as integer ID 1.
- The -- path (or - p) option specifies the project directory's location. The directory is created if it doesn't exist.
- The - -activity (or -a) option specifies the name for the default activity class. The resulting classfile is created inside */path/to/your/project/project_name/src/your_package_namespace/*, and is used as the .apk filename if —name (or -n) isn't specified.
- The —package (or -k) option specifies the project's package namespace, which must follow the rules for packages that are specified in the Java language.

Assuming a Windows XP platform, and assuming a C: \pr j \dev hierarchy where the Java7MeetsAndroid project is to be stored in C: \prj\dev\Dava7MeetsAndroid, invoke the following command from anywhere in the filesystem to create Dava7MeetsAndroid:

```
android create project -t 1 -p C:\prj\dev\3ava7MeetsAndroid -a
Dava?MeetsAndroid -k*-ca.tutortutor.j7ma
```

This command creates various directories and adds files to some of these directories. It specifically creates the following file and directory structure within C: \pr j\dev\Java7MeetsAndroid:

- AndroidManif est. xml is the manifest file for the app being built. This file is synchronized to the Activity subclass previously specified via the - -activity or -a option.
- bin is the output directory for the Apache Ant build script.
- build. properties is a customizable properties file for the build system. You can edit this file to override default build settings used by Apache Ant, and provide a pointer to your keystore and key alias so that the build tools can sign your app when built in release mode (discussed in *Android Recipes).*
- build. xml is the Apache Ant build script for this project.
- default. properties is the default properties file for the build system. Don't modify this file.
- libs contains private libraries (when required).

- local. properties contains the location of the Android SDK home directory.
- proguard. cf g contains configuration data for *ProGuard,* an SDK tool that lets developers obfuscate their code (making it very difficult to reverse engineer the code) as an integrated part of a release build.
- res contains the project's application resources.
- src contains the project's source code, res contains the following directories:
- drawable-hdpi contains drawable resources (such as icons) for high-density screens.
- drawable-ldpi contains drawable resources for low-density screens.
- drawable-mdpi contains drawable resources for medium-density screens.
- layout contains layout files.
- values contains value files.

Also, src contains the ca\tutortutor\j7ma directory structure, and the final j7ma subdirectory contains a skeletal Java7MeetsAndroid.Java source file.

Before you can create this app, you need to perform the following tasks:

- Replace the skeletal Java7MeetsAndroid. Java source file with Listing 12-3.
- Replace the layout subdirectory's skeletal main. xml file with Listing 12-4.
- Replace the values subdirectory's skeletal strings. xml file with Listing 12-5.
- Create a drawable directory underneath res. Copy the dukeo. png through dukeg.png images located in this book's code file along with listing's duke_wave.xml file to drawable.

The generated AndroidManif est. xml file should be fine, although you can replace it with listing if desired. Assuming that C: \prj\dev\Java7MeetsAndroid is current, build this app with the help of Apache's ant tool, which defaults to processing this directory's build. xml file. At the command line, specify ant followed by debug or release to indicate the build mode:

- *Debug mode:* Build the app for testing and debugging. The build tools sign the resulting APK with a debug key and optimize the APK with zipalign. Specify ant debug.
- *Release mode:* Build the app for release to users. You must sign the resulting APK with your private key, and then optimize the APK with zipalign. (I discuss these tasks in *Android Recipes.)* Specify ant release.

Build Java7MeetsAndroid in debug mode by invoking ant debug from the C: \prj\dev\Java7MeetsAndroid directory. This command creates a gen subdirectory containing the ant-generated R. Java file (in a ca\tutortutor\j7ma directory hierarchy), and stores the created Dava7MeetsAndroid-debug.apk file in the bin subdirectory.

Installing and Running Java7MeetsAndroid

If you successfully created Dava7MeetsAndroid-debug.apk, you can install this APK on the previously started AVD. You can accomplish this task by using the adb tool, as follows:

```
adb install C:\prj\dev\Dava7MeetsAndroid\bin\Dava7MeetsAndroid-debug.apk
```

After a few moments, you should see several messages similar to those shown here:

```
325 KB/s (223895 bytes in 0.671s)
pkg: /data/local/tmp/DavaTMeetsAndroid-debug.apk Success
```

You might have to repeat the aforementioned command line a few times should you encounter a "device offline" error message.

Select the app launcher (grid) icon at the bottom of the home screen.

You can uninstall this app by clicking the MENU button (on the app launcher screen), selecting Manage apps from the pop-up menu, highlighting Java7MeetsAndroid in the apps list, clicking this entry, and clicking the Uninstall button.